THE
TRAGIC STORY
OF THE
EMPRESS
OF
IRELAND

THE *EMPRESS OF IRELAND*

One of the finest ships of the Canadian line. Soon After leaving Quebec on her voyage to Liverpool with over 1300 souls on board, she was struck by the Norwegian collier *Storstad* off Father Point, Quebec, on May 29, 1914, at 2:10 A.M., and sank about fifteen minutes later, carrying a thousand passengers down with her.

THE
TRAGIC STORY
OF THE
EMPRESS
OF
IRELAND

Logan Marshall

BERKLEY BOOKS, NEW YORK

THE BERKLEY PUBLISHING GROUP
Published by the Penguin Group
Penguin Group (USA) LLC
375 Hudson Street, New York, New York 10014

USA • Canada • UK • Ireland • Australia • New Zealand • India • South Africa • China

penguin.com

A Penguin Random House Company

Berkley trade paperback ISBN: 978-0-425-27354-8

PUBLISHING HISTORY
Previously published as *The Tragic Story of the Empress of Ireland and Other Great Sea Disasters* by L.T. Yers in 1914.
Berkley trade paperback edition / April 2014

Cover art and design by Oyster Pond Press
Interior text design by Tiffany Estreicher

CONTENTS

Foreword by S. Thomas Russell   ix

Introduction   xv

I.   The *Empress of Ireland* Sails to Her Doom   1

II.   Captain Kendall Blames the *Storstad*   15

III.   Captain Andersen's Defense   21

IV.   Miraculous Escape of the Few   25

V.   The Stricken Survivors Return   33

VI.   Heroes of the *Empress* Disaster   52

VII.   The Surgeon's Thrilling Story   58

VIII.   Ship of Death Reaches Quebec   63

IX.   Solemn Services for the Dead   71

X.   Crippling Loss to Salvation Army   81

XI.   Notable Passengers Aboard   99

XII.   List of Survivors and Roll of the Dead   107

Contents

XIII.   The *Storstad* Reaches Port   118

XIV.   Parliament Shocked by the Calamity   125

XV.   Messages of Sympathy and Help   127

XVI.   Placing the Blame   134

XVII.   *Empress* in Fact, as in Name   151

XVIII.   The Norwegian Collier *Storstad*   155

XIX.   The St. Lawrence: A Beautiful River   157

XX.   The Tragic Story of the *Titanic* Disaster   169

XXI.   The Most Sumptuous Palace Afloat   173

XXII.   The *Titanic* Strikes an Iceberg!   182

XXIII.   "Women and Children First!"   192

XXIV.   Left to Their Fate   217

XXV.   The Call for Help Heard   226

XXVI.   In the Drifting Lifeboats   231

XXVII.   The Tragic Homecoming   250

XXVIII.   Other Great Marine Disasters   280

XXIX.   Development of Shipbuilding   288

XXX.   Safety and Lifesaving Devices   295

XXXI.   Seeking Safety at Sea   302

Afterword   315

FACTS ABOUT THE WRECK OF THE
EMPRESS OF IRELAND

Number of persons aboard: 1,477

Number of persons saved: 465

Number of persons dead: 1,012

Total number of first-class passengers: 87

Total number of second-class passengers: 253

Total number of third-class passengers: 717

Total number of crew: 420

The Salvation Army delegation numbered 150; of these 124 were lost.

The *Empress of Ireland* was a twin-screw vessel of 14,500 tons.

The vessel was built in Glasgow in 1906 by the Fairfield Company, Ltd., and was owned by the Canadian Pacific Railway.

The *Storstad* was a single-screw vessel, registering 6,028 tons.

The vessel was built by the Armstrong, Whitworth Company at Newcastle in 1911, and is owned by the Dampsk Aktieselk Maritime of Christiania, Norway.

FOREWORD

In May of 1914 the world did not appear to be on the verge of cataclysm. March of that year saw Babe Ruth play his initial game as a professional. Charlie Chaplin appeared in his first film, and a few months later, the Tramp made his debut. The last-known passenger pigeon did die in the Cincinnati zoo, bringing that once-numerous species to its final end, but apparently few saw this as an omen of things to come. Richard Patrick Russ was born, though he would not change his name to Patrick O'Brian and begin living the famous lie for some time. William S. Burroughs and Sonny Boy Williamson made their appearance on the planet, as did Dylan Thomas, Hedy Lamar, Jackie Coogan, and Dorothy Lamour. Given that list of luminaries (and it is far from complete), one would think it was in fact an auspicious year. A year that marked great things to come. But then, 1914 also saw the introduction of the "hobble skirt" (wide at the hips but so narrow at the ankles it made a normal stride impossible). Like the fashion world, mankind stumbled, guilelessly, into the summer of that year and the opening weeks of the War to End All

Wars. In the next few years over sixteen million would die as a direct result of that conflict and twenty million more would be wounded.

It is not surprising, given the early date—May 28—that the passenger liner *Empress of Ireland* departed her berth in Quebec City with the usual fanfare, goodbyes, and excitement. She was not new to the route, having crossed the Atlantic numerous times, and her captain, though new to the ship, was an experienced officer of good reputation and many years' experience. Twelve hours later the *Empress* was lying on the bottom in relatively shallow water and over a thousand people, who had waved to friends as they boarded, were dead. Her position, unlike more famous wrecks, was never a great mystery, and she has been reachable by divers from fairly early days. Had she sunk by daylight, land would have been visible, and had the waters been warm, a strong swimmer could have reached the shore.

The loss of the *Empress of Ireland* followed on the heels of the sinking of the *Titanic* two years earlier, on April 15, 1912, and preceded, by three years, the loss of the *Lusitania*, May 7, 1915. Over 3,700 lives were lost from the three ships, 1,012 from the *Empress* alone. (A fourth sinking, less well known, was the SS *Eastland*, which rolled over in her berth in Chicago, drowning over 800 passengers and crew.) From the vantage of a century later, the sinkings of these passenger liners in the early years of the twentieth century seem like a warning of the limits of technology and science, but then usable radar had not yet been developed, which almost certainly would have prevented two of the accidents. (Several inventors, including Marconi and Tesla, had suggested that radio waves could be used to detect and determine the course and speed of ships but no one seemed to take this idea seriously for many years.)

The sinking of the *Lusitania*, by a German submarine off the coast of Ireland, evokes, even today, deep feelings of anger and outrage, though divers have established beyond all doubt that she did carry war munitions. She was the swiftest, and briefly, largest liner of her time but went to the bottom in fewer than twenty minutes after being struck by a torpedo.

The *Titanic*, certainly the most famous loss of a ship in modern times, has been the subject of countless movies, books, and documentaries. The largest ship of her day, and advertised as unsinkable, her loss became a story of hubris, tragedy, and oddly, romance. The sinking of the *Titanic* seemed to signal the end of an era, with images of those first-class passengers in black tie, kicking bits of the iceberg about the deck and having a good laugh. Every film seems to have a romance, the most recent featuring the young Kate Winslet and Leonardo DiCaprio engaged in their doomed love affair. The fact that the *Titanic* took almost three hours to sink lends itself to drama in a way that the other tragedies do not, and also preys upon some dark part of the human imagination. The *Empress* and *Lusitania* took fourteen minutes and eighteen minutes to disappear beneath the surface, which has made them challenging subjects for dramatists (though, in the case of *Lusitania*, it has not stopped them from trying).

There is a certain sad irony that, only days before the *Empress of Ireland* was lost, the British Parliament had passed the bill establishing Irish Home Rule. The *Empress* lost her country and her life in a few short days. The assassination of Archduke Franz Ferdinand, which set in motion events that led to World War I, occurred exactly one month later and the outbreak of that terrible conflict was only two months distant. The loss of a thousand lives on the *Empress*, though a terrible tragedy and news all over the world at the time, became quickly insignificant when men were marched, by the tens of thousands, across no-man's-land and into the waiting machine-gun fire. The sinking of the *Empress of Ireland* was lost in a whirl of more momentous events. Machines designed to kill were so much more efficient than those that merely killed by accident.

That the *Empress* went down in the middle of the night (2 A.M.) and so quickly meant that many of her passengers never reached the decks and even fewer made it into the boats that were launched before she listed too far to make further launchings possible. The officers of the *Empress* had spotted the Norwegian collier *Storstad* at a distance of five miles, and the officers of the collier had seen the *Empress* at the same time. Had they followed the established rules for approaching ships, when the fog set in, they would likely have passed each other safely. Both captains deviated from these rules and it is apparent that both men subsequently lied during the inquiry. If one were to believe the two captains, both ships were at a standstill, or nearly so, when the bow of the *Storstad* penetrated the side of the *Empress* to a depth of twelve feet. Captain Kendall of the *Empress* claimed that he called out to the *Storstad* to keep moving forward so that her bow would partially plug the hole she had created in the liner's side. Captain Andersen of the *Storstad* reported that he attempted to do just that, but because the *Empress* was moving so quickly, her bow was torn free of the other ship. The Canadian inquiry exonerated Kendall and placed the blame on poor weather and the actions of the Norwegian ship and her captain. A Norwegian inquiry found the opposite. Had both ships altered course to pass port to port, collision would almost certainly been avoided.

Today the sinking of the *Empress of Ireland* is far less well known than the *Titanic* and the *Lusitania*. It happened in Canadian waters and Canadians, unlike their American cousins, are not great constructors of myth or creators of heroes. The founders of the American republic are mythical figures; the men who created Canada out of the various British colonies were simply men, and some very flawed men at that. Patton, Bradley, and MacArthur were mythic and heroic, whereas Canadian general Curry, who was very likely a military genius, is a man who returned to Canada after World War I to bad debts and some dubious financial dealings. He was human.

The *Empress of Ireland* and her loss have never attained the mythic stature of the loss of the *Titanic* or *Lusitania*, yet there was horrible loss of life, tragedy, and human complicity (and, like *Titanic*, the *Empress* had watertight bulkheads that did not save her). In some ways the tragedy is even greater, for the accident should have been easily avoided.

The great loss of life on the *Empress* will always make her memorable, at least to maritime historians, and the number—1,012 dead—will always horrify the rest of us. It is, however, worth noting that deaths on America's roads are so much greater than this (over 34,000 last year alone) that it makes one wonder why we should even notice the loss of a thousand lives, it is so paltry by comparison. Somehow, sinkings, and the great loss of life in a single event, will always have a hold on the human imagination. Images of the great ships slipping beneath the sea, and the passengers thrown into the frigid waters, are the stuff of nightmare, and the fear of drowning is so very primal that we are all in its grip. In the history of maritime tragedies the *Empress of Ireland* will always loom large, and it is fitting that we should remember her and the people who did not survive. These accidents changed the design of ships and all of their safety precautions so that such accidents seldom occur, and when they do, boats and rafts, with capacity for all passengers, can be launched in minutes.

The loss of these classic liners taught us another lesson—which should never be forgotten: we are only human and the sea remains a great, indifferent God.

S. Thomas Russell
S. V. Watersmeet
August 2013

CANADA MOURNS

INTRODUCTION

T hose who go down to the sea in ships" was once a synonym for those who gambled with death and put their lives upon the hazard. Today the mortality at sea is less than it is on common carriers on land. But the futility of absolute prevention of accident is emphasized again and again. The regulation of safety makes catastrophes like that of the *Empress of Ireland* all the more tragic and terrible. A blow, a ripping, the side taken out of a ship, darkness, the inrush of waters, a panic, and then in the hush the silent corpses drifting by.

So with the Canadian liner. She has gone to her grave leaving a trail of sorrow behind her. Hundreds of human hearts and homes are in mourning for the loss of dear companions and friends. The universal sympathy which is written in every face and heard in every voice proves that man is more than the beasts that perish. It is an evidence of the divine in humanity. Why should we care? There is no reason in the world, unless there is something in us that is different from lime and carbon and phosphorus, something that makes us mortals able to suffer together—

Introduction

"For we have all of us an human heart."

The collision which sent the *Empress of Ireland* to the bottom of the St. Lawrence with hundreds of passengers in their berths produced a shudder throughout the civilized world. And the effect on the spirits of the millions who received the shock will not soon pass off. The *Titanic* tragedy sat heavy on the minds of the people of this generation for months after it happened.

There is hardly anyone in touch with world affairs who will not feel himself drawn into the circle of mourners over such a disaster. From every center of great calamity waves of sympathetic sorrow spread to far-distant strangers, but the perishing of great numbers in a shipwreck seems to impress our human nature more profoundly than do accidents or visitations of other kinds in which the toll of death is as great. Our concern for those in danger seems to turn especially to those in peril on the sea.

Science has wrought miracles for the greater protection of those afloat. Wireless telegraphy, airtight compartments, the construction which has produced what is called "the unsinkable ship," have added greatly to the safety of ocean travel. But science cannot eliminate the element of error. None of the aids that the workers for safe transit have bestowed on navigation could avail to prevent what happened in the early hours of May 29, 1914. The *Empress of Ireland* was rammed by another vessel, and so crushed as to be unable to remain afloat for more than fifteen minutes after the impact.

Overwhelmed by the catastrophe, we fall back upon that faith in the Unseen Power which is never shaken by the appearance of what seems to be unnecessary evil or inexplicable cruelty. Trust in God involves the belief that behind the stupendous processes of natural life there is a divine wisdom so deeply grounded upon reality that no human mind can comprehend its precepts and a divine love so boundless in its compassion that no human heart can measure its scope. We concede the knowledge of the divine mind to be "too wonderful" for our understanding. "It is high: I cannot attain unto it."

Therefore we are prepared for the awful, the mysterious, and even the terrible. Nothing in the universal process can disturb or confound us. If a thing appears to be evil it is wisdom which is at fault. If an event seems to be cruel it is our love which is blind. We look upon the chances and changes of human experience even as we gaze at night upon the movements of the heavenly spheres; we would as little think of questioning the beneficence of the one as of the other.

Come sorrow or joy, failure or success, death or life—it is all the same. We trust God, and therefore we trust life, which is simply the thing that God is doing. "Though he slay me, yet will I trust in him!" Yea, it is only when God seems to slay us that we *can* trust in Him, for trust begins only when knowledge fails; just as the stars shine only when the sun is gone!

HE IS THE PILOT IN A FOG

1

The *Empress of Ireland* Sails to Her Doom

ANOTHER TOLL OF THE SEA—THE *EMPRESS* SAILS FROM QUEBEC—
THE HOLIDAY HUMOR OF THE PASSENGERS—CAPTAIN KENDALL
WARNED OF FOGS—THE *STORSTAD* SIGHTED—FOG SUDDENLY
SETTLES—THE *STORSTAD* CRASHES INTO THE *EMPRESS*—INJURY
ON STARBOARD SIDE—A MORTAL BLOW—WIRELESS CALLS FOR
HELP—HUNDREDS DROWN IN CABINS—NO TIME TO ROUSE
PASSENGERS—LIFEBOATS LAUNCHED IN RECORD TIME—
THE *EMPRESS* GOES DOWN

Once again an appalling sea disaster comes to remind us that no precautions man can take will make him immune against the forces that nature, when she so wills, can assemble against him. It is a truism to say that the most recent marine disaster was preventable. An accident suggests the idea of preventability. The *Empress of Ireland* was equipped with modern appliances for safety. She had longitudinal and transverse watertight steel bulkheads and the submarine signaling and wireless apparatus. She was being navigated with all the precaution and care which the dangers of the course and the atmospheric conditions demanded. The *Storstad* had been sighted and signaled. The *Empress* was at a standstill, or slowly moving backward in response to a hasty reversal of the engines. Nothing apparently that those responsible for the lives of their passengers could do to safeguard those lives was left undone, and yet hundreds of people perished miserably.

The *Empress* Sails from Quebec

Proudly the *Empress of Ireland*, under the command of Lieutenant Henry George Kendall of the Royal Navy Reserves, moved from her dock at Quebec, about half past four on the afternoon of Thursday, May 28, 1914, bound for Liverpool. Amid scenes that are ever new and full of deep feeling to those who are taking their leave or bidding Godspeed to dear ones, the majestic ship began what her hundreds of lighthearted passengers anticipated as a bon voyage. The last "Goodbye, and God bless you!" had been said; the last embrace had been bestowed; the last "All ashore that's going ashore" had been called out; the last home stayer had regretfully hurried down the gang board; and then, while hands, hats, and handkerchiefs were waved, with the ship's band playing a solemn hymn, distance grew apace between the *Empress* and the land.

The Holiday Humor of the Passengers

Fainter and fainter the crowd on the dock appeared to the passengers on board, until finally the dock itself was lost to view as the graceful vessel gained headway. Some of the passengers remained long at the ship's rail, held by the fascination of the water, which seemed swiftly to approach, and as swiftly to move away. Others, singly or in groups, left the rail to arrange their belongings in their staterooms, to inspect the magnificence of the vessel's equipment, and to accustom themselves to their new surroundings.

Twilight settled without dampening the gay humor of the throng. The first meal on board was eaten with a relish which only the occasion could impart, and the passengers disposed themselves for the full enjoyment of the evening.

Captain Kendall Warned of Fogs

Captain Kendall had been warned of the prevalence of fogs in the lower river, and information had reached the liner also that there were forest fires in Quebec which were throwing smoke blankets over the St. Lawrence. Having experienced such conditions before, the commander of the *Empress*, while quite unalarmed, took the usual precautions.

As night came on he reduced the liner's speed. The night was still clear when the incoming Alsatian passed so closely that her passengers had a fine view of the big Canadian Pacific Railway ship, which showed beautifully and majestically as she swung by with her decks blazing with electric lights.

Captain Kendall stopped his ship at Rimouski, a town of 2,000 inhabitants, on the New Brunswick shore, about 180 miles northeast of Quebec as the channel flows. It is a mail station, the last outpost of the Dominion mail service. Bags of mail were loaded aboard, and the *Empress* moved steadily out into the broad river.

At this point the St. Lawrence, leading into the inland sea, which is the Gulf of St. Lawrence, is thirty miles wide. The channel runs about ten miles from the New Brunswick shore and about twenty miles from the Quebec shore.

At midnight the tide was running in strongly. The weather was cold and there was a piercing sting to the air. The mercury had fallen to just above the freezing point. Few passengers were stirring after midnight. It was too cold on deck to make late vigils pleasurable.

There were a few parties in the smoking room at bridge and poker, but the great majority of the passengers were in their berths.

The *Storstad* Sighted

At half past one o'clock Friday morning the *Empress* reached Father Point, where the pilot was dropped. The vessel then proceeded at full speed. After passing the Cock Point gas buoy, Captain Kendall sighted the Norwegian collier *Storstad*. To quote from his own story, as he has told it in another chapter: "The *Storstad* was then about one point on my starboard bow. At that time I saw a slight fogbank coming gradually from the land and knew it was going to pass between the *Storstad* and myself. The *Storstad* was about two miles away at the time.

Fog Suddenly Settles

"Then the fog came and the *Storstad* lights disappeared. I rang full speed astern on my engines and stopped my ship. At the same time I blew three short blasts on the steamer's whistle, meaning 'I am going full speed astern.' The *Storstad* answered with the whistle, giving me one prolonged blast. I then looked over the side of my ship into the water and saw my ship was stopped. I stopped my engines and blew two long blasts, meaning 'my ship was under way but stopped and has no way upon her.' He answered me again with one prolonged blast. The sound was then about four points upon my starboard bow. It was still foggy. I then looked out to where the sound came from. About two minutes afterward I saw his red and green lights. He would then be about one ship's length away from me.

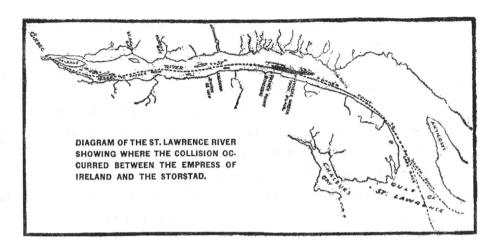

DIAGRAM OF THE ST. LAWRENCE RIVER
SHOWING WHERE THE COLLISION OC-
CURRED BETWEEN THE EMPRESS OF
IRELAND AND THE STORSTAD.

The safety of the St. Lawrence has long been the subject of debate. Certainly it has certain natural features which make it dangerous at some seasons of the year; and of course lack of knowledge of its waters and the absence of aids to navigation were the cause of wrecks in the early stages of its navigation. But the same might be said of any other great route of trade; and there can be no question whatever that the various governments of Canada have for many years been wide-awake to adopt means of protecting mariners on this greatest water route into the heart of the American continent. Today, so great has been the progress made, that it is a common opinion of shipping men that it is almost as safe to navigate the ship channel up to Montreal by night as in the full light of day.

The *Storstad* Crashes into the *Empress*

"I shouted to him through the megaphone to go full speed astern as I saw the danger of collision was inevitable. At the same time I put my engines full speed ahead, with my helm hard aport, with the object of avoiding, if possible, the shock. Almost at the same time he came right in and cut me down in a line between the funnels."

Captain Thomas Andersen, who commanded the *Storstad*, gives a different explanation of the approach of the two ships. According to his version, which is given elsewhere under his own name, "The vessels sighted each other when far apart. The *Empress of Ireland* was seen off the port bow of the *Storstad*. The *Empress of Ireland*'s green or starboard light was visible to those on the *Storstad*. Under these circumstances the rules of navigation gave the *Storstad* the right of way. The heading of the *Empress* was then changed in such a manner as to put the vessels in a position to pass safely. Shortly after a fog enveloped first the *Empress* and then the *Storstad*.

"Fog signals were exchanged. The *Storstad*'s engines were at once slowed and then stopped. Her heading remained unaltered. Whistles from the *Empress* were heard on the *Storstad*'s port bow and were answered. The *Empress of Ireland* was then seen through the fog close at hand on the port bow of the *Storstad*. She was showing her green light and was making considerable headway.

"The engines of the *Storstad* were at once reversed at full speed and her headway was nearly checked when the vessels came together."

Injury on Starboard Side

The horrible fact, about which there can be no dispute, is that the *Storstad* crashed bow on into the side of the big Canadian liner, striking it on the starboard side about midway of its length. The steel-sheathed bow of the collier cut through the plates and shell of the *Empress* and penetrated the hull for a distance of about twelve feet, according to the best testimony.

The water didn't flow in. It rushed in. From such stories as could be gathered from survivors and from members of the crew, it appears that Captain Kendall and his officers did all that was humanly possible in the fourteen minutes that the *Empress* hung on the river.

Captain Kendall said that he rang to the engine room for full speed ahead, with the object of trying to run ashore and save the passengers, but almost immediately after the engines stopped and the ship began to list rapidly. The captain of the *Storstad* declares that it was this action of Captain Kendall that prevented him from holding the bow of the *Storstad* in the gaping hole it made and that it was the *Empress* herself, with the way upon her, following the order "full steam ahead," which drew away from the *Storstad*, bending the collier's bow out of the great gash in the liner's side, and disappeared in the fog. What further damage may have been done as the vessels parted no one seemed to know certainly.

Fought for Life in Darkness

Instantly, it seemed as though there was a nightmare of sounds, cries of fear and agony that were too awful to be real. All lights went out almost at once. More than 1,400 persons were fighting for life in the black dark; yet for the most part the flight was not one of panic, but grim determination to find, if possible, some means of safety.

Wireless operator Bomford and others who managed to win a way to the top deck saw scores leap into the sea. They saw hundreds trying to crawl up decks that were sloping precipitously, lose their balance, and fall backward into the rising water. Passengers who couldn't get to the few lifeboats in time seized chairs, anything loose they could find, and leaped into the river.

Very many persons perished in the cold water while clinging to bits of wreckage and praying for help.

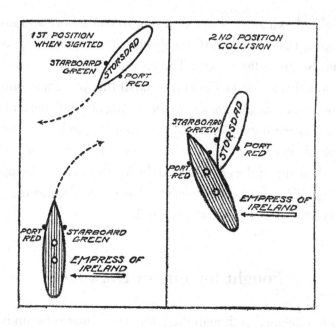

THE COLLISION ON THE ST. LAWRENCE

To make clear the somewhat contradictory testimony of Captain Kendall, of the *Empress of Ireland*, and Captain Andersen, of the collier *Storstad*, as to what took place just before and at the time of the fatal collision, diagrams Nos. 1 and 2, which are based on their statements, tell their own story. In No. 1 the vessels are shown in the position in which they were when first sighted, about which position both captains agree, the *Storstad* coming up the river on the starboard, or right side of the *Empress of Ireland*, so that those on the *Storstad* saw the green, or starboard, light of the *Empress of Ireland* over the port, or left, bow of the *Storstad*. The collier was in such a position that those on the *Empress of Ireland* could see both its red, port, light and its green, starboard, light. If the rules of the sea had been observed, the *Empress of Ireland* would have gone off to the right or steered to starboard so that the vessels would have passed each other easily. Instead, both vessels took a course which finally ended in position No. 2, in which the *Storstad* struck the *Empress of Ireland* between the funnels on the right, or starboard, side, hitting it a glancing blow with its starboard, or right, bow. As to how this fatal position was reached, the captains disagree, the question of the kind of signals and what response was made, or should have been made, being in dispute.

A Mortal Blow

In a moment the fate of the *Empress* was known to all. The one smashing blow had done for her and the great bull nose of the 3,500-ton freighter had crashed through the ribs and bulkheads. The one pithy sentence of Captain Kendall summed all. "The ship is gone," he said. "Women to the boats."

Kendall was hurt and in great pain, but he showed the pluck and decision of a naval officer. In the first minute of the disaster he ordered young Edward Bomford, the wireless operator, to flash the SOS call, the cry for help that every ship must heed. He ordered officers and stewards to collect as many passengers as could be found and hold them for the boats. He had nine lifeboats overboard within ten minutes.

Wireless Calls for Help

The SOS call was ticked out by Edward Bomford, the junior wireless operator. Bomford had just come on duty to relieve Ronald Ferguson, when the *Storstad* rammed the *Empress*. Both young men were thrown to the deck. As they picked themselves up they heard the chorus of the disaster, the cries, groans, and screams of injured and drowning passengers.

An officer came running to the wireless house with orders from Captain Kendall, but Bomford, at the key, didn't have to wait for orders. He began to call the Marconi Station at Father Point, and kept at it desperately until he had the ear of the Father Point operator.

Then young Bomford turned his wireless to search the river and gulf, and he hurled the news of the *Empress*'s fate for 500 miles oceanward. Many steamships picked up the call, but they were hours away. They started for the position given, but long before they had made any progress the *Empress* and two-thirds of her ship's company were under fifteen fathoms of water. Fourteen minutes is too brief a time for much rescue work.

Hundreds Drown in Cabins

Had there been time, hundreds who went down with the ship would have survived. A thousand men and women who had been asleep awoke too late to scramble to the decks. They were crushed or mangled by the bow of the *Storstad*, injured by splintered timbers, or overwhelmed in the terrific rush of water.

It is probable that scores who were asleep were killed instantly, but hundreds perished while feebly struggling for doorways, or while trying for a footing on sloping decks. The terror and confusion of the few minutes, while the *Empress* staggered, listed, and sank, can hardly be put in words. The survivors themselves could not describe those minutes adequately.

In the brief space of time between the shock of the collision and the sinking of the liner, there was little chance for systematic marshaling of the passengers. Indeed, everything indicates that hundreds of those on the steamer probably never reached the decks.

No Time to Rouse Passengers

The stewards did not have time to rouse the people from their berths. Those who heard the frenzied calls of the officers for the passengers to hurry on deck lost no time in obeying them, rushing up from their cabins in scanty attire. They piled into the boats, which were rapidly lowered, and were rowed away. Many who waited to dress were drowned.

The horror of the interval during which the *Empress of Ireland* was rapidly filling and the frightened throngs on board her were hurrying every effort to escape before she sank was added to by what seemed like an explosion, which quickly followed the ripping and tearing given the liner by the *Storstad*'s bow. As Captain Kendall afterward explained, this supposed explosion was in reality the pressure of air caused by the inrushing water. The ship's heavy list as the water pouring in weighted her on the side she was struck, made the work of launching boats increasingly difficult from moment to moment, and when she finally took her plunge to the bottom, scores still left on her decks were carried down in the vortex, only a few being able to clear her sides and find support on pieces of wreckage.

In Their Nightclothes

Many passengers fortunate enough to get into the lifeboats found themselves garbed only in their nightclothes. No baggage was saved. The condition of the survivors was pitiable. Some had broken arms and legs, and all had suffered terribly. L. A. Gosselin, a prominent lawyer from Montreal, saved himself by clinging to a raft.

Picked Up the Captain

Ernest Hayes, an assistant purser, said that he leaped from the promenade deck a minute or two after the collision. He climbed into No. 3 lifeboat, which, a few minutes later, picked up Captain Kendall.

J. W. Black and his wife, who live in Ottawa, jumped together before the ship sank. They got on deck too late to find places in a lifeboat. They decided to jump and take their chances. Fortune was with them, for it sent wreckage to Mr. Black's hand, and he kept his wife above water until a lifeboat reached them.

William Measures, of Montreal, a member of the Salvation Army band, jumped overboard and swam to a lifeboat. A young Englishman said there was a terrific shock when the *Storstad* struck. He had time only to throw a dressing gown over his pajamas and to awaken two of his friends.

To pluckily leap from the deck of the sinking liner and swim around for nearly an hour in the river, and then to fall dead from exhaustion on the deck of the *Eureka*, was the fate of an unknown woman.

Fourteen minutes settled the whole affair. With the decks careening, the captain, officers, and crew strove like fiends to release the boats. One after another, laden with a mass of humanity, sped away. The *Storstad* followed suit with as much ability, but the time was brief.

Boats there were aplenty, but time there was none.

When the listing increased and the nose of the ill-fated liner twisted skyward, panic seized upon the horde of persons, and once more a loud, prolonged burst of agony from several hundred throats vibrated through the fog.

Lifeboats Launched in Record Time

It takes five minutes to launch boats during a drill in harbor, when everything is calm and collected and the crews are all at their proper stations. The tarpaulin covering has to be removed, the falls cleared away and carefully tendered, and the boat fended off as it goes down the side.

But no more unfavorable conditions could be imagined than

those prevailing when the order "stand by to abandon ship" rang out from the bridge. The ship was listing over at a terrifying rate. The seas were flooding her aft, and in addition to the list she was sinking stern first.

Men hurled from sleep by the shock of the collision had to hurry to their stations in the confusion that must have been inseparable from such an accident. Precious moments inevitably were lost in getting the boat crews to their post, and all the time the ship was going down. Once the crew members were at their stations, the launching of the boats must have gone on with the precision of clockwork. It was all done in twelve minutes. That was remarkable discipline. That these nine boats were lowered successfully in the few minutes remaining before the ship made her final plunge is something that will be remembered forever.

The *Empress* Goes Down

While these frantic attempts at rescue were going on, the doomed ship was rapidly settling. Her decks were awash, and then, with a spasmodic heave, as if giant hands from below were pulling her down, the massive sea castle tilted to the bottom. Wreckage, spars and bobbing heads, and the few small boats trying to escape the vortex—with the slow heaving bulk of the collier in the background—alone marked the scene of the catastrophe.

SIR THOMAS SHAUGHNESSY, PRESIDENT OF CANADIAN PACIFIC, DEPLORES LOSS OF LIFE

Sir Thomas Shaughnessy, president of the Canadian Pacific Railway, issued the following statement on the morning of the *Empress* accident:

"The catastrophe because of the great loss of life is the most serious in the history of the St. Lawrence route. Owing to the distance to the nearest telegraph or telephone station from the scene of the wreck there is unavoidable delay in obtaining official details, but we expect a report from Captain Kendall in the course of the afternoon.

"From the facts as we have them, it is apparent that about two o'clock this morning the *Empress of Ireland* when off Rimouski and stopped in a dense fog was rammed by the Norwegian collier *Storstad* in such a manner as to tear the ship from the middle to the screw, thus making the watertight bulkheads with which she was provided useless. The vessel settled down in fourteen minutes.

"The accident occurred at a time when the passengers were in bed and the interval before the steamship went down was not sufficient to enable the officers to rouse the passengers and get them into the boats, of which there were sufficient to accommodate a very much larger number of people than those on board, including passengers and crew. That such an accident should be possible in the river St. Lawrence to a vessel of the class of the *Empress of Ireland* and with every possible precaution taken by the owners to insure the safety of the passengers and the vessel is deplorable.

"The saddest feature of the disaster is, of course, the great loss of life, and the heartfelt sympathy of everybody connected with the company goes out to the relatives and friends of all those who met death on the ill-fated steamship."

2

Captain Kendall Blames the *Storstad*

(Statement of Captain Kendall, Commander of the *Empress of Ireland*, Made at the Coroner's Inquest at Rimouski)

SLIGHT FOGBANK—NEARNESS OF STORSTAD—SIGNAL
GIVEN AND ANSWERED—SHOUTED TO COLLIER—SHIP BEGAN
TO FILL—LIFEBOATS OUT—DISTRESS SIGNALS—SHIP FOUNDERED
QUICKLY—CAPTAIN SHOT INTO THE SEA—RESCUED—WORK
TO SAVE OTHERS—NO PANIC ABOARD

After passing Cock Point gas buoy, I sighted the steamship *Storstad*, it then being clear.

The *Storstad* was then about one point on my starboard bow. At that time I saw a slight fogbank coming gradually from the land and knew it was going to pass between the *Storstad* and myself. The *Storstad* was about two miles away at that time. Then the fog came and the *Storstad*'s lights disappeared. I rang full speed astern on my engines and stopped my ship.

At the same time I blew three short blasts on the steamer's whistle, meaning "I am going full speed astern." The *Storstad* answered with the whistle, giving me one prolonged blast.

I then looked over the side of my ship into the water and saw my ship was stopped. I stopped my engines and blew two long blasts, meaning "my ship was under way, but stopped and has no way upon her."

He answered me again with one prolonged blast. The sound was then about four points upon my starboard bow.

Shouted to Collier

It was still foggy. I looked out to where the sound came from. About two minutes afterward I saw his red and green lights. He would then be about one ship's length away from me. I shouted to him through the megaphone to go full speed astern, as I saw the danger of collision was inevitable; at the same time I put my engines full speed ahead, with my helm hard aport, with the object of avoiding, if possible, the shock. Almost at the same time he came right in and cut me down in a line between the funnels.

I shouted to the *Storstad* to keep full speed ahead to fill the hole he had made. He then backed away. The ship began to fill and listed over rapidly. When he struck me, I had stopped my engines. I then ran full speed ahead again when I saw the danger was so great, with the object of running her on shore to save passengers and ship. Almost immediately the engines stopped, the ship filling and going over all the time, on the starboard.

In the meantime I had given orders to have the lifeboats launched. I rushed along the starboard side of the boat deck and threw all the grips out of numbers 1, 3, 5, and 7 boats; then I went back to the bridge again, where I saw the chief officer rushing along to the bridge. I told him to tell the wireless operator at once to send out distress signals. He told me that this had been done.

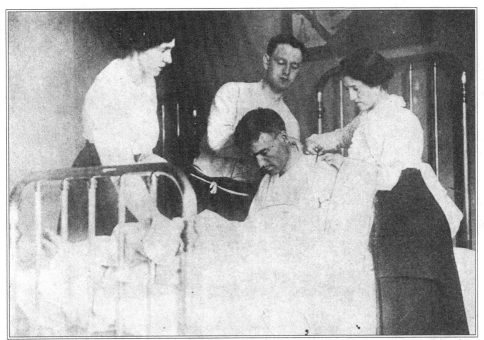

Photo by Underwood & Underwood, NY

ONE OF THE SURVIVORS

Many of those rescued were injured either in the collision or the rush that
followed it. This survivor's wounds are being dressed by the surgeon of the
lost ship, who also had a narrow escape.

RESCUED CREW OF THE *EMPRESS OF IRELAND*

A group of the crew on board the *Storstad* which sent the *Empress* to the bottom.

Ship Foundered Quickly

I said: "Get the boats out as quick as possible." That was the last I saw of the chief officer. Then, in about three to five minutes after that, the ship turned over and foundered. I was shot into the sea myself from the bridge and taken down with the suction. The next thing I remember was seizing a piece of grating. How long I was on it I do not know, but I heard some men shout from a lifeboat, "There is the captain, let us save him."

Work to Save Others

They got to me and pulled me in the boat. The boat already had about thirty persons in it. I did my best with the people in the boat to assist in saving others. We pulled around and picked up twenty or thirty more in the boat, and also put about ten around the side in the water, with ropes around their waists, hanging on.

Seeing that we could not possibly save any more, we pulled to the *Storstad*, which was then about a mile and a half away. I got all these people put on board the *Storstad*, then left her with six of the crew and went back and tried to save more. When we got back there everybody had gone. We searched around and could not see anybody alive, so then we returned to the *Storstad*.

No Panic Aboard

I had full control of the crew, and they fought to the end. There was no panic among the passengers or crew. Everybody behaved splendidly. As the ship sank and the water rose the boats floated away. The people who were saved were saved by the *Empress*'s boats and by the wreckage.

The *Storstad* had three or four of her boats out and they pulled around and took people off the wreckage. They did not get many.

3

Captain Andersen's Defense

(Captain Andersen's Account of the Accident, Contained
in a Statement Issued by the Agents of the *Storstad*)

A TERRIBLE AFFAIR—*STORSTAD*'S RIGHT OF WAY—FOG SIGNALS—
STORSTAD DID NOT BACK OUT—TO THE RESCUE—INJUSTICE TO
CAPTAIN—PLEA FOR SUSPENDED JUDGMENT

A fogbank settled down and we met. The *Empress* was struck amidships on her starboard side, listed, and filled rapidly. When we got clear I ordered all boats lowered, and we succeeded in taking off between 350 and 400 people with our crew of twenty-seven men. We transferred them to the *Lady Evelyn* and *Eureka*, and they steamed with them to Rimouski. Then we limped along under our own power to Montreal. It is a terrible affair. We did all in our power.

The fact that the *Storstad* only reached port on Sunday, May 31, made it impossible to give an authentic statement on her behalf before that. All connected with the *Storstad* deplore most deeply the terrible accident which has resulted in the loss of so many valuable lives. It is not with any desire to condemn others, but simply because it is felt that the public is entitled to know the facts, that the following statement is put forward:

Storstad's Right of Way

The vessels sighted each other when far apart. The *Empress of Ireland* was seen off the port bow of the *Storstad*. The *Empress of Ireland*'s green, or starboard, light was visible to those on the *Storstad*. Under these circumstances the rules of navigation gave the *Storstad* the right of way.

The heading of the *Empress* was then changed in such a manner as to put the vessels in a position to pass safely. Shortly after, a fog enveloped first the *Empress* and then the *Storstad*.

Fog signals were exchanged, the *Storstad*'s engines were at once slowed and then stopped. Her heading remained unaltered. Whistles from the *Empress* were heard on the *Storstad*'s port bow and were answered. The *Empress of Ireland* was then seen through the fog, close at hand on the port bow of the *Storstad*. She was showing her green light and was making considerable headway.

The engines of the *Storstad* were at once reversed at full speed, and her headway was nearly checked when the vessels came together.

Did Not Back Out

It has been said that the *Storstad* should not have backed out of the hole made by the collision. She did not do so. As the vessels came together, the *Storstad*'s engines were ordered ahead for the purpose of holding her bow against the side of the *Empress* and thus preventing the entrance of water into the vessel.

The headway of the *Empress*, however, swung the *Storstad* around in such a way as to twist the *Storstad*'s bow out of the hole, and to bend the bow itself over to port.

The *Empress* at once disappeared in the fog. The *Storstad* sounded her whistle repeatedly in an effort to locate the *Empress of Ireland*, but could obtain no indication of her whereabouts until cries were heard. The *Storstad* was then maneuvered as close to the *Empress* as was safe, in view of the danger of injury to the persons who were already in the water.

To the Rescue

The *Storstad* at once lowered every one of her boats, and sent them to save the passengers and crew of the *Empress*, though she herself was in serious danger of sinking. When two boats from the *Empress* reached the *Storstad*, the *Storstad*'s men also manned these boats and went in them to the rescue.

Her own boats made several trips and, in all, about 250 persons were taken on board and everything that the ship's stores contained was used for their comfort. Clothes of those on the *Storstad* were placed at the disposal of the rescued and every assistance was rendered.

Injustice to Captain

The statements which have appeared in the press, indicating that there was the slightest delay on the part of the *Storstad* in rendering prompt and efficient aid, do a cruel injustice to the captain, who did not hesitate to send out every boat he had in spite of the desperate condition of his own ship.

The owners of the *Storstad* ask of the public that, in all fairness to both the company and their commander, judgment as to where the blame for the disaster should rest be suspended until an impartial tribunal has heard the evidence of both sides.

When Captain Kendall shouted through the megaphone, I shouted back, but I did not have the megaphone at hand, so I shouted as loud as I could; our man on the lookout heard me call. I did go full speed ahead. I kept my hand on the telegraph to the engine room, and the very moment we touched the other ship I rang the engineer full speed ahead, but the *Empress* was going at a good speed and it was impossible for me to keep our bow in the hold. She disappeared from this ship and for a long time I kept my whistle blowing, but I heard nothing until the cries.

4

Miraculous Escape of the Few

HEROIC DEMEANOR OF CAPTAIN KENDALL—RESPONSE TO
WIRELESS CALLS FOR HELP—*EUREKA* AND *LADY EVELYN* ON
SCENE OF DISASTER—THE SEARCH FOR THE QUICK AND THE
DEAD—TERRIBLE PLIGHT OF SURVIVORS—SAD SCENES AT
RIMOUSKI—WILLING HANDS HELP—TWENTY-TWO DIE
AFTER BEING RESCUED—TALES OF NARROW
ESCAPES—THOSE WHO DIED BRAVELY

Amid the terrifying confusion, the awful darkness, and the harrowing scenes of death and despair, Captain Kendall bore
himself like a true sailor as long as his ship stood under him. He
retained such command of the situation that while the *Storstad*'s
stem still hung in the gap it had made in the *Empress*'s side, Captain
Kendall begged the master of the collier to keep his propellers going
so that the hole might remain plugged.

Captain Kendall stood on his bridge as the ship went down. One
of the boats from the liner picked him up, and he directed its work
of saving others until the craft was loaded. The captain was injured
in the crash and suffered from exposure.

Response to Wireless Calls for Help

Brief as was the time in which the SOS calls could be sent out from the wireless on the stricken *Empress,* they were caught by Crawford S. Leslie, the assistant wireless operator at Father Point. Leslie roused Whitehead, the chief operator, and John McWilliams, the manager of the telegraph company. Whitehead at once took charge of the wire, while McWilliams and Leslie notified the government boats *Eureka* and *Lady Evelyn.* The *Eureka* had steam up, having taken the mails to the *Empress* shortly before, and got under way at once, followed quickly by the *Lady Evelyn.*

Eureka and *Lady Evelyn* on the Scene of Disaster

The *Eureka* and *Lady Evelyn* found, on reaching the point where the *Empress* sank, a scene not dissimilar to that which greeted the liners which rushed to the *Titanic's* aid. They found the ship sunk, and the surface of the water, fortunately calm, dotted with lifeboats and smeared with floating debris from which many poor souls had been forced by exhaustion to loosen their hold.

In the lifeboats were huddled the survivors, dazed and moaning, some then dying of injuries sustained in the crash or in the rush of leaving the sinking *Empress.* Crushed by the collision, injured in their efforts to leap into lifeboats, or suffering from immersion in the icy water and exposure in the lifeboats in which they escaped, the survivors presented a pitiable condition.

The Search for the Quick and the Dead

The government steamships worked rapidly and took on the survivors from the lifeboats and a few persons that were clinging to bits of wreckage. Fifty dead bodies were picked up and the women cried aloud as they were brought aboard, some eagerly scanning the faces of the corpses for lost relatives and friends. Several of them walked around wringing their hands in a wild hysteria, and even the hardened members wept at the terribly pathetic scene.

One woman, whose identity was not established, let go her hold on a broken timber and tried to swim to the *Lady Evelyn*. She was nearly naked and too far gone from exposure to reach the steamship.

The *Eureka* picked up thirty-two of the survivors who were injured, and recovered a number of dead bodies. The *Lady Evelyn* rescued the great majority of the survivors. She also saved Captain Kendall.

The government boats, *Lady Grey* and *Strathcona*, on arriving later, found the *Eureka* and *Lady Evelyn* lying to in proximity to the *Storstad*, picking up scattered boats and searching among the scraps of floating debris.

Terrible Plight of Survivors

Many of the survivors were in a terrible condition following the exposure; the heartrending shock had driven some of them to the verge of hysterical insanity. Others, with the echo of the death screams ringing in their ears, were gathered in a dazed and pathetic condition. The fact that they were saved did not seem to be appreciated. The vision of death stayed with them for hours, and in many instances utter nervous collapse followed.

SECTIONAL VIEW OF THE EMPRESS OF IRELAND

Early impressions of the injury to the *Empress of Ireland* were that a large portion of the starboard side of the liner was torn open, as shown by the dotted line in the illustration. The testimony before the Royal Commission of Inquiry, however, gives no basis for this hypothesis, going to show only that the *Storstad* cut a great gash in the *Empress* on the starboard side near the forward funnel.

Photo by Bain News Service

THE WIRELESS STATION AT FATHER POINT

The first report of the disaster came to this station from the sinking ship.
"S. O. S.," came through the night again and again, and then suddenly ceased.
All was over, but the station saved many lives by calling ships to the rescue.

The *Eureka* and the *Lady Evelyn* cruised at the scene of the disaster for half an hour, until their commanders were certain that there were no more survivors to be picked up.

Sad Scenes at Rimouski

When the tug *Eureka*, with thirty-nine survivors, came up to the Father Point wharf, an agent of the Canadian Pacific Railway advised Captain Boulanger, of the tug, to put in at the Rimouski wharf for the reason that better care could be given to the survivors there. Rimouski is a town of 2,000, with doctors and medical facilities.

The Canadian Pacific official telephoned to Rimouski ahead of the *Eureka* and ordered all the cabs and doctors that could be obtained. Within an hour the *Eureka*'s rescued were being cared for at Rimouski. There were distressing, unforgettable scenes as the living and dead were delivered to the shore.

The *Lady Evelyn*, with survivors and corpses, arrived at the Rimouski wharf later. Among the rescued were men and women who had not had time to bring with them more than their nightclothes. The officers and crew of the mail tender had done what they could in providing coats, but their supply was not ample for the hundreds, and many suffered terribly from the cold.

The mercury was down to a few degrees above freezing and these wretched ones had endured exposure for more than two hours.

Willing Hands Help

At 6:10 A.M. the Norwegian collier *Storstad*, coal-laden from Sydney, Nova Scotia, for Montreal, came along slowly. When her bow was seen smashed in it became known that she was the vessel that had struck the *Empress of Ireland* the fatal blow. The *Storstad* was not too much damaged to allow her to proceed on to Quebec under her own steam. She also had some survivors and dead bodies, which were taken from her by the steamers *Eureka* and *Lady Evelyn* and landed on the Rimouski wharf.

Most of the population of Rimouski were at the wharf, ready and eager to do what was possible. They carried blankets, clothing, hot coffee, food, and medicines. The mayor, H. R. Fiset, was in charge of the relief work, acting with the local Canadian Pacific agents.

McWilliams, the wireless man from Father Point, had hurried over to assist in the relief work, and few gained more praise than was accorded to him. Every doctor in the town was hard at work for hours, going from house to house where the survivors were quartered.

Twenty-two Die After Being Rescued

Two relief stations were established, one at the wharf and one at the Intercolonial Railroad station, but these were not adequate for the care of so many. The grave problem was solved by the openheartedness of the townspeople, who turned over their own homes to the suffering. Of the survivors, it was found that forty-seven were from the second cabin. In this class had traveled about 150 Salvation Army delegates, who were on their way from the Dominion cities to attend a great international conference in London. Only a few of these were rescued.

Twenty-two persons died of their injuries or from exposure after being taken out of the lifeboats or from floating wreckage. One man suffered from broken legs. A woman was found who had a leg and arm broken. Others were crushed or injured internally. Many of the survivors were rushed to Quebec after they had had preliminary care at Rimouski.

Tales of Narrow Escapes

Some of the survivors were able to give snatches of their experience. One explained quietly that he had made up his mind that he had to die. The boats had gone. He could find nothing that promised to support him in the water. He made his way to the rail of the ship and waited until it sank.

As he went down he held his breath, held it for an age, it seemed to him, but finally he came to the surface and luckily near a lifeboat. A sailor seized him by the collar and hauled him in.

Those Who Died Bravely

The penetrating, lasting grief is that the fortunates who escaped were but few of the 1,475 souls that set sail on the *Empress*. Death's threatening wave engulfed almost all of them, but we may be sure that whether in the isolation of their cabins or in the crowded confusion of the final plunge on deck, they died bravely. That, indeed, seems to be the outstanding feature of this terrible tale of the sea. To face death unafraid, whether it comes in the sickroom, in tempest, fire, or flood, is the supreme test of fortitude. In our sorrow for those who died and for those who were bereaved let us remember that a thousand Canadians went to their deaths—as Britons for centuries have gone—masters of themselves, with head erect and spirit unconquered by the king of terrors.

5

The Stricken Survivors Return

EXTREME SUFFERING AMONG SURVIVORS—FEW WOMEN AND
CHILDREN SAVED—CROWD GREETS SURVIVORS—MANY INJURED—
EXPERIENCES OF SURVIVORS

A grim reminder of the fact that even the most perfect of modern Atlantic liners is subject to the dangers of the sea was given when the survivors of the passengers and crew who so gaily sailed from Quebec on Thursday returned to that city, ragged, exhausted, and wounded, leaving hundreds of their shipmates dead in the river or strewing the shore with their corpses.

Extreme Suffering Among Survivors

The survivors were carried by the special Intercolonial Railway, and a more mixed, worn-out crowd of passengers never appeared on a train in Canada. It was more like a relief train after a battle than a returning party from a steamship. The men were weary and worn, dressed in anything that could be secured at Rimouski to cover them, most of them having been rescued either nude or in their nightclothes.

Few Women and Children Saved

The women in the party were few, it being evident that the terrible experiences of the early part of the day, when the *Empress of Ireland* went to the bottom of the St. Lawrence, had claimed a far greater toll of the weaker sex.

Such few women as were left showed shocking traces of the hardships and anguish they had endured. Most of them were supported by men and, after disembarking from the train, walked through the lane of curious sightseers with drawn features and the utter indifference of suffering and fatigue.

A pathetic contrast was furnished by the presence of a few children in the sad procession, who had with the buoyancy of youth recovered from the shipwreck and prattled merrily to mothers or to their protectors when their mothers were not there, evidently enjoying the excitement of the rescue.

Crowd Greets Survivors

The crush about the train, notwithstanding the lateness of the hour, was tremendous. A huge crowd gathered in and near the station, which resounded with a cheer as the survivors filed on the platform. The latter experienced difficulty in passing through the portals to the waiting civic motorcars.

Some of the spectators endeavored to sing the Doxology, but it was a feeble effort. Heartbroken relatives sobbed, while others wandered aimlessly in and out of the crowd looking for an absent face. Three young girls were seen crying piteously for their parents who were drowned. They were taken in charge by a Salvation Army officer and conveyed to the Training Home.

Throngs surged forward and defied the policemen in an endeavor to snatch a glimpse of the saved ones. Leaning on the arm of a friend, a tall woman wearing huge bandages stepped first to the platform and her profound sigh of relief was heard by everyone in the hushed assemblage. Around her forehead was strapped a bandage. The chin bore a large zigzag of court plaster and a heavy black welt under the eye showed what painful injuries she had received. She was Mrs. Eddy from Birmingham, England. At the crash she had rushed to the deck in night attire, and this action resulted in her rescue.

Many Injured

Then came the long row of stretchers with their inert occupants. Every man was alive, but in many cases that was all. In spite of arms and legs broken in the grinding of wreckage, many of these cripples had remained afloat long enough to be seen and gathered in.

Every one of the invalids was rushed in a special ambulance to the Jeffrey Hale Hospital, while the slightly injured were allotted to quarters in the Chateau Frontenac.

Touching in its pathos was the contingent of third-class passengers. In little groups they huddled about the stateroom of the ferry, gazing at each other in dumb thankfulness, and rarely expressing a syllable. There were nine Russians and two Poles bound for their homeland. In the hour of peril they had leaped from the reeling decks, in many instances grasping to the end the little carpet and bandanna bundles which represented all their worldly effects.

Experiences of Survivors

The stories that were related by the survivors of the horrible disaster were dramatic, pathetic, and touched here and there with grim humor.

"All Over in Fifteen Minutes"

"It was just like walking down the beach into the sea. As the boat went over we climbed over the rail and slid down the stanchions onto the plates, and walked into the sea."

In this matter-of-fact manner did J. F. Duncan, of London, England, describe how he left his cabin on the promenade deck, in his pajama suit, and how he parted company with the ship.

When asked what he had to say about the disaster, he replied: "There is nothing to tell; it was all over in fifteen minutes. The signals woke me up and I lay in my berth amidships on the starboard side. That was the side the collier ran into us, but she was a low boat, and so my cabin was not crushed in as were some of those immediately below me. Directly [after] the collision occurred the *Empress* began to list, and I immediately went on deck.

"When I once got out of the cabin I could not get back, but fortunately I had taken my overcoat out of my baggage the previous night, and I slipped this on.

Knew It Was the End

"It was pretty rotten on deck. We simply stood there, we knew we were going down, there was no question about that from the first, and it was no good struggling. The poor women were hysterical, but there was no chance to do anything for them. When the steamer heeled over we walked into the water, and I struck out for the rescuing steamer, which was standing about half a mile off.

"Somehow or another the lifeboats appeared and began picking us up. I was in the water a jolly long time: it seemed like an hour and I believe it was an hour. It was terribly cold and I am stiff all over this morning. I eventually got into a lifeboat and was taken on board the collier. They told me there were fifty-three on the lifeboat—it was quite full up. Dr. Grant was on the collier, and he patched us up until the *Lady Evelyn* took us ashore.

"Like a Lot of Indians"

"We were like a lot of Red Indians when we got on the wharf—all wrapped up in blankets. I never saw such a big supply from so small a ship. They looked after us like princes at Rimouski. The local people were most kind—in fact, when you see me put on my clothes you won't think I had ever been shipwrecked. They got the clothes from the stores and fitted us all out—it was the most wonderful place in the world.

"Let me introduce you to my toilet," continued Mr. Duncan as he held up a toothbrush and a tube of toothpaste. "I do want a bath."

Mr. Duncan paid a high tribute to Dr. Grant. "He stood out as a typical Anglo-Saxon, calm, commanding, looking after the injured. He is a magnificent man."

Four Climbed on Upturned Lifeboat; Saved Many Lives

The sensation of sinking with the suction of the leviathan steamship as she went down, of being pulled down for fathoms underwater, and of rising on the crest of the reacting swell to catch the keel of an upturned skiff was the night's adventure of Staff Captain McCameron, of the Salvation Army, Toronto. The story as told in the captain's words is as follows:

"What an unspeakable confusion there was on the listing decks! With every lurch of the steamer we had to take a step higher and higher to the upper side, and finally I gained the rail, and stuck to it. I could swim, but I knew the mad folly of jumping into that swirling cataract at the side of the ship. She was sinking, inch by inch, now faster and faster. In a breathless moment, I felt the last rush to the bottom. A moment we hung on the surface. Then an endless, dreadful force dragged us down. How deep I went I cannot know, of course. It was yards and yards. Then came the cresting of the wave, and I was buoyed up on it. I had clutched tight at my senses meanwhile, and strove not to lose my head. The moment my head emerged, I saw a dark object on the water. I struck out for this, and soon was grasping the keel of an overturned ship's boat. I clambered aboard, not much the worse, and not very unduly excited.

"Three or four more men also managed to get on the rocking back of the boat, and we then got to another, which we righted and got into. The canvas covering had not been taken from this boat, and a member of the crew, who was of us, ripped this open and enabled us to board it. The oars were intact. Within a few minutes, therefore, we were at work rescuing the people whose bodies eddied about us in circles.

"One man grasped the end of my oar. He slipped. Again I reached his hand with it. Then he sank out of sight. A woman, a foreigner, had better fortune. The third time she did not slip off, and we managed to get her aboard. She was saved. I do not know her name. She was a steerage passenger.

"The ship's surgeon saved dozens of lives by his work of resuscitation on land. No sooner had we got to shore than he had us at work manipulating the chests and limbs of the apparently drowned in efforts to save them. He was a heaven-sent messenger to many stricken souls."

Salvation Army Lassie Rescued When About to Sink

Tales of each other's heroic rescues, and shuddering accounts of their own mishaps and fight for life in the swirling St. Lawrence, were told.

With a blanket thrown around her shoulders, her eyes lit with the wild excitement of the night of horror, Miss Alice Bales, one of the young women Salvationists who was saved, recounted how her struggles finally brought succor and safety. Her cheeks were successively hectic and pallid as she told the hideous story. She said:

"I thought we had struck an iceberg when I heard the fearful grinding in the bows. With a cry to the girls who were with me, I stumbled out of the narrow stateroom and groped up to the deck. Here was chaos. The ship was listing, listing, listing. Every step I took to the uppermost part of the deck, I seemed to be slipping back into that maelstrom of water and falling bodies. Finally, I gained the rail. I climbed up on the rail, and with a prayer in my heart I jumped into the blackness. The water surged over my head. Down, down, I went. I could not swim a stroke. But I remembered that you should keep the air in your lungs, and as I sank I clenched my jaws, determined to stay with the battle as long as strength lasted. After long, long periods of struggle and fainting and renewed struggle, I saw a man, not far off, swimming with a life belt. I forgot to tell you that I fastened a belt around my waist when I jumped.

"I reached my hand toward this hope of rescue, the man's belt. It eluded me. Finally I grasped it. Then I saw how the man made the swimming motions, like a frog. I tried to do the same. I used every fiber and nerve to make the motions. I knew this was the chance for life.

"Then, when my energy was going fast, I heard a faint cry. There was a cluster of people. It was a lifeboat.

"The next few moments are indistinct in my memory. Someone was lifting me, dragging me over something hard. Now they were speaking to me. They revived me, and I was got aboard the *Storstad*, the ship that struck us.

"I can't tell you any more. The scenes on the deck, ah—"

Climbed Up Side of Liner as She Keeled Over

A dramatic escape was related by Major Atwell of the Salvation Army, Toronto. Major Atwell lost all his belongings in the disaster. When he reached Montreal his clothing told of the struggle and its sequel. Peculiarly enough, as was the case with the *Titanic*, the shock of the collision was scarcely felt by a number of the passengers.

"My experience," said Major Atwell, "was that the slight shock scarcely worried me at all. I had an idea at the time that we had perhaps struck the tender, so slight appeared the shock. I did not look upon it as anything serious, but my wife thought I had better get up.

"My wife and I went on deck and we found that the vessel was listing and the list was increasing. It was all over in a few minutes. The list grew greater. It was so great that I could see no chance of getting into a lifeboat, even if one was launched, and I did not see how one could be launched. So I fastened a life belt round my wife and put one on myself.

"As the vessel heeled over, we clung to the rail and finally clambered over it on the side of the ship. As the boat sank, we clambered farther and farther along the side in the direction of the keel, until we had climbed, I think, a third of the way.

"Finally we jumped into the water and were picked up by one of the lifeboats."

Husband Gave Wife Belt; Plunged Out to Save Himself

Mrs. Atwell gave a graphic account of the struggle she and her husband, Major Atwell, had in the seething waters, narrating how with the one life belt between them her husband chivalrously placed this around her and himself struck out boldly into the waves.

"I was just lightly sleeping when I heard a slight crash," she said. "We thought the ship had struck the tender or pilot boat. Then I heard the engines start, going as hard as they could. I tried to rouse my husband. We got up almost directly, but by that time the water was coming in, and we climbed up on deck. My husband secured one life belt and placed it around me. We climbed over the rail, for the ship was listing heavily, but we hung on to the porthole for a few minutes, and then I heard a slight explosion. Then the water seemed to gush up, and my husband said, 'Jump!'

"In the water I grasped my husband's clothing and held on to his back; and there we just hung together and swam. My husband swims, but I just kicked and struggled and held on to him, and eventually I found my limbs very stiff, so that I had to be helped into the boat. We were put on the *Storstad* for a time and then on the *Lady Evelyn* and put into the cabin.

"One man who had a broken leg went insane. There was very little screaming, and there was nothing in the way of unseemly struggles."

Boat Listed So Badly People Could Not Get Up Deck Stairs

As Adjutant McRae, of the Salvation Army, Montreal, walked down the aisle of a sleeping car, a curtain rustled and parted.

"Oh, Adjutant! Alf! Look!"

"My boy!" came the adjutant's earnest answer as he reached upward to bury one of Captain Rufus Spooner's hands in both of his, and then turned to murmur broken words of cheer to Lieutenant Alfred Keith, who lay in the opposite bed. Both had escaped by a hairsbreadth.

"The awful thing," said Captain Spooner, "was to see the people trying to get up the staircase. The ship had listed so far over by the time we got up that to try to get upstairs was almost impossible. We got up a few steps, only to fall back again. All round me were frantic men and women, and then, before I could fairly realize where I was or what I could do next, I seemed to be lifted right up and carried forward off the ship into the water."

"I was rolled over and over, twisted round and round, banged against bits of wreckage, and got my foot caught in something of iron and rope. I thought I was gone then, for I'm not a great swimmer; but I managed to get free. I swam round till someone got me by the neck and I felt my head going under. I thought again I was gone for certain; but I got free the second time and started out again to try for a boat. It was a narrow shave."

"Yes, it was," put in Lieutenant Keith, "and mine was like it."

"The third time," went on the captain, "I had sense enough not to spend the little strength I had left, and I got hold of a spar and rolled over on it to keep myself up. I drifted like that for a long time till I was picked up and taken to Rimouski. All I've got left is my bunch of keys, which stuck in my pocket." He produced them and jingled them affectionately. "I'm going to hang on to them as a souvenir."

Picked Up by Boat Filled with Members of Crew

A member of the staff band of the Salvation Army, J. Johnson, of Toronto, got hold of a boat as it was drifting away from the steamer and hung to the side, and was saved in his night attire.

"We were all asleep in the second cabin when the crash came," he said. "I went upstairs to see what had happened and the other three fellows in the cabin stayed behind. Two of them were drowned and one got out. When I got up on deck I found the boat listing over and I ran back and told the others to come out.

"I saw the people struggling along the corridors to get on deck, but it was awkward because the water was coming into the vessel. Commissioner Rees and some others were just going along in front of me and I assisted them up as well as I could, and eventually we got to the deck, where I lost sight of them.

"The boat was listing so badly that I slid down to the lower end, nearest the water, and caught hold of the rails. I saw they were cutting away the boats, and by this time the steamer was nearly flat on its side. They had no time to launch the lifeboats, and as one went loose I jumped over and hung on to the side, and then got in. I hardly thought they would let me in at first, there were so many in it already. But every one was helpful. The desire to save themselves did not prevent the occupants of the boat from reaching out a helping hand to others.

IDENTIFYING THE DEAD AT QUEBEC

Salvation Army officers identifying their comrades. One hundred and fifty members of the organization were on the *Empress.*

THE SADDEST SIGHT OF ALL

Sailors taking the bodies of children from the *Lady Grey*, one of the government vessels.

"When I did get in all the ropes were not quite cut, and the liner was nearly on top of us. We seemed to be getting underneath the davits again, and expected every moment to go under. We managed to get away just in time, just as she was sinking, and we were only ten feet away from the steamer when she turned over and went under. While we knew there was no hope for us on the doomed vessel, it was a horrible sight to see her go down.

"There was not so much suction as I thought there would be. We were lifted up, the boat being on the top of a wave. We hung around quite a bit to see what the other boats were doing, and then we went to the collier.

"I think I was the only passenger in the boat. All the rest were from the crew. I don't know why this was so, but all the people were holding so to the higher side of the ship, and when the boat was cut free there was no one to get in her except the crew.

"We pulled two other men out of the sea—they were also members of the crew. There were nine saved out of the staff band of thirty-nine players. The bandmaster and his wife were drowned, but their little girl of seven was saved."

Toronto Woman Spent Long Time in Water Before Rescue

The highest tributes were paid by all to a brave woman who spent a longer time in the water than almost any other of the rescued. In telling her story, she said:

"I and my daughter were helped to the side of the ship by Bandsman McIntyre, of the Salvation Army. We crawled to the side, and as the ship leaned over we slid over the edge of the deck into the water.

"Oh, it was cold. I began to be numbed and lost track of my

daughter, of whom I have heard no news since. I don't know how long I was in the water; it was so cold, I had almost given up hope, when I seemed to feel arms lifting me out. Then it seemed to get colder than ever for a moment, and the next thing I remember I was on the collier with a crowd of other draggled individuals. From then on, everything was done for me, and even during the train journey up I managed to get rested up a little."

Unknown Member of Crew Saved Several Lives

Staff Captain McAmmond, of Toronto, relates how attempts were made by one of the crew of the *Empress* to pick up survivors from the water. Who the man was Captain McAmmond did not know, but he evidently saved several lives.

"As the *Empress* went down," said he, "I clung to the taffrail and hung over the vessel's stern. As she sank, I was dragged down into the water, but was immediately forced up again. Down I went again; again, I came up. Finally I managed to swim clear and succeeded in reaching an overturned lifeboat.

"There were several such. A man was already clinging to the boat and he helped me to get a firm hold. We floated along with the boat until we reached another. Holding to this, we found a member of the crew. It was a collapsible boat and under his instruction we were able to get it righted and use the oars.

"It was terribly cold in the water. Some of the people we assisted were so numbed that it was only with the greatest difficulty we succeeded in saving them."

Ottawa Man Put Wife in Boat; Was Saved Later

"Thank God I saved my wife; for myself I am not anxious," said John W. Black, of Ottawa, when he painfully limped across the platform of the Grand Trunk Station, carrying a little paper bundle— all his belongings—under his arm. His left leg was badly lacerated and he had much difficulty in walking to St. James Street, where a cab took him and his wife to the Windsor Station for the first train to Ottawa. Mrs. Black was cheerful and smiling in spite of bruises and scratches and the terrible exposure of the water and the cold night.

And this is the story, interrupted at times, as Mr. Black told it:

"I was asleep in my bunk when I felt the terrible impact of the collision. At first I thought it must be an evil dream and I saw visions of doomsday. But, looking out through the skylight, I saw frantic seamen rushing to the ship's side, sliding down, and, as often as not, being dashed headfirst into the sea. The *Empress of Ireland* was then keeling over.

"In a flash I saw that the thing had happened. Literally tearing my wife from her berth, I dashed onto the deck, and we both slid down the deck and were projected into the water. Then followed moments that no man could ever describe. Half drunk as I was with sleep, the sudden and terrible awakening produced an indescribable effect on me. For a moment I saw nothing but dirty gray. I struggled wildly for the surface, and the time seemed like years.

"As soon as I got to the surface I saw my wife struggling beside me. Right at our side was a deserted lifeboat which must have broken from its davits. I managed to push my wife into it, but was unable to follow myself. So I shouted to my wife to sit tight, and that I would swim until I was picked up.

"The last lifeboat was only a few yards away from me, passing by the side of the sinking *Empress*, when suddenly a huge, heavy super-structure broke from the steamer's side, falling with a terrible crash into the boat. I shut my eyes in horror. When I looked up again all that was left of the lifeboat and her forty-five occupants were a few stumps of wreckage. Poor people, they had gone to their doom! Fortunately death was sudden and merciful.

"A few minutes afterward I was picked up by one of the boats from the *Storstad*. I cannot express the joy and relief I felt when I saw my wife half seated, half lying in the boat. She was not badly hurt, however, and we soon were crying in each other's arms.

"The men of the *Storstad* treated us well the little time we remained on her. Not long after the rescue we were taken aboard the government vessel *Lady Evelyn*.

"At Rimouski we were treated and helped in every possible way by Mayor Fiset of Rimouski. He did all that could be done to help us."

Saw Collision; *Empress* Was Sounding Her Siren

A steerage passenger, John Fowler, was one of the few who actually saw the collision between the *Empress* and the *Storstad*. Fowler was from Vancouver, and immediately on arriving at Quebec rushed off to catch another train.

"I actually saw the *Storstad* approaching the *Empress*," Fowler affirmed.

"Was there any fog at the time?" he was asked.

"Yes," he replied, "there was fog, but it was not very thick."

"Did you notice whether the *Empress* had her siren going?"

"Yes, she had," was the reply. "I noticed it just before the collision."

"The shock," Mr. Fowler continued, "did not seem to be at all severe. I just felt it and had no idea the result had been so serious.

"The water came into our porthole, and reached above my shoulders before I could shut it. By that time the ship was heeling over so badly that it was difficult to get out. I heard the siren blowing a great deal, and got up to look out to see whether we were passing another vessel or were whistling for a pilot. I had just got my head out through the hole when the collier drove right into us just beyond me. And then we gradually went over to one side.

Fell into Water

"I tried to quiet the people when I got out," continued Fowler, "by telling them that it was all right, and that the boat would right herself. I saw a lady with two children, a small baby and one little girl of six, and I put on them a life belt each, which I grabbed from the spare ones by the side of the stairs. I took them on deck and in a kind of panic we lost each other, and I don't know if any of them were saved. Everyone was struggling to get on deck, and if I had not had strength I could not have got away. I climbed up to the second-saloon deck and went along there and saw Miss Wilmot struggling to get up the steps. She could not do so, as the boat was listing so badly and there was a lot of water in the passage, into which she fell back.

"The ship was so much to one side that you could walk on her plates as on a floor."

Montreal Man Saw No Life Belts

"When the boat commenced to slide over I looked for a life preserver, but found that someone had taken every one of them from the promenade deck. So I went back to my cabin and took the life preserver on the top of the wardrobe. The majority of passengers did not seem to know that there were life preservers in their cabins, and although they were easily accessible they were not conspicuous and many could not find them in the confusion, although they looked."

Thus did Lionel Kent, of Montreal, tell of the sinking of the *Empress*:

"I was in Cabin 41, which was aft on the promenade deck, and my traveling companion was Mr. Gosselin. He woke me about an hour after I had retired and told me there had been a collision. I did not feel it at all. I went on deck at once in my night attire and my bathrobe, and I saw the two boats just drifting apart. At that time there were no lights on the deck, and very few people were about, but they soon began to appear.

"I remained on the port side of the boat as the list continued until the starboard side was underwater. Then I jumped into the water with many other people, and was picked up ten minutes later by one of the lifeboats. Those in her, numbering about thirty, were mostly members of the crew, with four or five women.

"The boats on the port side of the liner could not be launched because, owing to the list of the ship, they swung inward on the davits instead of out over the sea. The only boats that could be launched were those on the starboard side.

"I think a good many people were injured by the sliding of the port lifeboat when it was released, for it slid along the deck to the starboard side and crushed many people against the railings.

"I think they did marvelously well considering the short time they had to work in. They could not get a foothold on the sloping deck, and there was very little confusion under the circumstances."

6

Heroes of the *Empress* Disaster

DR. GRANT THE CHIEF HERO—SIR SETON-KARR GAVE UP LIFE FOR
STRANGER—LAURENCE IRVING DIED TRYING TO SAVE HIS WIFE—
H. R. O'HARA DIED FOR FAMILY—CAPTAIN KENDALL SAVED
BELLBOY—HOW CHIEF OFFICER STEEDE DIED—HERO SAVED WEE
GIRL—GAVE UP HIS LIFE BELT

I n the luxurious Hotel Chateau Frontenac, in the seamen's mission, in the hospitals, and on ships, where the survivors of the *Empress of Ireland* disaster were cared for and nursed, they spoke of their dangers. There were stories of self-sacrifice in which men died that women might live, of battles in the water, of lifeboats falling on struggling men and women in the water.

Every such disaster as that which befell the *Empress of Ireland* seems to bring out at least one man who stands out above all others for coolness, resourcefulness, and courage. These are men who control mobs and who bring order out of chaos.

Dr. Grant the Chief Hero

The survivors united in laying such honor on the shoulders of Dr. James F. Grant, a 1913 graduate of McGill, the ship's doctor, who calmed the terror-stricken, kept hope alive in the breasts of those who felt themselves bereft of loved ones; who quieted the ravings of those whom the shock had, for a time, made insensible to those human attributes which make heroes; who went about among the rescued and gave them treatment, not only for their physical injuries, but for the awful mental shocks which had been endured.

Miss Grace Kohl, of Montreal, was among those who heralded the heroism of Dr. Grant. When she was asked to tell her story, she said:

"Miss Brown, the stewardess, wakened me and helped me put on my shoes and coat and a life belt. I went up on the promenade deck, but there was scarcely anyone there. Then the boat began to list in a really dangerous way, or so it seemed to me, and I jumped overboard. I swam around for about five minutes, and someone picked me up and placed me in a boat. That was all.

"But there was something else," she continued. "You must say something very, very nice about Dr. Grant. He was quite wonderful. The way he took charge of things on the *Storstad* and controlled the situation was marvelous. I think he deserves the thanks of everyone, and there is no doubt but that for his skill and quickness in tending people, many more would have died."

Sir Seton-Karr Gave Up Life for Stranger

M.D.A. Darling, of Shanghai, was saved by the life belt that might have saved Sir Henry Seton-Karr. Darling said:

"My cabin was opposite Sir Henry's, and when I opened my door he opened his, and we bumped into each other in the passageway. He had a life belt in his hand and I was empty-handed. Sir Henry offered me the life belt and I refused it.

"He said, 'Go on, man, take it or I will try to get another man.' I told him to rush out himself and save his own life while I looked after myself.

"Sir Henry then got angry and actually forced the life belt over me. Then he pushed me along the corridor. I never saw him after that. He went back to his cabin, and I believe he never came out again, because the ship disappeared a few minutes later.

"I owe the fact that I am alive to Sir Henry, and while I believe he lost his life because he wanted to give me the life belt, I am certain that he would have given it to someone else."

Laurence Irving Died Trying to Save His Wife

Laurence Irving, the noted actor, son of the late Sir Henry Irving, died trying to save his wife. F. E. Abbott, of Toronto, was the last man to see Irving alive.

"I met him first in the passageway," he said, "and he said calmly, 'Is the boat going down?' I said that it looked like it.

"'Dearie,' Irving then said to his wife, 'hurry, there is no time to lose.' Mrs. Irving began to cry, and as the actor reached for a life belt, the boat suddenly lurched forward and he was thrown against the door of his cabin. His face was bloody and Mrs. Irving became frantic. 'Keep cool,' he warned her, but she persisted in holding her arms around him. He forced the life belt over her and pushed her out of the door. He then practically carried her upstairs."

Abbott said: "Can I help you?" and Irving said, 'Look after yourself first, old man, but God bless you all the same.'" Abbott left the two, man and wife, struggling. Abbott went on deck and dived overboard. He caught hold of a piece of timber, and holding on tight, he looked around. Irving by this time was on the deck. He was kissing his wife. And as the ship went down they were both clasped in each other's arms.

H. R. O'Hara Died for Family

H. R. O'Hara, of Toronto, died that his wife and child might live. There were two life belts for three of them. He fixed the belts on the two, hoping that there would be buoyancy enough to hold up all three. Not one of them could swim. O'Hara bobbed in the water, resting on the belts to keep himself afloat. He saw the two sinking, and then slipping a little behind them, he disappeared beneath the water. Mrs. O'Hara was found afterward hysterically clinging to the keel of an overturned boat by Henry Freeman, of Wisconsin.

Captain Saved Bellboy

Charles Spencer, a bellboy on the *Empress*, told of the manner in which Captain Kendall of the *Empress* saved him. Still hysterical from the suffering he endured, he cried as he told of his experiences.

"When the crash came I ran down to the steerage to wake up the boys there and get them to go the bulkheads and turn them. They are closed by handwheels. I did not have much time, because when I reached there the water was two feet deep and I could hardly get through it. I know two of the boys were drowned there. I and another, Samuel Baker, were the only bellboys saved out of the dozen on the vessel. When I woke the boys below I ran to the boat deck, where the men were trying to put the lifeboats overboard. The *Empress* had a list to starboard and the top deck was down to the water. She was going very fast. One of the funnels toppled into the water and almost fell on a lifeboat. When the boat made a final lurch I dived into the water, because I felt I could get somewhere. When I came up Captain Kendall was near me. He caught hold of me and helped me along, and we were in the water about twenty minutes when we were picked up and taken to the coal boat."

How Chief Officer Steede Died

"There are few people," said one survivor, "who really know how the chief officer, Mr. Steede, died. He was at his post to the last and was killed by tumbling wreckage.

"Each man has his post at a certain boat, and his was at boat No. 8, on the port side. The ship was struck on the starboard, but an effort was made to launch the port-side boats at once after the collision. But the list on the vessel made it impossible to get away these boats.

"We went over to the port side. 'No good, boys, on this side,' said he. 'Go to the starboard.' We went there, but the chief officer remained at No. 8, directing passengers, until he was swept from his post either by falling ropes, boxes, or perhaps a boat, for the starboard boats broke loose and did a lot of damage to life. No one actually saw Steede disappear."

Hero Saved Wee Girl

The description of the wreck and the heartrending scenes that followed, given by Robert W. Crellin, of Silverstone, British Columbia, was graphic.

Crellin is a prosperous farmer. He was one of the heroes of the wreck. He saved Florence Barbour, the eight-year-old daughter of a neighbor, by swimming with the child on his back, and, with the aid of another rugged passenger, pulled two women and several men into a collapsible boat.

Clad only in a nightshirt, Crellin said the water and air were as cold as winter, chilling all hands to the bone.

Despite the peril and exposure, flaxen-haired Florence Barbour clung to Crellin's neck and never even cried.

"The child was pluckier than a stout man," said Crellin. "She never even whimpered, and complaint was out of the question. You should have seen how the girls and women in the little village of Rimouski hugged her when we got ashore.

"Time and time again I feared Florence would lose her hold, and I would speak to her when my mouth and eyes were clear. Each time her little hands would clutch me tighter, until it seemed she'd stop my breath, but I welcomed the hold because it showed she had the pluck and courage needed.

"Poor child! She lost her mother and sister, and only a year ago her father, William Barbour, of Silverstone, was killed. She's alone in the world, but Florence will never need a friend or home while I have breath in my body."

Big and rugged as he is, Crellin's eyes grew moist as he recalled how the child's mother and three-year-old sister, Evelyn, were drowned.

Gave Up His Life Belt

A well-built young fellow, Kenneth McIntyre, was disinclined to go into the part he had played, but a Salvation Army officer, also a survivor, related how McIntyre had taken his own life belt off a few minutes before the *Empress* took her last plunge, and put it about a woman close by. The woman was picked up later by one of the lifeboats.

7

The Surgeon's
Thrilling Story

BY DR. JAMES F. GRANT

(Ship's Surgeon on the *Empress of Ireland*)

HAD DIFFICULTY REACHING DECK—MANY PLUNGE
INTO ICY WATER—WEIRD SHRIEKS OF TERROR—PASSENGERS
CAUGHT LIKE RATS

I was in my cabin, and heard nothing until the boat listed so badly that I tumbled out of my berth and rolled under it. I concluded that something had gone wrong and tried to turn on the light, but there was no power. I tried to find the door bolt, but the list was so strong that it took me considerable time to open the door.

Had Difficulty Reaching Deck

When I reached the alleyway it was so steep, due to the way the ship was canted, that my efforts to climb up were rendered impossible by the carpet, which I was clinging to, breaking away. I then scrambled up, and managed to get my head through a porthole, but I was unable to get my shoulders through. At that time the ship was lying almost flat in the water on her starboard side, and a passenger who was standing on the plated side of the ship finally managed to pull me through the porthole.

About a hundred passengers were standing on the side of the ship at the time, and a moment after I had joined them the ship took another list and plunged to the bottom. I next found myself in the water, and swam toward the lights of the steamer *Storstad*, and when nearly exhausted from the struggle and the exposure, I was picked up by a lifeboat, which went on to the scene of the disaster, and was loaded with survivors, who were pulled out of the water and taken on board the *Storstad*. Then we were heated and wrapped in blankets, and I was provided with the clothes which I now wear, and which enabled me to do what I could to help the other survivors.

Many Plunge into Icy Water

There was no disorder among the crowd. The captain and other officers remained on the bridge until the vessel sank. It was just seventeen minutes from the time she was rammed until she sank below the surface. Comparatively few were able to obtain lifeboats, and practically were forced in their night attire into the icy water.

Several hundred clung to the ship until she sank, holding to the rail until the vessel canted over so far that it was necessary to climb the rail and stand on the plates of the side. Then they would slide down into the water as she keeled over farther as though they were walking down a sandy beach into the water to bathe.

Photo by Bain News Service

CAPTAIN KENDALL

The commander of the ill-fated ship. His reputation for seamanship and ability was unexcelled, and he stayed with his ship until the last, being thrown from the bridge as she turned over. Fortunately he was picked up by a lifeboat from a piece of floating wreckage.

ON THE PIER AT QUEBEC

The sad-faced crowd of friends and relatives awaiting the arrival of the bodies.

Weird Shrieks of Terror

Then there were several hundred souls swimming around in the water screaming for help, shrieking as they felt themselves being carried under, and uttering strange, weird moans of terror.

The lifeboats of the *Storstad* were launched and came rapidly to the rescue. One went back that was not well loaded. About five of the *Empress*'s boats got away.

Passengers Caught Like Rats

The catastrophe was so sudden that scores never left their bunks. They were caught there like rats in a trap. Added to this was the fact that passengers had been on the ship only a day and were not familiar with their surroundings.

In the confusion and the semipanic, many could not find their way to the decks, and only a few knew where to reach the boat deck. This was largely responsible for the terrible toll of death.

The survivors were taken on board the *Storstad* and the *Lady Evelyn*, which was summoned by wireless. There everything possible was done for them, but in at least five cases the shock and exposure were too severe. Four women perished after they reached the *Storstad*. In each case I was called and the unfortunates died before anything could be done. The last spark of energy had been exhausted. One other woman died just as she was being taken ashore.

8

Ship of Death Reaches Quebec

THE GHASTLY CARGO—ESCORTED BY BRITISH CRUISER *ESSEX*—
SMALL WHITE COFFINS—PATHETIC SEARCH FOR RELATIVES AND
FRIENDS—WRETCHED CONDITION OF BODIES—LOST HIS ENTIRE
FAMILY—TWO CLAIM SAME BABY—"JUDGMENT OF SOLOMON"—
BODIES BRUISED AND MUTILATED

In the full sunlight of a perfect summer day, with church bells chiming and people trooping to early Mass, the government steamer *Lady Grey* slowly steamed into Quebec Sunday morning with the most ghastly cargo ever brought to that port—188 coffined corpses of the victims from the *Empress of Ireland* wreck.

In spite of every effort sufficient coffins could not be secured at Rimouski, and a score or more victims had to be brought in hastily constructed wooden boxes. The *Lady Grey* looked like a lumber vessel with a heavy deck load, every inch of deck space being covered with coffins of all sorts piled three and four deep.

Escorted by British Cruiser *Essex*

On her melancholy journey the *Lady Grey* was escorted by the British cruiser *Essex*, which had been cruising 348 miles below Quebec, and received a wireless order from the Admiralty to make all speed to the scene of the collision and render every possible assistance.

The *Lady Grey* at five minutes past eight proceeded to pier No. 27, where the huge shed was transformed into a mortuary chamber. The entrance was draped with black and purple, while inside three long counters had been constructed to accommodate the bodies.

As the *Lady Grey* drew up with the Union Jack half-masted at the stern, her bulwarks were lined with a hundred blue jackets and marines from the *Essex*, under Commander Tweedie, who had been detailed to remove the coffins from the death ship. This was most fortunate, for the British seamen not only lent the necessary touch of dignity to the scene, as without a word and scarcely a sound they carried the dreadfully long row of bodies ashore, but they did the work with most impressive skill. The men were evidently weighted with this terrible illustration of the dangers of the sea, and worked with solemn intentness during the long hour and a quarter it took to get the dread cargo from the *Lady Grey*.

Inside all was gloom, tears, and death, while outside the sun shone gloriously as the marines continued at their task, the silence broken only by the busy clicking of moving-picture machines and the snapping of many cameras. The arrival of the corpse-laden vessel had driven home the whole horror of the catastrophe, and people moved around on tiptoe, talking in hushed whispers as the place became more and more populous with its load of coffins.

Small White Coffins

When a group of marines passed by, each carrying a tiny white coffin, the strain became too much, and many men were moved to tears, while the few women present were openly crying. One little coffin opened, disclosing a beautiful baby girl of about four, with golden curls clustering around her ears, looking as though happily asleep—stark naked. Even hardened newspapermen were overcome at the sight.

Dead silence reigned as the slow minutes went by, each recording the advent of the marines' load of horror, until the long counters were filled and the last score of bodies had to be laid on the floor.

Pathetic Search for Relatives and Friends

At the heads of the lines of coffins stood anxious men and women, many of them survivors, looking for relatives and friends. Each coffin lid was lifted by one of the searchers while others crowded close to get a glimpse at the body inside. The line moved constantly. One lid would be dropped with a low-toned "no" and the searcher would raise the lid of the next coffin, just dropped by the person ahead.

Occasionally a low moan of a man or the muffled scream of a woman broke the silence. "Oh, Mary!," "My husband!," or some name of endearment was uttered.

One particularly pathetic figure was an elderly Australian named Byrne, who had after years of saving started out with his wife and daughter on a tour of the world. He had been saved, but both wife and daughter had met their death. He seemed too overcome even to realize his loss, and rambled about, aimlessly looking at the tagged numbers on the coffins and muttering, "Would to God I had gone with them." Their bodies were not found in the list.

Another old man sat beside the coffins silently weeping, and asked all he met if they would not get him a newspaper so that he might find what had become of his family.

Wretched Condition of Bodies

Some few of the bodies had been prepared for burial at Rimouski, but so great was the work that most of them had to be put in the coffins as they were found, the women in shreds of clothing, some absolutely naked, as were most of the children, with anything available wrapped over them, while most of the men were in trousers and undershirts. Every undertaker in Quebec and Point Lévis had been engaged by the Canadian Pacific Railroad with instructions to embalm all the bodies and prepare them for burial. Each body was also photographed for its identification.

Many of the coffins were of the crudest make; some had this inscription: *Ne pleurez pas sur moi!* (Do not shed tears over me), but as the sailors arranged the coffins and the marines took their station, tears were visible in the eyes of many. Coffin No. 1 had a card bearing these words: "Woman on bottom, baby on top." There were two in the coffin. The only other writing on the boxes were words indicating that within were *"fille," "fils," "femme,"* or *"homme."* With the bodies were in some instances the articles found on them, such as watches, pocketbooks containing money, letters, or other things that might help in the identification.

Solemnly the search continued. A man would find the bodies of his wife and children. A woman would identify the body of her husband. In the hunt for bodies of the victims there was no distinction of class. Every person, whether finely dressed or roughly clad, took his turn in the line that moved constantly from coffin to coffin. The great majority of persons, however, were disappointed in their search.

Lost His Entire Family

At times a frantic man would hurry from coffin to coffin looking over the shoulders of persons near it and trying to satisfy himself by a quick glance that the body was not that of the loved one—most of the bodies were so marred that quick identification was impossible—and then dash to the next. The most pathetic is the experience of C. W. Cullen, a candy merchant of Montreal, who had sent his wife, two children, and a maid, Jennie Blythe, on the *Empress of Ireland* for a summer trip to England. The maid alone survived.

Cullen ran from one coffin to another looking for his wife, but in vain. Then he turned to gaze on the coffins of children. He quickly found the body of his daughter, Maude, six years old, who in the excitement following the collision had been seized by the mother. The search among the babies ranging from twelve months to three years then went on. Some of the babies lying in the coffins looked as if they were asleep, with their hair curled or ruffled by a light breeze. Others had bruised foreheads, suggesting vividly how they had been hurtled against stanchions or the sides of their cabins and killed before the water came upon them. The legs and arms of others were cut and bruised terribly. Upon the little ones Cullen gazed and finally picked out one baby with blond hair.

He turned to Canon Scott, rector of St. Matthew's Episcopal Church, and said: "That is my boy." Then Cullen turned again to search through the bodies of the adults for his wife.

Two Claim Same Baby

Scarcely had he turned away when T. H. Archer, who had lost wife and baby in the wreck and had escaped himself, began to study the

faces of the babies. He had found the body of a woman that he supposed to be his wife. He came upon the body of a child marked No.
118, which had been identified only a few minutes before by Cullen
as the body of his baby. Archer insisted that the body was that of his
baby Alfred. He was told that Cullen had decided that the boy was
his own child.

The two men were brought together by Canon Scott. Both were
gracious and affable and both consented to study the features of the
face again. A police officer lifted up the coffin in his arms and held
it while the two men scanned the face of the child. Cullen decided
he would go and get the maid. He disappeared. Then Archer asked
the officer to carry the baby to a window, where he looked again at
the face of the baby. He wanted to see the knee of the baby, but that
was so bruised and discolored that the little knee proved no help.
He insisted, however, that the baby was his, and accompanied by the
clergyman, he took it back to Coroner G. Will Jolicoeur and had the
child registered as his. Canon Scott, feeling that there might be a
mistake, counseled the man to make a study of the features of his
wife and compare them with those of the child. Archer consented to
do so. While that was going on Cullen returned with the maid, who,
after a quick glance, agreed that the baby belonged to Cullen. Each
bereaved father clung to the belief that the child was his.

"Judgment of Solomon"

There came a deadlock and finally someone suggested that the decision be left to Mayor Napoleon Drouin of Quebec. The mayor was
called and each father presented what he considered proof that the
child belonged to him. The mayor, however, after a study of the features of Mrs. Archer and those of the child, decided that the baby
was not the Archer child, and he finally awarded the baby to Cullen.

While the controversy between Cullen and Archer was going on a woman attired in clothes of coarse texture wandered past the bodies of the children, stopping to lift up the coffin lids and gaze tenderly on the little faces. She was a survivor and was looking for the baby that had been torn from her arms.

One child with dark hair and features of a cherub, bearing many bruises, attracted her attention. She believed the baby was hers, but she was not sure. "My child," she said, "has one tooth on the right side." Bending over she reverently opened the mouth of the tot and then a moan escaped her.

"It's mine," she whispered, and untied a black baby ribbon that ran around the neck. Weeping, she was helped to the office of the coroner, where she obtained a burial certificate and received permission to have the body shipped to her home.

Bodies Bruised and Mutilated

Many similar tragic incidents were enacted in the course of the day, and by nightfall there were twelve other bodies of which identifications were made but of which the relatives were not sure because of their bruised and mutilated condition.

A glance at the corpses taken in a walk along the line revealed the story of the collision and the incidents following. Almost all bore marks of violence inflicted by contact with parts of the wrecked ship or in struggles in the water. There were bodies of women whose heads were split open or gashed. It is possible that women running from their staterooms in the darkness following the collision ran against stanchions or were hurled against the walls of the sides of the corridors. The wounds also indicated that some of the women had been crushed when the collier buried her steel nose in the side of the *Empress*.

Officials in Rimouski have said also that the bodies of the women showed that several of them had been stabbed, that bodies of men had been found with knives in their hands. At any rate, it was apparent by a glance at the shrouds that had been placed on the bodies of both men and women that there were other wounds not disclosed on the faces.

In addition to the bodies received in Quebec, a number had been identified at Rimouski and shipped to the homes of relatives. If the *Empress* is raised, many other bodies trapped in their staterooms will probably be obtained.

The bodies which were not identified in Quebec on Sunday were embalmed and kept for a few days longer. Then they were photographed by representatives of the Canadian Pacific and buried in graves marked "unknown."

9

Solemn Services for the Dead

MEMORIAL SERVICES THROUGHOUT CANADA—TRUST IN GOD—
AT ST. JAMES'S CATHEDRAL—RABBI JACOBS'S TRIBUTE—
WHOLE CITY HONORED THE ARMY DEAD—SERVICES IN
THIRTY-FOUR LANGUAGES

In every church in Canada, Protestant, Catholic, and Jewish alike, reference was made on Sunday, May 31, to the disaster that had at one blow bereaved hundreds of Canadian homes. Many congregations had suffered to the extent of losing one or more of their members, and these held memorial services of an impressive character. The first news of the sinking of the *Empress* came with such suddenness that few people were at once able to appreciate the appalling nature of the tragedy. But by Sunday, when the full significance had impressed itself upon them, the effect was apparent. An air of sadness filled the churches, and the faces of those in the congregations were grave and drawn. Outside, scores of flags floating at half-mast bore mute testimony to the catastrophe.

Trust in God

Reverend Dr. W. G. Wallace, of the Bloor Street Presbyterian Church, made reference to the tragedy as a preface to his sermon. "Our spirits are hurt and our hearts are sore," he said, "in the presence of the great bereavement that has come with such tragic suddenness to thousands of our fellow Canadians."

Reverend J. W. Aikens, of the Metropolitan Methodist Church, said: "There is a mystery in the relation of God to happenings such as this disaster. We cannot understand His relation to them, but there are some things which He permits but does not cause."

Reverend Dr. W. F. Wilson, of the Elm Street Methodist Church, said: "Man, with all his imperial power of mind and genius, must sooner or later learn the great laws of nature. They are fixed and irrevocable."

Reverend T. T. Shields, at Jarvis Street Baptist Church, made a touching reference to the disaster, seeking to show that such occurrences have an object. "Sometimes," he said, "the newsboy is a better preacher than the minister."

At St. Paul's Church, Bloor Street, Archdeacon Cody devoted his sermon to the loss of the *Empress*. He made particular reference to the death of Mr. H. R. O'Hara, who was one of the sidesmen at St. Paul's, speaking of his connection with the church and of his life in the community. Special music was rendered, including the "Dead March" from *Saul*.

At St. James's Cathedral

Reverend Canon Plumptre preached at St. James's Cathedral from the text "Ye shall receive power when the Holy Ghost is come upon you, and ye shall be my witnesses." With reference to the disaster in the St. Lawrence, he said the collect for Whitsunday struck exactly the note desired. He said that in our perplexities and bewilderment at the ways of God we should rest assured that He would "give right judgment in all things," and prayed that the bereaved might be given grace to "rejoice in His holy comfort." Canon Plumptre spoke of the comfort in the memory of lives consecrated to the service of God and fellow-men and of the acts of heroism that had illumined the darkness of the night. "Whether death comes to us," the preacher concluded, "as a lightning stroke in the darkness or amid the calm of a peaceful destiny, may it be said, 'We died like men and fell like one of the princes.'"

Rabbi Jacobs's Tribute

"It is with difficulty," said Rabbi Jacobs, of the Holy Blossom Synagogue, "that I can trust myself to speak on that sad calamity which has touched the heart of Canada and other parts of the civilized world so deeply in the past two days. Ah, it is such blows as these which teach us how fleeting is all human existence, how uncertain the span of life, how our earthly days are measured, our only hope in God. May this sad event remind us of the uncertainty of life and stir us all to a greater sense of our duty to the Great Creator and to each other. Events such as this have a great spiritual purpose to accomplish. They show how weak, how unstable, all our calculations are—how man proposes, but God disposes. May the Lord take into His safekeeping the souls of the departed."

Throughout the churches of England and America similar references were made to the catastrophe that carried so many souls swiftly to their doom and sympathy expressed for those who had suffered the loss of dear ones. To the bereaved Salvation Army especially was a wealth of Christian love and fellowship extended.

Whole City Honored the Army Dead

With the heavily draped standards of their late corps massed before, and amid the solemn notes of the funeral dirge, the dead of the Salvation Army were on the following Saturday borne in melancholy state through the streets of Toronto to their final resting place in Mount Pleasant Cemetery. The procession followed an impressive and soul-stirring service in the Arena, attended by a sorrowing multitude which crowded the vast building to its utmost. The service was under the direction of Colonel Gaskin and Commissioner McKie, successor to Commissioner Rees. Lying in heavily draped caskets, covered with the world-renowned colors of the Army, emblazoned with the motto "Blood and Fire" and surrounded with handsome wreaths, tokens of love and esteem sent by sorrowing comrades and friends, the bodies lay in state in the Arena. The mute evidence of the terrible disaster which had overtaken the Army on the "Black Friday" of the week before, when the *Empress of Ireland* was swept beneath the waters of the St. Lawrence River, drew a vast concourse of people.

Long before the service commenced the streets were lined with the grief-stricken citizens who desired to pay their last respects to those silent Soldiers of the Cross. With sorrowing faces and tear-glistening eyes they reverently passed through the heavy banks of floral tributes encasing the catafalque, on which rested the caskets in three long rows, and gazed for the last time upon the still forms of the sixteen victims who had done so much for the uplift of humanity in the city and whose labors were so suddenly ended.

A Striking Service

The most striking feature of the service was its wonderful revelation of the common brotherhood of humanity. In the face of the great calamity which had befallen the Army, men of every religious denomination and every sphere of life were present to bow their heads in humble submission to the will of the Almighty Father. A still stronger and deeper note was struck by two of the survivors of the disaster, who, in simple, eloquent words, brought home to all anew the great truth of the Resurrection. The wonderful sustaining power of Christianity, they said, was shown in the early morning hours when the vessel sank, and when the sudden call came none was afraid to answer the summons. They knew that it was a call to Glory!

Although a pitifully small remnant of the Army dead had been recovered, the service was also an affectionate and reverent memorial for the great majority whose remains still lay engulfed in the St. Lawrence River. Many were the sorrowing tributes paid by the speakers to those missing comrades and friends, and deep regrets were voiced that the waters had not given them up so that they might lie in state beside the silent forms with whom they had in former days toiled together to accomplish God's work.

Messages of Sympathy

The sorrow which the great tragedy had aroused throughout the entire Army world was made public by Commissioner McKie, who read numerous telegrams from Army officers in the farthermost corners of the world, from Japan and India, from Australasia and Africa, and from Northern and Southern Europe.

Photo by Bain News Service

PROMINENT ACTOR WHO WENT DOWN

Laurence Irving was the second son of the late Sir Henry Irving, the famous English actor, and was himself well-known on the stage.

Photo by Underwood & Underwood, NY

MABEL HACKNEY

The young and charming wife of Laurence Irving, who also went down with the ship.

In an eloquent address the commissioner paid a tribute to his dead comrades on behalf of the general and of the British corps. "At this moment I stand before you as the representative of General Booth and Mrs. Booth," he said, "to express for them and for all our comrades their deepest sympathy for you in this your great hour of sorrow.

"I should also like to say a few passing words about those whose remains lie in our midst, and to assure the bereaved relatives and friends that the sorrow is international. In the death of Mrs. Commissioner Rees we have lost a good worker, and the loss is a heavy one. Mrs. Rees was a good mother and helpmeet to her husband. I cannot speak of her without making a reference to the commissioner. Great as is our sorrow at his being called home, and heavy as we will feel his loss, it would be a source of great consolation to us if we but had his remains with us to lay beside those of his brave wife."

With the conclusion of the service the massed militia bands, under the conductorship of Lieutenant Slatter, of the Forty-eighth Highlanders, began to play Chopin's "Funeral March," and the sad duty of removing the caskets to the funeral vans commenced. Between the long rows of mourners the pallbearers silently passed with their mournful burdens, while the drawn faces and dimmed eyes spoke eloquently of the pangs suffered as the remains of their loved ones passed from their sight forever. It was a moment filled with the tense current of emotion—a moment as impressive as any that has followed the tragic *Empress* disaster.

Impressive Procession

Headed with the heavily white-draped standards of the Army from all the city corps, at the slow march, and followed by the first section of the massed bands playing the "Dead March," the cortege presented a melancholy and impressive sight. The funeral cars, draped heavily with crepe and purple, and each drawn by four black horses caparisoned with black-and-purple trappings, and each led by an attendant, were preceded by two draped cars heavily laden with the beautiful floral tributes. Behind came the mourners and farther in the procession the survivors, many of whom came from sickbeds to attend the service, while at the rear walked the lodges, the massed military bands, and the various representatives of the local militia in full regimentals. The procession was one of the largest known in the city, almost 6,000 marching.

People Lined Streets

Tens of thousands of citizens lined the streets to witness the passing of the funeral cortege. The crowd was densest on Yonge Street, both sides of the thoroughfare from Wilton Avenue to the cemetery gates, a distance of three miles, being crowded with humanity of every nationality. As the remains of the unfortunate victims were borne past on the heavily draped drays, every man bared his head in solemn reverence, while hundreds of women were observed wiping their stained eyes. There was a solemn silence that seemed strange at such an hour of the busiest day of the week.

Services in Thirty-Four Languages

On the following Sunday, in sixty-nine countries and colonies the world over, 200,000 soldiers of the Salvation Army, speaking thirty-four different languages, conducted impressive memorial services in honor of those of the *Empress* dead who belonged to that organization. It is estimated that upward of 2,700,000 people gathered in all the citadels and buildings of the Army to mourn for the 138 of the Army that went beneath the waves in the St. Lawrence.

In a special memorial service held in Albert Hall, London, General Booth paid special tribute to those who had perished for their lives of service to the cause and for the many sacrifices they had made. Their trials were now over, their warfare had ceased, he said, and victory was theirs. He spoke in highest terms of Commissioner Rees and of Colonel and Mrs. Maidment. While the Army had been deprived of some of its most valuable officers, and while he, above all others, felt the great blow, yet there seemed no limit to the evidences that good fruit would follow from the sorrowful trial.

10

Crippling Loss to Salvation Army

JOY OF FAREWELL SERVICE TURNED TO GRIEF—SCENES AT
HEADQUARTERS AS SAD NEWS CAME—REUNIONS THAT FAILED—
HEARTBREAKING RETURN OF THE FEW—REVERENT CROWDS
WAITING—ENSIGN PUGMIRE'S STORY—STORY OF BANDSMAN
GREEN—"IN GOD'S HANDS"—REDEDICATION TO WORK—
SALVATIONISTS BRAVE TO THE END—MAJOR ATWELL'S
EXPERIENCE—SUNDAY SERVICES IN TORONTO—FLOWER OF
ARMY AMONG THE LOST—HUNDREDS SAIL ON *OLYMPIC*—LOSS
TO ARMY IN CANADA

On the night before the *Empress of Ireland* sailed for the last time from Quebec a thousand people thronged the body of the spacious hall in the Salvation Army Temple in Toronto. Before them, ranged in tiers on the platform, sat almost a hundred men and women, their hearts beating high with the supreme happiness of meeting loved ones in the homeland. They were the envied of all. Not a soul of the thousand friends but wished himself in their place, but longed to join them on their trip to the International Congress in London.

The service was arranged as a farewell—for a short space. And none dreamed that the chasm of eternity yawned between the last sad parting and a meeting that will never take place on this side of the grave. That little uniformed band had done their work; Toronto would know them no more.

"God be with you till we meet again," sang the throng of spectators, and the Staff and Temple Bands tuned their instruments to the refrain. As the strains of the solemn melody died away, the last note was sounded that man will ever hear played by those devoted men.

Scenes at Headquarters as Sad News Came

Another crowd thronged the Temple two days later—an anxious, fear-haunted crowd, awed into an ominous silence by the dreadful news of the loss of the *Empress of Ireland*. Round the doors the press of men and women blocked the street, each anxious to catch a glimpse of the bulletins posted up every few minutes.

Colonel Rees, who was temporarily head of the Army in Canada, paced the room with hasty steps. His eyes were dim with tears, and his voice trembled slightly as he said, "This suspense is the worst of all. We can only wait and pray till the news comes." The other officers were holding themselves well in hand, but the atmosphere was one of tense anxiety and unrelieved strain.

"It is terrible; we are almost driven distracted," declared Major McGillivray, who was left in charge of the immigration department. "It does not seem possible that it can be true. All our best men in the Dominion were on board that vessel, and it does not seem possible that they can be drowned."

At first the messages delivered to the waiting crowd were hopeful; then one came saying that all the passengers were saved. As its purport became known a wave of combined relief and thankfulness swept the crowds. A sigh went up, a sigh which breathed aloud the inward, pent-up feelings of the palpitating hearts of men and women.

Many sank on their knees and with bared heads poured out their thanks to God.

But the report was only the preliminary to a more cruel blow, for scarcely had they risen to their feet when the crushing news of the loss of nearly the whole ship's complement stared at them from the bulletin boards.

Inside the building deeper feelings were stirred. There sat those whose nearest and dearest lay sunk in a watery grave. Dry-eyed, silent, hoping against hope, they sat—young, fresh maidens, round whose grief-stricken faces the Army bonnet threw a shadow of gathering sadness, young men, buoyed up only by physical strength, and old men with drawn faces and aureoles of snow-white hair. Silent as ghosts, the stream of humanity, picking its way around them, passed unnoticed.

Reunions That Failed

One of the saddest features of the wreck and its dreadful loss is the number of men and women, separated from their family for many years, who sailed in the confident hope of uniting long-broken family ties.

Other shattered ties swelled the burden of grief. Commander David M. Rees, with his wife, two daughters, and son perished with over one hundred others—the very flower of the Salvation Army in Canada.

One sobbing girl said the most distressing thing to her was the number lost who were looking forward to seeing their parents. "They left them years ago," she said, "to work in Canada, and just when their reunion seemed assured death severed them forever."

Two newly married couples belonging to the Salvation Army were on the *Empress of Ireland*. They were Captain and Mrs. E. J. Dodd and Mr. and Mrs. Thomas Greenaway, all of Toronto.

"It is a horrible honeymoon," said a Salvation Army officer as the list of the Army people on board was eagerly scanned at the Army headquarters.

Heartbreaking Return of the Few

A small group of survivors, including Major and Mrs. Atwell, Staff Captain McAmmond, and Ensign Pugmire, reached Toronto on Saturday. When seen by a party of reporters who met the train at Atha Road Station, twenty-five miles east of the city, some of the party were just finishing dinner, others were sitting about in listless attitudes, while evidences of their recent terrible experiences were clearly marked on the faces of all.

They were met at Locust Hill Station by some of their friends, and it was then that deep emotion stirred the little band. A silent handclasp was all the greeting that passed between survivors and friends for some moments; then came a half-whispered inquiry about some friend, often receiving for reply only a wistful shake of the head.

Mr. Aldridge, whose brother, Mr. Ernest Aldridge, was lost, speaking to Major George Atwell, asked in a low voice, "Did you see Ernie?"

"I never saw him," replied Major Atwell.

The bereaved brother, without a word, turned aside to hide the strong emotion that the simple words aroused in him. Similar scenes took place in various parts of the car, until gradually a natural conversation about the wreck was in progress.

Reverent Crowds Waiting

An enormous crowd surrounded the Union Station long before the train arrived, those who were unable to gain admission crowding the streets outside and lining the sidewalks along Front Street. The platforms swarmed with hundreds of friends of the returning Salvationists and others, the Army uniform dotting the crowd here and there.

When the train drew up, a feeble cheer, dying almost as soon as it began, was heard, and then a hush fell on all, unbroken till the first survivor appeared on the steps. One by one the little band stepped down, to be instantly surrounded by friends and relatives.

The meeting was a profoundly touching one. Hardly a word was spoken, for the sight of familiar faces revived too keenly the memory of those who stood on the same spot but a few days before. Little groups of Army girls moved about, many of them weeping silently.

Just before the survivors walked out, the crowd parted to make way for the truck bearing a dead body. As it passed, the entire body of Salvationists uncovered and sang the hymn "O God, Our Help in Ages Past." The effect on the listening spectators was marked by the hush which followed.

Several automobiles were in waiting outside and the survivors were quickly placed in these and driven off.

Ensign Pugmire's Story

Ensign Pugmire, connected with the financial department in Toronto, calmly told the tale of his survival to the tearful friends who asked for last tidings of their beloved Commissioner Rees. In describing his impressions more in detail, Ensign Pugmire said that there was no shock at the time of the collision.

"I heard a grazing sound as if we were touching a berg," he said, "and as the sound continued I went up on deck, curious to see what was wrong. I never got back to my cabin. The life belts were all there. The ship was already listing over dangerously. It was all the work of a moment.

"Yes, there were a number of passengers on deck with me at the time, but when I looked over my shoulder as I grabbed the rail, I could see the gangways jammed with people. I passed Major Simcoe's berth going up and asked her if she was not coming. She told me to leave her and find out what the matter was. Her body was among the first picked up on shore.

"Shouting? None at all. Every one was orderly and quiet. No one had time to realize what was going on. We could not launch the boats because we could hardly stand up, so heavy did the list become. We had to take the side, and only the swimmers like myself are left of those who went over with me.

"I saw Commissioner Rees when he ran back to get his wife. Major Frank Morris tried hard to save him, for he carried him on his shoulders as long as he could. Morris was a hero.

"There was an explosion just as the ship went down, and that must have killed hundreds outright. The shock of it blew Morris right overboard. Morris's arm was badly scalded with the steam.

"We saw the ship heeling over when we were in the water, but there was no outcry until she had disappeared. The swimmers then shouted to attract the lifeboat that was already coming. My comrades died like Salvationists."

Story of Bandsman Green

The satisfaction of Bandsman Green of the Salvation Army in finding himself alive and without a scratch was darkly clouded by the loss of his father, Adjutant Green, his mother, and his sister Jessie.

"It was not a great blow we felt," he volunteered. "Just a little jar. You could not say that it was severe, not enough to throw you against the side of your bunk, for instance. But we guessed when the engines stopped and then began to go again fast, that something had happened. I tell you that to get out was like climbing up a straight wall, the *Empress* listed so.

"And then, when she sank, I could think of nothing but a village suddenly flooded and all the people floating in the water. It was awful to see those faces bobbing up and down with the ship gone underneath and only water.

"But a wonderful thing happened. You know it is not light at that time in the morning, and when we were thrown out it was quite dark. But all of a sudden it got light very quickly and we could see well. That was wonderful!" The voice softened into reverence. "Like Providence, as I don't believe it usually gets light as early.

"In God's Hands"

"When I last saw my father, he said, 'Well, boy, we are in God's hands'; and I said, 'Yes, Father.' In a second I was parted from all forever. They were all standing together, my father and my mother and my sister Jessie.

"I must say that all, or nearly all, the men behaved like men and all the women like women."

"Was there great panic?" he was asked.

"No," he replied. "It was surprising how little panic there was. They were all so gritty. You saw men and their wives being saved together, or standing to die together. Many did not part. And the Salvationists stood up and sang 'God Be with You till We Meet Again,' as long as they could. I did see one man in the water try to push into a lifeboat ahead of a woman, but another struck him in the face and sent him back. I did hear, too, that there were other cases of this kind, but not many, and I didn't see them. The only real panic was among the foreigners. Most of the others were very calm."

Hymn the Salvationists Sang
While the *Empress of Ireland* Was Sinking

God be with you till we meet again!
By His counsels guide, uphold you,
With His sheep securely fold you,
God be with you till we meet again!

Chorus

Till we meet, till we meet,
Till we meet at Jesu's feet;
Till we meet, till we meet,
God be with you till we meet again.

God be with you till we meet again!
'Neath His wings securely hide you,
Daily manna still provide you;
God be with you till we meet again!

God be with you till we meet again!
When life's perils thick confound you,
Put His loving arms around you,
God be with you till we meet again!

God be with you till we meet again!
Keep love's banner floating o'er you;
Smite death's threatening wave before you;
God be with you till we meet again!

—J. E. Rankin, D.D.

Rededication to Work

To a running accompaniment of half-smothered ejaculations, Kenneth McIntyre, a member of the Salvation Army, in New York on the following Sunday told of the way in which, while swimming for his life in the icy waters of the St. Lawrence River, he had rededicated himself to work for his Maker and his organization.

"God bless you," "The Lord be praised," "Thy will be done," in women's voices full of emotion would be answered by "Amen" in the deeper bass of some of the men officers. For the greater part of the time Mr. McIntyre's audience hung breathless on his words.

Mr. McIntyre was the first survivor from the *Empress of Ireland* disaster to arrive in New York City. He was a member of the Canadian staff band of the Salvation Army.

He was telling some of his experiences and some of his thoughts at a meeting of members of the Salvation Army, at the organization's headquarters, No. 120 West Fourteenth Street. Mr. McIntyre is well known among Salvationists. His father, Colonel William A. McIntyre, is one of the leading officers in the Salvation Army in New York. Mr. McIntyre himself has been active in the movement for many years and joined the Canadian staff band in the autumn of 1913, when he went to take up electrical work in Toronto.

"When I was nine years old, in Boston, I was at death's door for months," he said. "My father and mother never expected that I could live, but in their prayers they said to God that they were resigned and were willing that His will should be done. If there was something in store for me, they told Him, they hoped that I might be spared.

"While I was swimming in the water I thought of this again, and I said practically the same thing my father and mother had said. Now that I am here and alive and comparatively well I want to repeat to you my pledge that I will devote myself and my life to God's work.

"Somehow or other when I was on the ship I didn't pray. I don't know whether I hadn't time or whether I didn't think of it. It's always the other ship that's going down. You never think that the one you're on will sink.

Salvationists Brave to the End

"Those of the Salvation Army who reached the deck after the collision made no outcries," he said. "None of them seemed afraid, and I heard only a low moan from one woman. There was no trampling of children on the part of anyone on the ship that I saw. Of course, in the rush to the deck everyone wanted to get up, but many helped others on the way. There was no great excitement.

"We didn't know for hours after the wreck how many of our party had been saved. All I had on when I reached the rescue ship was an undershirt and a piece of canvas, and I didn't have the latter until some hours after the accident. One of our men was upon two different pieces of wreckage before being picked up by a boat. One woman, Mrs. Greenaway, on being pulled into a boat exclaimed, 'Why did you save me? Tom is gone!' When she was taken to shore she found that Tom had been saved. Husband and wife were reunited. Tom Greenaway had sent her up to the deck and waited to dress. When he got on deck he could not find his wife, and thinking she was dead, said, 'I don't want to live.' He clung to the railing as the ship went down. The water tore him loose and he rose to the surface. A table floated under him. Thinking it was not intended he should die, he hung on and was picked up to find that his wife, Margaret, had also been saved.

Major Atwell's Experience

"Major Atwell hunted for a life preserver for his wife and finally found one in a lifeboat that was out of commission. He strapped it around her and then went to look for something for himself. He found a water cask, emptied the water out, and clung to it as he and his wife went overboard. The waves tore the cask away from him and he, with his wife near, went under three times. On the third rising he found somebody's air cushion in his hands. It saved his life.

"As I swam away from the ship I heard him calling as he and his wife floated in the water. I thought he was sinking and said to myself, 'There goes poor Major Atwell.' When he had seen me go over the side he had said, 'There goes poor Kenneth.' I swam a mile and a half before being picked up.

"Bert Greenaway, one of the bandsmen, had taken time to put on his trousers and a sweater and tennis shoes. He put the sweater on a woman on deck. He couldn't swim ten strokes, he told me. He slid down over the side of the ship into a lifeboat, being saved without even getting wet or his tennis shoes dirty. Every Salvation Army husband who had his wife with him went down into the water with her, and not one was saved without his wife."

Sunday Services in Toronto

There was much sorrow in the hearts of those who attended the three services held on Sunday, May 31, in the Salvation Army

WHAT HAPPENED TO THE STORSTAD

The Norwegian collier which sent the *Empress of Ireland* to the bottom, showing her crumpled bow plates caused by the collision. The ship was attached by the owners of the *Empress of Ireland* immediately upon her arrival at Montreal.

Photo by International News Service

CAPTAIN ANDERSEN

The master of the Norwegian collier *Storstad* which rammed the *Empress of Ireland* in the fog. Captain Andersen is seen on the bridge of his ship after she reached Montreal.

Temple in Toronto. Many pitiful scenes were witnessed, when those who had lost dear friends and comrades broke down; and it was with tender faces and gentle words that the brave soldier lassies went about doing their utmost to bring hope and peace into hearts dark with despair.

The meetings were in charge of Colonel Chandler and Colonel Brengle, who came to Toronto on Saturday with Colonel French of Chicago to convey the sympathy of the Army in the United States to those who suffered bereavement in the loss of the *Empress of Ireland*. Colonel Brengle was the principal speaker at each service.

When Colonel Chandler introduced Colonel Brengle at the morning service, he clasped him in his arms and kissed him. Before his sermon the colonel spoke a few words of condolence to the sorrowing audience, which filled the large assembly hall to overflowing. Proceeding to his discourse, Colonel Brengle spoke feelingly of the beautiful lives that had been, in God's good pleasure, lost to the world.

Flower of Army Among the Lost

"Those who have died were prepared," he said, "and we believe that our dear ones have gone home, so have no fear or sorrow, because Jesus would have it so.

"God," he continued, "whenever He finds it necessary to speak to His people very loudly through the medium of what men call a great disaster, chooses those best fitted to cope with the temporary pain and sorrow entailed thereby. Though for the time being the way may seem very dark, we must trust God to make the purpose plain and look forward to a glorious future of happiness, united once more with our beloved comrades."

Gradually the sounds of grief that had been heard from all parts of the hall ceased as the colonel continued to point out the joy that is the portion of those who went out on that last short voyage prepared to meet their Maker.

A cable from General Bramwell Booth was read, which concluded with the words "Whether we live or whether we die, the Army must go forward." The whole gathering then rose, and with right hands upraised pledged themselves by singing:

> *"I will trust Him, I will trust Him,*
> *All my life He has proved true."*

Hundreds Sail on *Olympic*

Several hundred members of the Salvation Army, under the command of Miss Eva Booth, on Saturday, May 30, sailed from New York on the *Olympic* for their International Congress in London, mourning the fate of the fellow workers of Canada who were lost in the *Empress of Ireland* wreck and in full realization that they themselves had barely missed sharing that fate.

Miss Booth said: "We all came within an ace of sailing on board the *Empress of Ireland*. They offered us special rates and we thought it would be a good thing to go with our Canadian leaders. It was just by chance that we happened to change our minds and take passage on the *Olympic* instead. The terrible disaster, in which it is reported so few of our Salvation Army comrades survived, cannot fail to make us sorrowful and very serious as we sail this morning."

Loss to Army in Canada

Commander Booth said that the loss of Commissioner Rees left the Army in Canada without a head, and added that most of those who had perished belonged to the preaching staff.

Brief mention of some of the officers lost in the wreck follows:

Commissioner Rees came out from Reading in 1882, and in 1911 was put in charge of the work of the Salvation Army in Canada. He had been principal of the International Training College, London, field secretary of the United Kingdom, and territorial commissioner for South Africa and Sweden. In 1885 he married Captain Ruth Babington.

Colonel Sydney Maidment, chief secretary for Canada, had been stationed in Toronto since 1912. In 1887 he graduated from Pokesdown and was appointed as an officer. He had seen service in Denmark, Finland, South Africa, South America, Norway, and the West Indies. He married Captain Peckham in 1882.

Brigadier Potter was born in Scotland and had seen service in Great Britain, Japan, the United States, and Canada. He had been in Toronto since 1906 as financial secretary.

Brigadier Henry Walker, an Englishman, had been editor of the *War Cry* since 1912. He had served in Sweden, South Africa, and Great Britain.

Brigadier Hunter was in Canada on furlough after many years of service in India. He with his wife and family were going to the congress in London, on their way back to India.

Major David Creighton was born in Sussex, Ontario, and entered the Army nearly thirty years ago at St. John, New Brunswick. He had been assistant immigration officer, and previously was a field officer. His wife was also on the *Empress of Ireland*.

Major Nettie Simcoe for the past year had been in charge of the work in Vancouver. For a number of years she was assistant editor of the *War Cry*. She was born in England.

Major Findlay had been stationed in Toronto for the past five years. He was a member of the special-efforts department and had a long term of service in England before coming to Canada.

Staff Captain Emma Hayes had been in charge of the Temple Corps at the Army headquarters, Toronto, for the past three years. She had a varied career in different parts of Canada.

Staff Captain Arthur Morris had been stationed in Toronto for twenty years or more. He was assistant in the field department at the headquarters, James Street.

Adjutant Hanagan was bandmaster of the Territorial Staff Band and was a valuable officer. He had been in Toronto for the past eight years.

Adjutant Green had been in Toronto for the past two years only and was accompanied by his wife and daughter on the *Empress of Ireland*.

Adjutant Price was matron of the Hamilton Home.

Adjutant De Bow was private secretary to Commissioner Rees. He had been in Toronto for ten years.

Adjutant Stitt, secretary to the property board, had been in Toronto for six years.

Adjutant Edwards was in the department of the men's social work in Halifax.

Ensign Mardall was formerly in charge of the police court work in the Toronto courts, but in 1913 was removed to Vancouver, where he had charge of the entire police court and rescue work of Vancouver and New Westminster.

Ensign Jones was in command of the Calgary Rescue Home.

Ensign Bonynge had been in Toronto for five years and was secretary to Colonel Maidment.

Ensign Pattenden was the only Toronto-born officer of the Army on the *Empress*. He was connected with the immigration department. He entered the service of the Army in 1906.

Captain James Myers was connected with the financial department at the headquarters. He was born in England.

Captain Dodd, who was on the editorial staff of the *War Cry*, had served in Toronto for eight years. He had been married for only a few days and his wife was on the boat with him.

Captain McGrath was a member of the Headquarters Band and was well known in Toronto, where he had lived several years.

Captain Harding Rees came to Toronto with Commissioner Rees and was with the property department.

Captain Ruth Rees was connected with the divisional headquarters.

A list of the Salvationists aboard and of the survivors will be found in another chapter.

11

Notable Passengers Aboard

SIR HENRY SETON-KARR—LAURENCE IRVING—MABEL
HACKNEY—COMMISSIONER REES—MAJOR LYMAN—CANADIAN
GOVERNMENT OFFICIALS—LONDON CLERGYMAN—HALIFAX
PATHOLOGIST—AUTHORESS AMONG LOST—SOME OTHER
WELL-KNOWN PASSENGERS

The tragic loss of life was emphasized by the fact that many of the passengers were known around the world. Among these were Sir Henry Seton-Karr, English lawyer, traveler, and hunter, and the actor Laurence Irving, and his wife, Mabel Hackney.

Sir Henry Seton-Karr

Sir Henry Seton-Karr was born in India, on February 5, 1853, the son of G. B. Seton-Karr, of the Indian civil service and resident commissioner at Baroda during the Indian mutiny. He was educated at Harrow and at Corpus Christi College, Oxford, where he received an M.A. degree. In 1876 he took second-class honors in law. He was called to the bar in 1879.

In the next year he married Edith Pilkington, of Roby Hall, Liverpool, who died four years later. Then he married Miss Jane Thoburn, of Edinburgh. Two sons and a daughter are in his family. His work for the State Colonization Committee and the results he accomplished as a member of the Royal Commission on Food Supplies in Time of War won for him, in 1902, his place among the knights of England. He was created a commander of the Order of St. Michael and St. George. From 1885 to 1906 he represented St. Helen's, Lancashire, in Parliament. Sir Henry wrote many books on sports, as he took keen delight in shooting, golfing, salmon fishing, and yachting, and collected notable hunting trophies.

Laurence Irving

Laurence Sydney Brodribb Irving, actor, author, and manager, was the second son of the late Sir Henry Irving, born in London August 5, 1870. He was educated at Marlborough College and the New College, Oxford. Later he spent three years in Russia studying for the Foreign Office. He made his first appearance on the stage in F. R. Benson's Shakespearean company in Dundee in 1893, and for the next two years was with J. L. Toole's company. Mr. Irving played in provincial tours, appearing in *A Bunch of Violets*, *Trilby*, and *Under the Red Robe*, from 1896 until 1898. In the latter year he joined his father, for whom he wrote the play *Peter the Great*, which proved a disastrous experiment, although it was a work of considerable cleverness and force. He was the translator of *Robespierre*, written especially for his father by Sardou, and he himself played Tallien. He was the Junius Brutus in his father's unfortunate revival of *Coriolanus*, and later was Colonel Midwinter in *Waterloo*, Fouche in *Madame Sans-Gêne*, Antonio in *The Merchant of Venice*, Nemours in *Louis XI*, and Valentine in *Faust*. In all these diverse characters he manifested marked intelligence and ability, although his histrionic facility developed slowly. He then entered into management for himself, acting in England in *Bonnie Dundee* and *Richard Lovelace*, with moderate popular success, but no little critical approval, and later in *Raffles*. He had made great advancement as an actor, proving himself an eccentric comedian of fine finish and incisive force, when he and his wife (Mabel Hackney) appeared in New York in 1909–1910 in *The Incubus* (*Les Hannetons*), and *The Three Daughters of M. Dupont*. In both these plays he won critical and popular approval. Recently, he was the Iago in Sir Herbert Tree's revival of *Othello*.

Sir Herbert Tree's Tribute

Sir Herbert Tree has written the following tribute to Laurence Irving:

"We actors were proud of Laurence Irving in life and no less proud of him in death. There was always something fateful about his personality, and one feels that his end is in tragic harmony with his being. Irving was an idealist, fearless of standing by his ideals in any company. He was a scholar in knowledge as in expression, and as an actor had already attained to a great height. His work, like the man himself, was always original.

"Technically Irving stood at the very top of his profession. As an actor with power to thrill and hold his public, he had few equals and fewer superiors. Personally, he was a man of rare charm of manner, courteous, dignified, serious in conversation, and imbued with the highest ideals. His devoted wife, whose whole career was wrapped up in her husband's success, was herself an actress of distinction whose loss is deeply deplored.

"They did honor to their profession and added dignity to the stage upon which they had so often appeared together and from which they were destined, in the end, to pass—together, as they would have wished it to be."

Commissioner Rees

The late Commissioner David M. Rees entered the Salvation Army Service from Reading in 1882. He was at the time of his death territorial commissioner for Canada for the second time. He was at one time principal of the International Training College in London, and later became field secretary for the United Kingdom, assuming afterward the office of territorial commissioner for South Africa and Sweden. He married Captain Ruth Babington in the year 1885.

The last official function performed by Commissioner Rees was the conduct of the farewell service at the Salvation Army Temple on Wednesday night. On that occasion he was full of life and spirits. Every speaker on the platform was stimulated by his enthusiastic and delightfully humorous address. At the close he leaned over the desk during the singing of "God Be with You till We Meet Again" and shook hands with a group of young men in the front seats, perfect strangers to him, but brothers in their presence at the service.

Major Lyman

Major Henry Herbert Lyman, one of the passengers, was well known throughout Canada as head of the old established wholesale firm of Lyman, Sons & Co., and was also widely known for his former association with military affairs.

He was long connected with the Royal Scots, now the Royal Highlanders. He served from ensign up to senior major. He retired in 1891, but was afterward appointed to the reserve of officers. In religion he was a Congregationalist, a member of Emmanuel Congregational Church.

An ardent imperialist, Major Lyman supported every movement tending to a greater unity of the Empire. He held that to attain full citizenship in the Empire, Canada must bear her just share of imperial burdens. He was a strong advocate of imperial preferential trade. Politically, he was independent.

Mr. Lyman was one of the organizers of the Imperial Federation League in Canada and formed one of the deputation that waited upon Lord Salisbury and Mr. Stanhope in 1886 to ask that an imperial conference be summoned, which conference was held in the following year. He was treasurer of the league in Canada and was a member of the executive committee of the British Empire League in Canada.

He was also vice president of the Graduates' Society of McGill University; vice president of the Natural History Society; president of the Entomological Society of Ontario and Montreal; a fellow of the Royal Geographical Society; and a life governor of the Montreal General Hospital.

Canadian Government Officials

George Bogue Smart, superintendent of child immigration, was a well-known government official who was en route to England to accompany a party of British children to Canada. Mr. Smart was fifty years old and a native of Brockville, Ontario. He had been fifteen years in the government service, and his business took him frequently to the old country. He was a writer of articles and author of works dealing with immigration problems in Canada. He was well known as a lecturer. Recently he was elected a member of the Authors' Club in London.

R. A. Cunningham, of Winnipeg, was on his way to England as

representative of the Manitoba government in the immigration department. He was formerly a lecturer at the agricultural college.

London Clergyman

The Reverend J. Wallet, pastor of the United Methodist Church of Argyll Street, Westcliff-on-Sea, was returning from a holiday in Canada, paid for by his congregation. He gave up a good position in a shipbuilding yard in North England to join the ministry. He has a wife and one child. The story of his escape from the sinking vessel is told in another chapter.

Halifax Pathologist

Dr. Alexander Lindsay, of Halifax, pathologist at the Victoria General Hospital, was on his way to England to be married. His engagement to Miss Kathleen Webb, second daughter of Richard Webb, of Briarwood, Solihull, Warwickshire, was announced the day before he sailed, and the marriage was to have taken place the middle of June. He was also professor of pathology at the Dalhousie Medical College.

Authoress Among Lost

Mrs. Ella Hart Bennett, one of the passengers on the *Empress of Ireland* reported lost, was the wife of Honorable W. Hart Bennett, C.M.G., colonial secretary of the Bahamas, was president of the Nassau Dumb Friends' League, member of the Order of Daughters of the Empire, and prominent in social life of Nassau. As a girl, she lived in Japan; she was the author of the book *An English Girl in Japan.*

Some Other Well-Known Passengers

W. Leonard Palmer, of the London Financial News, was well known in Halifax. He came with his wife to Canada to complete the organization of a New Brunswick land colonization scheme on behalf of English capitalists. He organized a recent English manufacturers' tour in Canada on behalf of the *Financial News* and had organized a proposed Canada Confederation Exhibition in Montreal in 1917.

Alfred Ernest Barlow was a lecturer in geology at McGill University. The son of the late Mr. Robert Barlow, of the Canadian Geological Survey, he was born in Montreal in 1871. He entered the employ of the Geological Survey and was its lithogist from 1891 to 1907, when he retired. His wife was Miss Frances Toms, of Ottawa.

Mrs. F. H. Dunlevy, numbered among the lost, was prominent in Denver society. Her husband, whom she married seven years ago, is a well-known realty dealer. Mrs. Dunlevy's family home is in Portsmouth, near Quebec.

Henry Freeman and his wife were to spend two months abroad, visiting their old home in England. Freeman was head of the blacksmith department of the Allis-Chalmers Company and was to transact company business abroad. He refused to run for reelection as alderman of West Allis, Wisconsin, in April, because of his contemplated trip abroad. He was president of Common Council and one of the directors of the First National Bank of West Allis.

P. C. Averdierck and A. G. Brandon, of Manchester, England, had been in New York for several days regulating the business of the

American Thread Company, the American branch of Jones, Crewdson & Youatt, of Manchester, and were returning on the ill-fated steamer.

George C. Richards, president of Lower Vein Coal Company, of Terre Haute, Indiana, was born in England in 1843 and took a degree in geology and mineralogy at the Bristol School of Mines. Mrs. Richards, daughter of Ben J. Street, Sheffield, England, came to America in 1879.

12

List of Survivors and Roll of the Dead

M any and varied were the reports of the numbers lost and saved in the great disaster; but the final official figures were as follows:

	Total Sailing	Rescued	Dead
First Class	87	36	51
Second Class	253	48	205
Third Class	717	133	584
Crew	420	248	172
Total	1,477	465	1,012

The lists of survivors and dead have been compiled from all available sources.

List of Survivors

First Cabin

Abbott, F. E., Toronto.

Abercrombie, H. R., Vancouver.

Addie, J. P., Birmingham, England.

Addie, Mrs., Birmingham, England.

Atkinson, John, Vancouver.

Burrows, A. J., Nottingham, England.

Burt, C. R., Toronto.

Cash, Hardwood, Nottingham, England.

Cash, Mrs., Birmingham, England.

Clark, Charles R., Detroit, Michigan.

Cunningham, R. A., Winnipeg.

Darling, M. D. A., Shanghai.

Duncan, J. Fergus, London, England.

Fenton, Walter, Manchester, England.

Gallagher, Cedric, Winnipeg.

Gaunt, Doris, Birmingham, England.

Godson, F. P., Kingston.

Gosselin, L. A., Montreal.

Henderson, G. W. S., Montreal.

Hirst, A., Birmingham, England.

Hyamson, L. A., London, England.

Kohl, Miss Grace, Montreal.

Kent, Lionel, Montreal.

Lee, Ailsa, Nassau, Bahamas.

Lyon, C. B., Vancouver.

Malloch, C., Lardo, British Columbia.

Mullins, Mrs. A. E., London, England.

O'Hara, Mrs H. R., Toronto.

O'Hara, Miss Helen, Toronto.

Paton, Mrs. W. E., Sherbrooke.

Seybold, E., Ottawa.

Smart, G. Bouge, Ottawa.

Taylor, Miss H., Montreal.

Townsend, Miss T., New Zealand.

Wakeford, A. J., Liverpool.

Wallet, Reverend J., London, England.

List of Survivors—Second Cabin*

Archer, T. H., Winnipeg.

Barbour, Miss Florence, Silverton, British Columbia.

Black, J. W., Ottawa.

Black, Mrs., Ottawa.

Bock, Miss Edith, Rochester, Minnesota.

Byrne, E., Brisbane, Australia.

Crellin, Robert W., Silverton, British Columbia.

Court, Miss E., Liverpool, England.

Dandy, J. F., Pierson, Manitoba.

Erzinger, Walter, Winnipeg.

Freeman, Henry, West Allis, Wisconsin.

Freeman, Mrs., West Allis, Wisconsin.

Hunt, Dr. L. W., Hamilton.

Kruse, Miss Freda J., Rochester, Minnesota.

Kruse, Herman, Rochester, Minnesota.

Langley, J. W., Merritt, British Columbia.

Lennon, J., Winnipeg.

Oslender, J., London, England.

Patrick, J., Toronto.

Peterson, H., Winnipeg.

Peterson, Mrs., Winnipeg.

Shongutt, Miss, Montreal.

Simmonds, Reginald, London, England.

Simmonds, Mrs., London, England.

Weinrauch, B., Montreal.

Wilmot, Miss E., Campbellford, Ontario.

List of Survivors—Salvation Army

Atwell, Major George, Toronto.

Atwell, Mrs., Toronto.

Bales, Miss Alice, Toronto.

Brooks, Frank, Toronto.

Brooks, Mrs., Toronto.

Cook, Mrs. J. E., Vancouver, British Columbia

Delamont, Archie.

Delamont, Bandsman.

Delamont, Lieutenant.

Delamont, Mrs.

Fowler, Mr.

Green, Ernest, Toronto.

Greenaway, Herbert, Toronto.

Greenaway, Thomas, Toronto.

Greenaway, Mrs., Toronto.

---

* Names of other second-class passengers appear in the Salvation Army list.

Hannagan, Miss Grace, Toronto.

Johnston, J., Toronto.

Keith, Lieutenant Alfred,
Toronto.

McAmmond, Staff Captain D.,
Toronto.

McIntyre, Kenneth, Toronto.

Measures, William, Toronto.

Morris, Major Frank, London,
Ontario.

Pugmire, Ensign E., Toronto.

Spooner, Captain Rufus, Toronto.

Turpin, Major Richard, Toronto.

Wilson, Captain George, Toronto.

Roll of the Dead

First Cabin

Anderson, A. B., London,
England.

Averdierck, P. C., Manchester,
England.

Barlow, A. E., Montreal.

Barlow, Mrs., Montreal.

Bennett, Mrs. Hart, Nassau, New
Providence.

Bloomfield, Mrs. W. R.

Bloomfield, Lieutenant-Colonel
W. R., Auckland, New Zealand.

Brandon, A. G., Manchester.

Bunthorme, A., Santa Barbara,
California.

Cayley, J. J., Hamilton.

Cay, Mrs. C. P., Golden, British
Columbia.

Crathern, Miss Waneta, Montreal.

Cullen, Mrs. F. W., Toronto.

Cullen, Miss Maud.

Cullen, Master.

Dunlevy, Mrs. F. H., Denver.

Edwards, Cox, Yokohama.

Goldthorpe, Charles, Bradford,
England.

Graham, W. D.

Graham, Mrs., Hong Kong.

Hailey, Mrs. D. T., Vancouver.

Hisenheimer, W., Montreal.

Holloway, Mrs. C., Quebec.

Howes, F. W., Birmingham.

Hunt, Miss, Toronto.

Irving, Laurence S. B., London.

Irving, Mrs. Laurence (Mabel
Hackney).

Johnson, David Frederick.

Lindsay, Dr. Alex, Halifax.

Lyman, H. H., Montreal.

Lyman, Mrs., Montreal.

Maginnis, A. G., London,
England.

Marks, J., Gabriel.

LANDING THE BODIES

A gruesome feature. The dead are being transferred from the rescue ship to the wharf at Rimouski, Quebec.

CARRYING BODIES OFF THE *LADY GREY* AT QUEBEC

The sad return of those who had sailed so gaily such a short time before.

Marks, Mrs., Suva, Fiji.

Miller, Mrs., St. Catharines, Ontario.

Mullins, A. E., London, England.

Mullins, Miss E., London, England.

O'Hara, Mr. H. R., Toronto.

O'Hara, small son.

Palmer, Leonard, London, England.

Palmer, Mrs., London, England.

Price, Mrs. W. L., New Zealand.

Rutherford, F. J., Montreal.

Seton-Karr, Sir Henry, London, England.

Seybold, Mrs. E., Ottawa.

Stearns, Miss E.

Stork, Mrs. A., Toronto.

Taylor, J. T.

Taylor, Miss D., Montreal.

Tylee, C. G.

Tylee, Mrs.

Roll of the Dead—Second Cabin*

The list of second-cabin passengers is not perfect, owing to the impossibility of obtaining accurate information. Even the lists issued by the Canadian Pacific contained many inaccuracies, and did not agree with the official figures.

Assafrey, Miss A. S. M.

Atkin, Miss M.

Balcomb, Miss D.

Barbour, Mrs. W.

Barbour, Miss Evelyn.

Barker, Alfred.

Barrie, W.

Bawden, Miss Bessie.

Bawden, Miss Florence.

Baxter, Miss Mary.

Beale, Edward.

Berry, Miss E.

Birkett, Henry.

Birne, E.

Birne, Mrs. E.

Birne, Miss F.

Bishop, G. D.

Blackhurst, Miss I.

Boch, Reinholdt.

Boynton, Mrs. F. E.

Brown, Mr. O.

Buhler, Mr. Costa.

Buhler, Mrs.

Bulpitt, R. B.

---

* Names of other second-cabin passengers appear in the Salvation Army list.

Burgess, Mrs. S.

Caughey, A. E.

Caughey, Mrs.

Chignell, Mrs. E.

Clarke, Mrs. William.

Clarke, Miss Nellie.

Cole, Mrs. A.

Dale, Mrs. M.

Dale (child of Mrs. M.).

Dargue, Mrs. J.

Deats, A. S.

Elenslie, Mrs. J.

Farr, Miss K.

Farr, Miss N.

Farr, Miss B.

Finley, J. M.

Fisher, Mrs. John.

Ford, H. E.

Gray, Mrs. Charles J.

Gray, Miss Mary.

Gregg, James.

Gregg, Mrs.

Griffin, Mrs. W.H.

Griffin (child of Mrs. W.H.)

Hageston, Hilda.

Hakker, Mrs. J.

Hakker, Miss Judith.

Halliday, C.

Hart, William Mortlach.

Hart, Mrs. Mortlach.

Hart, Miss Edith.

Hart, Master William.

Heath, H. L.

Heath, J. R.

Hepburn, Mrs. M. K.

Hepburn, Miss B. M.

Hepburn, Master H. M.

Hoggan, Mrs. Robert.

Holcombe, Miss F.

Hope, Miss C.

Howard, Mrs.

Howard, (child of Mrs.).

Howard (another child of Mrs.).

Howarth, William.

Howarth, Mrs.

Howarth, Master Melvin.

Hudson, R. W.

Hunt, Miss E. De V.

Johnstone, George.

Kavalesky, Ivan.

Matler, A.

McAlpine, A.

Moir, Mrs. Charles.

Morgan, J.

Morgan, William.

Mouncey, Mrs. W.

Muttell, Mrs. T.

Muttell, Miss.

Muttell (infant).

Neville, Mr. Harold.

Neville, Mrs. Harold.

Newtons, Miss Jennie.

Oslender, Miss.

Patterson, John.

Patterson, Robert.

Patterson, Miss S.

Perry, W. H.

Priestly, Miss M.

Prior, George.

Quartley, Miss W. M.

Reilly, John.

Richardson, W. J.

Richardson, Mrs. W. J.

Richards, George C.

Richards, Mrs. George C.

Sampson, S. J.

Scott, John M.

Searle, Miss Eva.

Shattock, William N.

Smith, Miss E.

Stage, Miss.

Stainer, Mrs. E.

Stanon, M.

Stillman, A. E.

Swindlehurst, Miss A.

Taplin, Mrs. Eliza.

Veitch, Miss B.

Vincent, A.

Vincent, Mrs. A.

Voneley, Miss Alice.

White, Mrs. George.

White (infant of Mrs. George).

Whitelaw, Mrs. J.

Wood, Miss Mary.

Wood, Mrs. S.

Yates, Harry.

Yates, Mrs. H.

Zebulak, Josef.

Roll of the Dead—Salvation Army[*]

Aldridge, Bandsman.

Axton, Mrs., and son.

Becksted, Adjutant.

Bigland, Lieutenant Stanley.

Bonynge, Ensign George.

Braithwatte, Mr., and two children.

Brooks, Miss D.

Brown, Mr.

Clark, Mrs., and child.

Cooper, Mr.

Corsell, Mrs., and child.

Crafton, Mrs.

Creighton, Major David.

Creighton, Mrs. David.

Davidson, Mrs., and child.

Davies, Mr.

Davies, Mrs.

De Bow, Adjutant.

De Bow, Mrs.

Delamont, Leonard

Dixon, Mrs.

---

[*] This list was obtained through the courtesy of the Salvation Army officers in Toronto.

Dodd, Captain T. and Mrs.

Duffy, Mrs.

Dunn, Miss B.

Eastes, Miss T.

Edwards, Adjutant.

Evans, Bandsman.

Evans, Mrs., and baby.

Falstead, Mr. George.

Falstead, Mrs., and two children.

Fell, Miss.

Findlay, Major.

Findlay, Mrs.

Fishwick, Mrs.

Ford, Bandsman.

Ford, Mrs., and child.

Goddard, Mr.

Green, Adjutant Harry.

Green, Mrs.

Green, Miss Jessie.

Greenfield, Mrs.

Grey, Bandsman.

Groome, Captain C.

Hannagan, Adjutant.

Hannagan, Mrs.

Haules, Mr.

Haules, Mrs.

Hayes, Staff Captain.

Horward, Bandsman.

Humphries, Bandsman.

Hunter, Brigadier.

Hunter, Mrs.

Ingleton, Miss.

Jay, Mrs., and five children.

Jeffries, Mrs.

Jones, Bandsman.

Jones, Ensign Emily.

Kelly, Mr.

Kennedy, Mrs.

Knudson, Ensign.

Maidment, Colonel.

Maidment, Mrs.

Malone, Bandsman.

Mardall, Ensign.

Martin, Mrs.

May, Mr.

McEwan, Mr.

McGrath, Captain.

Meecher, Bandsman.

Morgan, Miss Lily.

Morris, Staff Captain.

Morris, Mrs.

Myers, Captain James.

Neeve, Bandsman.

Pantling, Mrs.

Pattenden, Ensign.

Perkins, Bandsman.

Perkins, Mrs.

Peryer, Mrs.

Potter, Brigadier Scott.

Price, Adjutant Hanna.

Raven, Mr.

Rees, Commissioner.

Rees, Mrs.

Rees, Captain Harding.

Rees, Captain Ruth.

Rees, Miss A.

Robert, Mr.

Simcoe, Major Nettie.

Simper, Mr.

Simper, Mrs.

Smedley, Mrs.

Smith, Mrs.

Stevenson, Mr.

Stevenson, Mrs.

Stitt, Adjutant.

Stitt, Mrs.

Wakefield, Bandsman.

Walker, Brigadier.

Watson, Mrs.

Whatmore, Captain.

White, Miss.

Wilkie, Mrs.

Woodward, Miss.

Woodward, Mr.

Woodward, Mrs.

Woodward, Mrs.

Wyetta, Mr.

13

The *Storstad* Reaches Port

BADLY DAMAGED, THE COLLIER DOCKS AT MONTREAL—SEIZED ON
WARRANT—CARGO UNLOADED—OFFICERS IN CONFERENCE—
THEIR VERSION OF THE ACCIDENT—ENGINEERS' STATEMENT—
HELPED RESCUE *EMPRESS* PASSENGERS—STATEMENT OF CAPTAIN
ANDERSEN'S WIFE—GAVE ALL THEY HAD TO RESCUED
PASSENGERS—*STORSTAD*'S OWNERS FILE COUNTERSUIT

With the Norwegian flag flying half-mast at her stern the collier *Storstad*, in charge of the tug *Lord Strathcona*, came into port at Montreal on Sunday.

The arrival of the *Storstad* at Montreal was awaited keenly from early morning. After leaving Quebec she was reported almost mile by mile by the Marconi and government signal stations. By early morning it was definitely known that she would arrive soon after noon, and the wharf where it was announced that she would warp in was soon crowded.

Newspapermen from all over the American continent had gathered to meet her. Obtaining information, however, was a difficult task. The Norwegian consul was one of the many on the pier, and he was appealed to, but explained that he understood several lawyers were on hand representing the owners of the vessel. The Black Diamond Line, a Norwegian firm, had several lawyers on the pier to meet the collier. The warping in was a slow process, but when it was safely accomplished a gap of fifteen feet was left between the ship and the wharf edge.

She bore the marks of her encounter with the big liner. Her bow was buckled and twisted. There was a hole in her side large enough for three men to stand in. Her anchors had cut their way through the heavy steel plates like a can opener through a sardine tin.

Rails had been torn away and huge plates of steel bent and twisted lay piled on the deck just at the bow. All the gaps were high above the waterline. Nevertheless, the *Storstad*, undoubtedly, was practically disabled and was able to reach port only with the assistance of the government steamer *Lord Strathcona*.

Seized on Warrant

In anticipation of the arrival of the Norwegian collier, W. Simpson Walker, registrar of the Admiralty court, was instructed by solicitors for the Canadian Pacific Railroad to issue documents for their seizure of the *Storstad* for damages by collision to the extent of $2 million. The warrant was executed by Acting Deputy Sheriff Marson.

Cargo Unloaded

No sooner was the vessel moored than the work of unloading her cargo of some 7,500 tons of coal started, and except for the battered condition of her bows it would have been difficult to imagine that the collier had but a few hours previously taken part in the worst marine disaster in the history of Canadian navigation.

The officers and men, however, bore traces of the harrowing experiences through which they had just passed. When questioned on the subject of the disaster, they were averse to entering into conversation.

Officers in Conference

Captain Andersen, immediately after the collier reached her pier, was in conference with Captain Ove Lange, American chief of the maritime steamship company of Norway, and John J. Griffin, attorney for the company, both of whom had come on from New York to get the report of the captain and sailors firsthand, and to look into the situation.

Their Version of the Accident

Captain Andersen declined at first to discuss the disaster, declaring that he would make a statement later in the evening. Subsequently a statement based on Captain Andersen's report as well as the reports of other officers to Messrs. Lange and Griffin was given out.

According to the captain and officers, contrary to what had been stated by the captain of the *Empress of Ireland*, the *Storstad* did not back away after the collision. On the contrary, she steamed ahead in an effort to keep her bow in the hole she had dug into the side of the *Empress*. The *Empress*, however, according to the *Storstad* officers, headed away and bent the *Storstad*'s bow over at an acute angle to port.

After that the *Empress* was hidden from the view of the *Storstad*, and despite the fact that the *Storstad* kept her whistle blowing she could not locate the *Empress* until the cries of some of the victims in the water were heard. The captain absolutely denied that he had backed away from the *Empress* after his vessel struck the passenger steamship. The *Storstad* had not moved. It was the *Empress* which had changed position, he declared.

Engineers' Statements

One of the most important statements was that of the third engineer of the *Storstad*, who was not averse to talking, but refused to give his name. He was on duty in the engine room when the collision occurred.

"How long before you struck was the signal given to go astern?" he was asked.

"It is impossible to say definitely, but it was about a minute; I should say a little longer than a minute," he replied.

"Are you positive that you got the signal to go at full speed astern?"

"I am certain the engines were going full speed astern when the collision occurred," he said.

The third engineer's statement was supported by that of the second engineer, who, however, was not on duty at the time of the accident. He said that at no time for several hours before the collision had the *Storstad* proceeded at greater speed than ten miles an hour. Thick fog had been encountered at intervals, he said.

"The shock of the impact was not very noticeable," he said. "I did notice, however, that the engines had been reversed, and we were going full speed astern. That was about one minute before the shock came."

Helped Rescue *Empress* Passengers

Another officer said he was awakened in his bunk by the clanging of bells in the engine room, and, hastily going on deck, noticed the ship was going astern. The collision followed almost immediately. He said he helped to lower one of the boats and started to pick up the passengers.

"It was no trouble to get a boatload of them," he said. "Altogether some sixty were saved on the first trip. So heavily was the boat loaded she all but sank on her return to the *Storstad*."

As far as this officer could tell, four other lifeboats were lowered from the *Storstad*, and most of those saved in the first trip belonged to the crew of the *Empress*. He could not account for this beyond the supposition that they were better able to endure shock and exposure than were the passengers.

Asked if he noticed the siren of the *Empress* sounding, he replied that he had heard nothing, but would not say that the *Empress* did not sound her siren.

Statement of Captain Andersen's Wife

Mrs. Andersen, wife of the captain of the *Storstad*, dressed in a blue cotton dress because she had given all her other clothes to the survivors, said that the captain was called from his bed Friday night by the mate because it was foggy. Her husband called her to come on deck, and while she was dressing the collision took place.

"I ran up to the bridge where Captain Andersen was," said Mrs. Andersen. "Everything was dark and quiet. There was no excitement among the crew and I was cool.

"'Are we going to sink?'

"'I think so,' he answered.

"I couldn't cry, although I felt like it. I said to myself, 'My place is here and I will die with my husband.'

"Captain Andersen told me he was trying to keep the *Storstad* in the hole and that if the other liner had not been speeding they would have stopped together for a time at least. My husband ordered two of the officers to go to the bow and see if there was any water pouring in.

"Again I asked him if we were going down and he answered, 'I can't tell yet.' He said he thought the *Empress* was all right.

Gave All They Had to Rescued Passengers

"I think it was five minutes later that I heard screams and cries, and I shouted to my husband, 'Oh, they are calling.' At first it seemed as if the cries were coming from shore. The captain gave orders to go in that direction and proceeded very slowly. Everywhere around me now I could hear screams. My husband gave orders to send out all the lifeboats, and that could not have been ten minutes after the vessels had collided.

"I gave all I had to the passengers and have only what I am standing up in. My husband gave two suits and other clothes away.

"The first woman to come on board was a Salvation Army member, clad only in her nightdress. When she was brought into the cabin she ran to me and, putting her arms around my neck, said, 'God bless you, angel, if you had not been here we would have gone to the bottom.'"

Mrs. Andersen went among the rescued passengers with stimulants. All the cabins were packed with shivering survivors.

Storstad's Owners File Countersuit

An unexpected development came in the *Empress of Ireland* disaster on Wednesday, June 3, when the *Storstad*'s owners entered a counterclaim against the Canadian Pacific Railway for $50,000 damages due to the collision, contending that the *Empress* was at fault and alleging negligent navigation on her part. This complicated the case still more, and counsel on both sides busied themselves searching for precedents in Canadian courts. There is a case, heard in Prince Edward Island in 1892, when the liability was limited to $38.92 for each ton of gross tonnage. On this basis the total liability of the *Empress of Ireland* would be $552,313 and of the *Storstad* $234,609.

14

❧❦❧

Parliament Shocked by
the Calamity

ST. LAWRENCE DISASTER DISCUSSED IN THE COMMONS—AN
APPALLING SHOCK—FATE'S HEAVY HAND—BORDEN AND
LAURIER EXPRESS SYMPATHY

Governments may seem a little aloof from their people in times
of prosperity; but not so in times of trouble. The Canadian
Parliament met on May 29 under the shadow of a great disaster. No
other business was discussed.

The extras issued early in the morning had been read by members, and when the orders of the day were called the premier rose
with a paper in his hand.

"I would like to say just a word," he said, "respecting the disaster,
tidings of which have been brought to us today in awful suddenness,
and in a dreadful toll of human lives taken. The disaster is one which
brings a shock such as we in this country have never felt before. I am
speaking of the earlier reports. Later reports are more reassuring. I
sincerely hope they are true. That this ship, only a few hours out from
Quebec, in the dead of night, and with 1,400 passengers on board,
should be so badly damaged as to sink in ten or twenty minutes
comes to us in this country and this House as a most appalling shock.

"I do not believe, from reports which have come in, that this is a disaster which could have been averted by anything the country could have done in rendering the navigation of the St. Lawrence more safe. It came in a fog, and could not have been prevented by any safeguards to navigation. In view of the magnitude of the disaster it is fitting that something should be said in this House, that we should express our deepest regret for the disaster and our profound sympathy for those bereaved."

"The hand of fate has been heavy against us during the past few months," said Sir Wilfred Laurier. "This is the third disaster on the St. Lawrence route since navigation opened two months ago, and in loss of life it has surpassed anything since the wreck of the *Titanic.* In proportion to the number of passengers carried, the loss of life in this event exceeds the *Titanic* itself.

"It is premature to express an opinion on the disaster, but it is difficult to believe that such an accident could take place in the St. Lawrence so near to Father Point and not be prevented. I will not pass judgment, and I hope it will turn out to be one of those disasters which could not have been prevented by human agency. The sympathies of all will go out to the victims, and perhaps in a more substantial way later on. I will join with the premier in extending to the families of those who have been lost our sincerest and deepest sympathy."

15

Messages of Sympathy and Help

NEARNESS OF THE *EMPRESS OF IRELAND* CATASTROPHE—
MESSAGE FROM THE GOVERNOR-GENERAL—GRIEF IN ENGLAND—
LORD MAYOR OF LONDON STARTS FUND—SYMPATHY EXTENDED BY
KING AND QUEEN—PRESIDENT POINCARÉ REGRETS LOSS—THE
UNITED STATES SYMPATHIZES—AMERICAN RED CROSS ACTS

W hat we do not see does not hurt us." We can endure a Balkan war or a Calabrian earthquake or a Kieff massacre with composure because the black print on white paper does not bring it alive before us. We have to be taken to the scene to realize it, and even then, unless we are trained observers, we stand with dull wits, not comprehending the full meaning.

Yet so far as we can, we seek to picture the calamities that happen even in the most distant parts of the world and to express our sympathy for those who are in trouble. In the case of the sinking of the *Empress of Ireland*, which the president of the Canadian Pacific Railway describes as "the most serious catastrophe in the history of the St. Lawrence route," the task is not so difficult because the scene of the disaster is comparatively near, and because, perhaps, some of the unhappy passengers were known to us. Canada, England, the

United States—these were the countries most deeply affected and the first to extend sympathy and offers of assistance.

Message from the Governor-General

The following message was sent Friday night by H.R.H. the duke of Connaught, governor-general of Canada, to Right Honorable R. L. Borden, prime minister:

"On behalf of the duchess and myself, I desire to express to you our deep grief at the terrible disaster to the *Empress of Ireland*, and our heartfelt sympathy with the families of those who have perished."

Grief in England

The British public, which went home Friday night believing that the greater part of the passengers on board the *Empress of Ireland* had survived the disaster in the St. Lawrence, was greatly shocked Saturday when it was learned that the loss of life had reached one thousand, and that many of the victims were from the United Kingdom.

King George early in the morning sent a messenger to the European manager of the Canadian Pacific Railway expressing his sorrow at the disaster and the great loss of life.

Lord Mayor of London Starts Fund

The lord mayor of London, upon learning of the extent of the disaster, decided to open a fund toward the relief of the widows and orphans as well as the dependents of those of the passengers and crew who had been lost. The king donated $2,500; the queen, $1,250; the prince of Wales, $1,250, and the queen mother Alexandra, $1,000. The Mansion House Fund was also turned to the aid of the sufferers, and a Liverpool Relief Fund started.

Sympathy Extended by King and Queen

King George cabled to the duke of Connaught, governor-general of Canada, as follows:

"I am deeply grieved over the awful disaster to the *Empress of Ireland* in which so many Canadians lost their lives. Queen Mary and I both assure you of our heartfelt sympathy with those who mourn for the loss of relatives and friends."

To Sir Thomas Shaughnessy, president of the Canadian Pacific Railway, His Majesty cabled:

"In the appalling disaster which has befallen your company by the loss of the *Empress of Ireland*, in which so many perished, I offer you my sincere sympathy."

The Irish Nationalist Convention at a meeting in London under the presidency of T. P. O'Connor, passed a resolution of sympathy with the relatives and friends of those who died when the *Empress of Ireland* sank and it was transmitted to Sir Thomas Shaughnessy.

President Poincaré Regrets Loss

King George received the following telegram from Raymond Poincaré, president of the French Republic:

"It is with profound emotion that I learn of the terrible catastrophe in connection with the *Empress of Ireland* which will plunge so

THE MAIN DINING SALOON

An example of the spaciousness and luxury of the *Empress of Ireland*. The late supper served in this saloon had been ended but a short time when the disaster occurred.

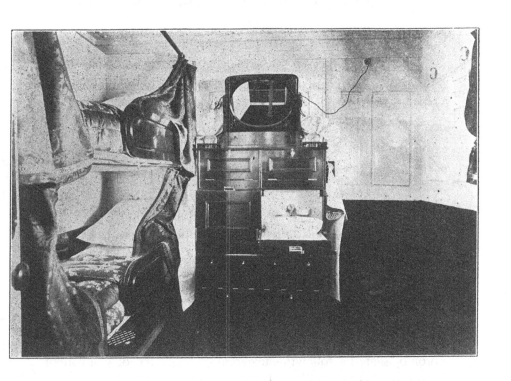

ONE OF THE LUXURIOUS CABINS

It was from such scenes of comfort that the passengers of the ill-fated ship were hurried to a scene of death and despair in which more than a thousand of them perished.

many families into mourning. From my heart I tender to Your Majesty the sincere regrets and keen sympathy of the French people."

The United States Sympathizes

President Wilson also sent a message of condolence to King George.

"I beg of Your Majesty," the president cabled, "to accept my deepest sympathy in the appalling catastrophe to the steamship *Empress of Ireland* which has brought bereavement to so many English homes."

Secretary Bryan instructed Ambassador Page in London to call at the British Foreign Office and express the United States government's condolences and his own.

The Transatlantic Society of America through its Secretary, E. Waring Wilson, cabled the United States ambassador in London, requesting him to transmit to King George a message of sympathy for the loss of life in the disaster to the *Empress of Ireland*. Condolences were also wired to the governor-general of Canada at Ottawa.

President McAneny, of the Board of Aldermen of New York City, who had just returned from a conference on city planning in Toronto, sent the following telegram to the duke of Connaught regarding the loss in the sea disaster:

"On behalf of those Americans who have just returned from the City Planning Conference at Toronto, and to whom the hospitality of Canada had so generously been given, I extend deepest sympathy to you and to the Canadian people upon your tragic loss of today."

Mayor Mitchel also forwarded his sympathy:

"The city of New York sends sincere sympathy to the people of Canada who have suffered through the tragedy on the Gulf of St. Lawrence."

American Red Cross Acts

While aid was not asked by Canadian and British organizations in behalf of survivors of the steamship *Empress of Ireland* and those dependent upon victims of the disaster, the American National Red Cross Society on Saturday, May 30, announced that it would forward to the proper authorities any contributions sent by Americans.

16

Placing the Blame

THE ROYAL COMMISSION OF INQUIRY—IMPORTANT DISCREPANCIES
IN THE TESTIMONY—DISAGREEMENT AS TO SPEED—
CONTRADICTIONS AS TO WHY THE STORSTAD BACKED—THE
CAPTAINS DIFFER—A SENSATIONAL CHARGE—QUARTERMASTER
GALWAY'S TESTIMONY—WHERE THE EMPRESS WAS STRUCK—
STORSTAD PORTED HER HELM—A HUMOROUS INCIDENT—THE
DIVERS TESTIFY—BOATSWAIN'S SENSATIONAL EVIDENCE—
TESTIMONY OF EXPERTS—ADDRESSES OF COUNSEL—COMMISSION
HOLDS STORSTAD RESPONSIBLE—RECOMMENDATIONS

The shock dealt to the civilized world by the news that a catastrophe in the St. Lawrence River had cost a thousand human lives was scarcely greater than the ensuing demand for a thorough investigation of all of the facts connected with the disaster.

The Royal Commission of Inquiry

The minister of Marine and Fisheries, the Honorable J. D. Hazen, acted promptly in appointing a Royal Commission of Inquiry, consisting of Lord Mersey (chairman), who had conducted the British inquiry into the *Titanic* disaster; Sir Adolphe Routhier, president of the Court of Admiralty for the Province of Quebec; and the Honorable Ezekiel

McLeod, judge of the Supreme Court and of the Vice Admiralty of New Brunswick.

The commission assembled on June 16, at Quebec, where it had the assistance, as assessors, of Commander Caborne, of the Royal Naval Reserve; Professor John Welsh, of Newcastle, England; Captain Demers, Dominion wreck commissioner; and Engineer-Commander Howe, of the Canadian Naval Service. Heading an illustrious array of counsel were E. L. Newcombe, K.C., deputy minister of justice, representing the government; Butler Aspinall, K.C., of London, representing the Canadian Pacific Railway Company; and C. S. Haight, K.C., of New York, representing the master and owners of the *Storstad*.

Important Discrepancies in the Testimony

The first two witnesses called were Henry George Kendall, master of the *Empress of Ireland*, and Alfred Tuftenes, chief officer of the *Storstad*.

The chief discrepancies in the stories of these opposing witnesses occurred in that portion devoted to the course of events which took place after the heavy fog rolled up from the shore and formed a barrier between the vessels. Captain Kendall stated decisively that there never was one blast alone sounded from the bridge of the *Empress*. Chief Officer Tuftenes declared with equal certainty that the first signal which came across the rolling bank of fog was one long blast, which he interpreted as meaning that the *Empress* was continuing on her way. He replied with a similar signal.

Both officers maintained that, had the vessels held to their courses set when they first sighted each other's lights, there would have been no collision. But Captain Kendall's asseveration was that he signaled three blasts, meaning that he ordered the ship full speed astern. This was the first discrepancy.

Disagreement as to Speed

The second discrepancy of outstanding importance was in regard to the speed at which the vessels were traveling when they came in sight of each other through the fog, one hundred feet apart.

Captain Kendall stated that as soon as he saw the collier he realized that a collision was inevitable, and he telegraphed "full speed ahead," but his ship had no way on her and the collision came. He stated that by the curling waters at the bow of the *Storstad* he was certain that she was traveling some ten knots an hour.

Chief Officer Tuftenes stated that he had stopped his ship and then, because she refused to answer to her helm, he had given the command "slow ahead," in order to prevent her shearing with the current. This was about a half a minute before the *Empress* was sighted one or two ship lengths away. When the liner was sighted, the engines were ordered "full steam astern," and this was the condition, according to this witness, instead of the ten knots an hour speed which was Captain Kendall's estimate.

Chief Officer Tuftenes also declared that when he sighted the *Empress*, she was moving ahead at a fast rate of speed, and it was this fact that made it impossible for the *Storstad* to hold her stem in the wound her anchors gashed in the starboard side of the liner.

Contradictions as to Why the *Storstad* Backed

The reason for the *Storstad*'s movement after she struck the *Empress of Ireland* was the third divergence of opinion. The evidence showed that both Captain Kendall and Captain Andersen realized the necessity of keeping the stem of the collier in the wound in the liner's side.

The divergence of opinion was about the reason why the desired position of the two vessels was not maintained.

Captain Kendall's explanation of the backing up of the *Storstad* was that she rebounded after the terrific blow, her engines were full speed astern, and she swung about because she lost her heading when her engines were reversed. This brought the two vessels side by side, and from this position, he claimed, the collier continued to draw away until a mile separated the two ships.

But Chief Officer Tuftenes stated that Captain Andersen gave the order "full speed ahead," as instructed by Captain Kendall, to keep her bow in the wound, and that it was because the *Empress* was moving ahead that the collier's stern was forced around in a half circle, still with her stem in the gigantic gash, and then, by the force of the water against her side, her bow was pulled out, and the vessels stood heading more or less in the same direction. Both officers agreed that the collier collided with the liner at something less than a right angle.

The Captains Differ

With the examination of Captain Andersen it became known what mistakes of judgment and navigation the masters of the *Empress* and the *Storstad* each thought the other made.

Captain Kendall, of the *Empress*, gave his opinion on varying points on the opening day of the proceedings. During the second day's session Captain Andersen, of the collier, named the three blunders which, in his idea, were made on board the *Empress*.

Briefly, Captain Kendall claimed that the *Storstad* seemed to have changed her course in a heavy fog, with another vessel in the vicinity, which, it is said, is against all the ethics of seamanship. He gave as his opinion that this was done probably to avoid Cock Point shoal. His charge, not made directly, was that the *Storstad* ran through the fog at ten knots an hour, which was said to be another infraction of the rules. These were the two chief points which, Captain Kendall submitted, were the most probable cause of the collision.

Captain Andersen, on the other hand, stated that three blunders, in his opinion, were made on board the *Empress.* The first was that, having ported her helm and brought the ships red to red, which means that the starboard light alone of each ship was visible to the other, the *Empress* starboarded, changing her course toward the south shore, "a very risky thing to do."

The second blunder, he believed, was that when two long blasts were sounded, meaning that the *Empress* was stopped, she was still under way, "a remarkable blunder," and the last blunder, in his opinion, was that some five or six minutes after blowing the three blasts, when she came in sight she was going eight or ten knots an hour, "an extraordinary blunder."

A Sensational Charge

The most sensational incident of the investigation into the circumstances attending the sinking of the *Empress of Ireland* occurred on Thursday, the eighteenth, when serious statements were made by Mr. Haight, counsel for the *Storstad*, to the effect that he had been informed by a quartermaster of the *Empress of Ireland* that for five minutes, while she was on her way down the St. Lawrence after leaving Quebec, the steering gear of the *Empress of Ireland* was out of order, and that during this period she nearly ran down another vessel. The quartermaster's name was James Galway.

Quartermaster Galway's Testimony

On the following day Galway was put on the witness stand. He was evidently unnerved by the quick fire of questions which assailed him after every answer he gave. As he paused to give his answer, first repeating the question like an echo, he glanced round the room at the gathering of shipping experts, started a reply, and in his nervousness, stopped again.

As he made some little slips, a titter ran round the room and the witness was more unnerved than ever.

He stated that on one occasion when the *Empress of Ireland* was in the Lower Traverse, below Quebec, she behaved in an extraordinary manner, swaying from side to side.

"Am I to understand," asked Lord Mersey, "that she turned to port or starboard at her own sweet will?"

"Yes, that is right," Galway replied.

Galway further declared that when he put the helm to starboard the head of the vessel went to port and then came back again.

"She changed her mind," jocularly commented Lord Mersey.

On the night of May 28, Galway added, between ten and twelve, he put the steering gear to port and it jammed for a few minutes.

George Sampson, chief engineer of the *Empress*, whose duty it was to examine the steering gear, testified in rebuttal to Galway. He was emphatic in his assertion that the steering gear was in proper condition on the day of the collision.

From the steamship *Alden*, however, there were witnesses who contended that the course of the *Empress* was somewhat erratic. The *Alden* was the third vessel which figured in the charges made by counsel for the *Storstad*. While she was on her way down the river, it was alleged, the *Empress* had answered her helm so badly that she had almost run down the *Alden*.

Where the *Empress* Was Struck

An interesting exhibit shown during the proceedings of the inquiry was a model of the bow of the *Storstad*, showing her twisted stem; another was that of a cabin plate from the *Empress*, found on the *Storstad* after the collision. The number was 382, and was that of a cabin on the saloon starboard deck, near the forward funnel.

The latter exhibit was particularly interesting as giving an indication of the point where the *Empress* was struck, and how far the stem of the *Storstad* plowed through her side.

When the officers and men from the *Storstad* continued their testimony before the Royal Commission of Inquiry on Saturday, the twentieth, some remarkable declarations were made.

Storstad Ported Her Helm

It was Jakob Saxe, the third officer of the collier, who provided the sensation of the session. He told how he was standing on the bridge of the *Storstad*, just before the collision, when the navigating officer gave the order to port the helm a little.

"But," Lord Mersey asked in surprise, "when he gave the order to change the course in a fog, did you think about it, remembering that you must not change course in a fog?"

Yes, the witness admitted, I thought about it. But, Saxe continued, he did not think it was dangerous.

Saxe then created a buzz of excitement in the courtroom by relating how, without any orders, he had put the wheel over hard aport.

"That," Lord Mersey continued, "to me is news."

Again and again the witness was pressed by counsel as to the effect of his putting the wheel of the *Storstad* hard aport, whether it might not have been responsible for the collision, but he strenuously denied this.

The evidence given on Monday, the twenty-second, threw little additional light on the disaster or its cause.

The second officer of the *Storstad* persisted that the *Empress* was moving rapidly. He had rushed on deck immediately after the collision, he said, and the *Empress* was moving forward. He could not remember whether the bow of the *Storstad* was held fast in the side of the *Empress*.

"But," Lord Mersey asked, "whether they were fast together or not, the *Empress* was moving forward. Is that right?"

"Yes," the witness insisted.

One witness heard during Monday's session gave a peculiar reason for the closing of portholes on a steamer.

A Humorous Incident

When there was a fog, he informed Lord Mersey, he would go and close the cabin portholes.

"But," said Lord Mersey, "that is for the comfort of the passengers, not for the safety of the ship?"

"There is no other reason that I can think of," was the reply, "except that it is a matter of form."

The little touch of red tape amused the court and sent a roar of laughter around the room.

"And," Lord Mersey drily added, "suppose you go into a cabin on a foggy night and you begin to close a porthole when a passenger wants it open, what do you do?"

"Oh, I close it," the witness replied, and again there were roars of laughter.

The Divers Testify

G. W. Weatherspoon, of the American Salvage Company, which conducted diving operations on the scene of the wreck, was closely examined on Tuesday, the twenty-third, in an effort to learn which of the two ships had changed her course. Counsel for the *Storstad* contended that the position of the *Empress* as she lay on the bed of the river was proof of his contention.

Weatherspoon was closely pressed by Mr. Aspinall on the question of the importance of the currents as the point where the *Empress* lay.

"There was always a current there," Weatherspoon said.

"And, therefore," Mr. Aspinall queried, "the heading of the vessel may have been affected?"

"Very possibly," the witness admitted.

Mr. Haight suggested that the influence of the currents might be scientifically determined by government surveyors placing down buoys.

"I must leave the government to make up its mind on that," Lord Mersey replied.

Weatherspoon spoke of the danger of his undertaking. Divers had attempted to ascertain the damage of the ship, but the hazard was very great. In his opinion it would be impossible to raise the vessel.

On the following day Winfrid Whitehead, one of the *Essex* divers, one of the men who cautiously made his way along the hull, related his experiences to the court. He told his story simply. He had gone down to find out in which direction the ship was lying. He descended onto the side of the vessel, felt at her plates, to determine the direction of her stem, and then walked forward. By this means the air bubbles rising from him told the officer above which way the vessel was lying.

This direction, Chief Gunner Macdonald informed the court, was northeast and southwest, the stem of the ship being northeast.

Boatswain's Evidence Sensational

Something of a sensation was caused shortly after the opening of Wednesday's session by the evidence of Alexander Redley, the boatswain's mate of the *Empress*. During a preliminary examination, it appears, Redley stated that he heard one long blast blown by the whistle of his ship ten minutes before the collision.

That such a signal was blown, a signal signifying "I am going ahead," was denied by Captain Kendall, when he was on the stand.

"Can you tell me," Lord Mersey asked counsel for the Dominion government, "why it is this evidence was not called sooner? It seems to me as if it were put in at the last moment. It is important whether such a blast was blown or not."

In reply to a direct question from Lord Mersey, Redley could not say definitely if or when he had heard the *Empress* blow one long blast.

Testimony of Experts

The afternoon's evidence was a maze of technicalities. The design of the steamer, the possible effect of such and such a blow, assuming the speed to be such and such, the effect of the collision on the heading of the *Empress*—all this was the trend of the questions asked of Mr. Percy Hillhouse, a naval architect employed by the Fairfield Shipbuilding Company, the builders of the *Empress*.

From the maze one learned that a foot had been added to the rudder of the *Empress of Ireland* in 1906.

"On the trials," said Mr. Hillhouse, "everybody was absolutely satisfied with her steering qualities. But sometime later the forepart of the rudder got carried away accidentally, and when that was being renewed advantage was taken of the change to slightly increase the area of the rudder."

A few calculations submitted by Mr. Hillhouse gave a graphic idea of the great gap in the side of the liner. He estimated, he said, that the area of the breach was 350 square feet, and that 265 tons of water per second poured through the hole. At this rate the boiler space would be filled in from one and a half to two minutes.

On the following day, John Reid, the naval architect, called by the owners of the *Storstad*, entered the box equipped with photographs and a model of the *Storstad*'s bow, made to scale. The most interesting assertion of Reid was that the rudder of the *Empress* was quite small.

"Do you know," Mr. Aspinall asked, "how the area of the rudder of the *Empress* compared with the area of the rudder of other ships?"

Mr. Reid replied, "It was considerably smaller, but there is no type of vessel with which you could accurately compare it, the *Empress* having the peculiar formation of fullness about the stern."

On this point, Percy Hillhouse, of the Fairfield Shipbuilding Company, the builders of the *Empress*, was recalled. He thought that Mr. Reid's criticism was not just. The area of the *Empress* in proportion to the size of the ship rudder compared very favorably with that of other large vessels. A mean percentage he had taken of thirteen large vessels gave an average of 1.265. For the *Empress of Ireland*, the figure was 1.53 percent.

Address of Counsel

After all of the testimony was in, George Gibson, counsel for the Seamen's and Firemen's Union of Great Britain and Ireland, made the first address of counsel. His speech was brief, Mr. Gibson making the recommendation that (1) the number of able seamen on passenger ships should be increased to two for each boat; (2) boat drill should consist of the lowering of every boat into the water; and (3) rafts or floats should be provided so that firemen and stokers, who would be the last to leave a ship, would have a better chance to escape.

Mr. Aspinall, in summing up, drew attention to the evidence of the *Storstad*'s officers which tended to corroborate the claims of the captain and owners of the *Empress*. "We were contending," he said, "that what caused the collision was a porting and a hard porting of the helm on the part of the other vessel. It is remarkable that as this case has been developed and the evidence has been sifted, it should be established that the helm of the *Storstad* was ported and hard ported, and without any orders to that effect having been given by her navigating officer. That is the whole feature of this case, and I submit it is of immense value in determining where the truth of this story lies."

Mr. Haight defined the accident as absolutely inexcusable. The whole world wanted to know who was responsible; and Mr. Haight unhesitatingly fixed the blame on the ship which, while running through a fog, changed her course. That ship, he argued, was the *Empress of Ireland*.

He could only think of three reasons. If the *Empress* had dropped her rudder entirely, she might have steered. There was no charge that the *Storstad* did not steer. Mr. Aspinall had fully recognized her

IN THE DRIFTING LIFEBOATS

Here the intense physical suffering from cold and exposure, added to the mental agony preceding and accompanying it, overwhelmed many of the boats' occupants. In consequence, the *Carpathia*, which rescued the survivors, was literally a floating hospital during her sad journey back to New York.

COMMISSIONER DAVID M. REES

Of Toronto, who was in command of the Toronto detachment of the Salvation Army on the *Empress of Ireland*, and was among those lost in the disaster.

steering qualities, and had indeed made them the basis of his argu-
ments. The *Empress* might not have steered well. They had direct
evidence that in some respects the *Empress* was an innovation. He
could never believe that Captain Kendall deliberately turned his
splendid ship straight across the bows of the *Storstad.*

There was a new note in the closing address of E. L. Newcombe,
deputy minister of justice, who represented the Dominion government. Mr. Newcombe argued that both vessels might have been at
fault—the *Empress* for lying dead in the water while entering fog
and knowing another vessel to be in dangerous proximity—the
Storstad for the hard-porting of her helm by her third officer, without instructions by her navigating officer.

Commission Holds *Storstad* Responsible

The report of the Royal Commission of Inquiry was filed on July 11,
the decision of the commission being as follows:

> First. The *Storstad* is responsible for the accident, because she
> changed her course. The helm of the *Storstad* was ported by order
> of Chief Officer Alfred Tuftenes, who thought the *Empress* was at
> port, whereas, in reality, she was on the starboard.
>
> Second. The first officer is also blamed for having failed to call the
> captain, Thomas Andersen, when the fog came on. There is noth-
> ing to blame in the course followed by the two ships before the fog
> came on.
>
> Third. It is virtually certain that some of the bulkheads of the
> *Empress* were not closed at the time of the collision.

Discussing the disaster, the report said:

It is not to be supposed that this disaster was in any way attributable to any special characteristics of the St. Lawrence waterway. It was a disaster which might have occurred in the Thames, in the Clyde, in the Mersey or elsewhere in similar circumstances.

There is, in our opinion, no ground for saying that the course of the Empress of Ireland *was ever changed in the sense that the wheel was willfully moved; but as the hearing proceeded another explanation was propounded, namely, that the vessel changed her course, not by reason of any willful alterations of her wheel, but in consequence of some uncontrollable movement, which was accounted for at one time on the hypothesis that the steering gear was out of order, and at another by the theory that, having regard to the fullness of the stern of the* Empress of Ireland, *the area of the rudder was insufficient. Evidence was called in support of this explanation.*

The principal witness on the point as to the steering gear was a man named Galway, one of the quartermasters on the Empress of Ireland. *He said that he reported the jamming incident to Williams, the second officer on the bridge (who was drowned), and Pilot Bernier. He said he also mentioned the matter to Quartermaster Murphy, who relieved him at midnight of the disaster. Pilot Bernier and Murphy were called, and they denied that Galway had made any complaint whatever to them about the steering gear.*

Galway gave his evidence badly, and made so unsatisfactory a witness that we cannot rely on his testimony.

On the whole question of the steering gear and rudder we are of the opinion that the allegations as to their conditions are not well founded.

Recommendations

The commission's report contained the following recommendations:

1. That a maritime rule be adopted compelling ships to close their bulkheads when fog comes on and also at night, whether the weather is foggy or not.

2. That different stations be established for the ships to take on and leave off pilots so that they would not be obliged to meet one another.

3. That more life rafts be put among the lifesaving equipment on ships so that if a boat sinks before the lifeboats can be lowered, the rafts will slip off and float in the water.

17

Empress in Fact, as in Name

THE EXPONENT OF SAFETY AND COMFORT—DIMENSIONS AND
ACCOMMODATIONS—PROVISIONS FOR COMFORT AND PLEASURE—
WEEKLY LIFESAVING DRILL—THE LOSS AND INSURANCE

The *Empress of Ireland* and her sister ship, the *Empress of Britain*, were in many respects fittingly called "the Empresses of the Atlantic." They stood as a synonym for all that is best, safest, and most reliable for the use of the traveling public. The *Empress of Ireland* was an example of the best in construction and a model of excellence and taste in furnishings. She was an exponent of the latest achievement in marine architecture, combined with all the newest devices for the comfort of passengers. A large, graceful ship, well proportioned, she was built to meet every possible requirement of the service and also was remarkably steady in rough weather.

Dimensions and Accommodations

The length of the *Empress of Ireland* was 550 feet, and her width 66 feet. Her gross register (a term used in marine nomenclature to describe the carrying capacity of a ship) was 14,500 tons; when loaded, her displacement (the weight of the volume of water displaced by a vessel when afloat) was 26,550 tons. She was equipped with twin-screw propellers, driven by triple-expansion, reciprocating engines generating 18,000 horsepower, and was capable of attaining a speed of 18 knots an hour, or approximately 20¾ geographical miles.

The *Empress of Ireland* contained accommodations for 350 first-cabin passengers, 350 second-cabin passengers, and 1,000 third-cabin passengers. Elaborate provision was made for the safety and comfort of the passengers.

Six transverse bulkheads divided her into seven watertight compartments, and before the *Titanic* disaster demonstrated that all safety devices have their weaknesses, the *Empress of Ireland* was regarded as approaching to the ideal of the unsinkable ship. After the *Titanic* disaster, the lifeboat accommodation of the *Empress*, in common with that of all other big liners, was overhauled and extended.

The *Empress* was built at the Fairfield Shipbuilding Company's works, Glasgow, and was regarded by seafaring men as being of thoroughly sound construction. She was not the largest ship running to Quebec, the *Calgarian* and *Alsatian*, of the Allan Line, being of about 18,000 tons.

Provisions for Comfort and Pleasure

There were five passenger decks, with a boat deck above. The upper deck was famous among travelers, affording a walk of about an eighth of a mile.

On the upper and lower promenade decks were a number of special rooms, single and en suite, with or without private baths.

The spacious dining saloon accommodated the entire complement of passengers, and an attractive feature was the arrangement of small round tables in alcoves which were usually assigned to families or parties traveling together.

The café situated on the lower promenade deck was sumptuously appointed, in keeping with its practical purpose to supply light refreshments at any time during the day.

The music room on the upper promenade deck, with its original decorations, cheery open fireplaces, and many cozy nooks and corners, was the acme of comfort and luxury, while the smoking room, library, and other public rooms were in every respect in keeping with the high standard maintained throughout the ship.

The *Empress of Ireland* had been on the Atlantic service of the Canadian Pacific Railway for eight years and was regarded as one of the finest ships on the Canadian route to England. Comfortable, fast, and considered to be as safe as any ship afloat, she was a favorite with travelers.

Weekly Lifesaving Drill

The usual lifesaving drill took place every Thursday when the boat was in port. Every man on board was mustered, and instructed in case of accident what he should do and where he must report for service. It was very interesting to see the lifeboats manned, lowered, and rowed around the ship, also to see the great collision mat quickly put over an imaginary hole in the side of the ship, and to watch the men rush with hose bucket and blankets to put out an imaginary fire. There was no hesitating or inattention: every man seemed to understand just what was expected of him and performed his part with precision and pride.

Watertight Compartments Tested

In this safety drill the watertight compartments were closed and opened a number of times to test their mechanism and to see if they were working properly. All of the lifeboats, of which there were enough to accommodate both passengers and crew, were kept provisioned with biscuits and water enough to last several days.

The Loss and Insurance

Incidental to the loss of the *Empress of Ireland* is the loss of the mails. The Toronto shipment alone comprised fifty-one bags of letters and fifty-eight of papers, while 805 registered letters went down with the ship. The money orders carried on the ship, as nearly as could be estimated, amounted to $160,000.

Both the *Empress of Ireland* and her cargo were fully covered by insurance, mostly in English and continental companies, Lloyd's being assessable for between 45 and 50 percent of the whole loss. The only Canadian company affected, as far as is known, is the Western Assurance Company, for $12,000 on a shipment of bullion from Cobalt to London.

Following is the insurance on the *Empress of Ireland*:

Empress of Ireland (valued at)	$1,750,000
Empress of Ireland (cargo)	$250,000
Empress of Ireland (baggage and passengers' effects)	$10,000
Total	$2,010,000

18

The Norwegian Collier *Storstad*

DIMENSIONS OF THE *STORSTAD*—A RECENT RESCUE—
PERSONALITY OF CAPTAIN ANDERSEN—INSURANCE

The *Storstad*, a twin-screw steamer, was built in 1910 at Newcastle, England, by Armstrong, Whitworth & Co., for A. F. Klaverness & Co. Her registered home port is Christiania, Norway, and she steams under the Norwegian flag. She is 440 feet long, 58 feet 1 inch beam, and has 24 feet 6 inches depth of hold. The *Storstad* is a craft of 6,028 tons, with triple-expansion engines.

A Recent Rescue

A brusque man is Captain Thomas Andersen, who commands the *Storstad*. It was scarcely three months before the collision with the *Empress of Ireland* that Captain Andersen with his vessel and crew was the means of rescuing six fishermen who had been fishing off Atlantic City, New Jersey. After they had fished for several days they decided to put farther out to sea.

Their engine was started and they sailed away. They had gone only a few miles when their engine broke with a snap. They drifted on at the mercy of the sea, for nearly a week, the food supply almost gone.

When their hope was about to give out they saw a passing steamship, which appeared as a speck upon the horizon. When she got near, the fishermen saw leaning over the side of the steamship a large man, smiling broadly, but with an expression of determination to land those in distress safely upon his vessel.

Personality of Captain Andersen

This man was Captain Andersen, master of the Norwegian steamship *Storstad*. Two days later he landed the men he had saved.

Captain Andersen is a typical captain of a tramp steamer. Modest and unassuming, he tells quietly of what he is asked to, his simple story of bravery being entirely without varnishing by him.

Insurance

The insurance of the *Storstad*, carried wholly by Norwegian underwriters, was as follows:

Storstad	$325,000
Storstad (cargo)	$60,000
Grand total	$385,000

19

The St. Lawrence: A Beautiful River

MEASURES TAKEN FOR SAFETY—FATHER POINT—PICTURESQUE
RIVER—GULF OF ST. LAWRENCE—HISTORICAL BACKGROUND—
TADOUSAC—CAP TOURMENTE—QUEBEC—MONTREAL—
GEOLOGY OF COUNTRY

T he St. Lawrence passage is one of the most beautiful in the world, and is also one of the safest and best marked of all interior waterways.

The improvement of the St. Lawrence, indeed, dates as far back as 1825. In that year the opening of the Lachine Canal gave connection with the Great Lakes and established a commercial basis for the route. In those days attention was turned chiefly to making the channel deeper. At that time light sailing vessels could come up as far as Montreal. In 1844 dredging was begun to give safe passage for vessels of 500 tons. The progress made in this fundamental of safe navigation may be strikingly shown by a few figures. The original depth of water in Lake St. Peter was ten feet six inches. Today there are thirty feet of water there and a channel it has been necessary to dredge seventy miles; and the cost of the work since 1851 has been $15.6 million.

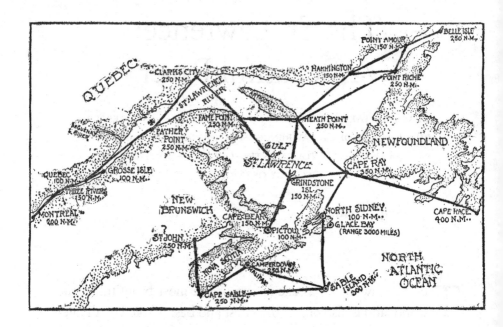

HOW THE ST. LAWRENCE GULF AND RIVER ARE
GUARDED BY WIRELESS STATIONS

The black dots represent government owned and operated wireless stations under the station name. The "N. M.'s" and the dots with the rings around them show stations operated by the Marconi company. The Gulf stations between Montreal and Point Riche are open permanently day and night during the season of navigation. The remainder of the stations, except Pictou, are open permanently day and night all the year round. Pictou is open permanently day and night during the winter season.

The deepening of the channel, the straightening of curves, and the removal of obstructions—these things have been but the beginning of measures taken for the safety of the St. Lawrence route by the Canadian government. The waterways have been charted. The tides have been measured. The darkness has been lighted and beacons erected to throw a warning or a welcoming flash across the waters. Fog alarms have been installed. Wireless and other signal stations have been erected, and a system of marine intelligence has been built up to warn the mariner of coming storms. Science has been enlisted in the cause, and the Dominion has in several directions been a pioneer in the worldwide work of providing for the safety of those who go down to the sea in ships.

Father Point

Father Point, near which the wreck of the *Empress of Ireland* occurred, is a small village on the south bank of the St. Lawrence and ten miles distant from Rimouski, where the transatlantic mails are transferred. It stands high above the water, and on clear days can be seen from a distance of twenty miles.

In 1859 the first telegraph line was connected with this point, and Robert E. Easson was the first operator. It was the first point in Canada to receive old-country news from the boats, and this was relayed to other parts. Messages for the old country were also wired there frequently and mailed on the boats.

The river in this neighborhood is approximately thirty miles wide. Rimouski is about 150 miles down the river from Quebec, and usually is reached in the early morning after an afternoon departure from Quebec.

Picturesque River

The St. Lawrence comes down to the gulf under various names. From the little River St. Louis it pours through the great inland sea of Lake Superior and the St. Mary's River, with its crowded canals, into Lake Huron; thence, in another outflow, through the St. Clair and Detroit rivers to Lake Erie, and from there by the Niagara River and its wonderful falls, to Lake Ontario. From Lake Ontario, for 750 miles, it rolls to the gulf and the ocean under its own historic name and is never less than a mile in width. As it broadens and deepens into beautiful lakes or narrows and shallows into restless rapids, as it sweeps past cliffs crowned with verdure or great natural ridges capped with dense forests, as these break frequently to reveal fertile valleys and a rolling country, or rise into rugged and yet exquisitely picturesque embodiments of nature such as the heights of Quebec, there comes the thought that here, indeed, is a fitting entrance to a great country, an adequate environment for the history of a romantic people, a natural stage setting for great events and gallant deeds.

Though greater than any other Canadian river, the St. Lawrence was, and is, a natural type and embodiment of them all. Sweeping in its volume of water, sometimes wild and impetuous, never slow or sluggish, on its way to the sea, ever changing in its currents and rapids and waterfalls, its lakes and incoming river branches, passing through varied scenery yet always preserving in its course a degree of dignity which approaches majesty, it reveals a combination of volume and vastness, beauty and somberness, which makes it in more senses than one the father of waters on this continent—"the great river without an end," as an Indian once described it to Cartier.

Gulf of St. Lawrence

The gulf into which the river broadens is more or less a landlocked sea, deep and free from reef or shoal, running 500 miles from north to south and 243 from east to west. In its center lies the once lonely and barren Isle of Anticosti; not far from Gaspé Bay, two miles out at sea, lies La Roche Percé, a gigantic pile of stone with perpendicular walls forming, in certain conditions of the weather, a marvelous combination of colors outlined against the blue sky and emerald sea. In this rock there is now an opening broken by the unceasing dash of the waves; according to Denys there were at one time three great arches, and seventy years before his time Champlain stated that there was only one but that one big enough for a ship to sail through; in still-earlier days Indian legends describe its connection with the shore.

Historical Background

Let us at this stage look lightly at some of the geographical and associated conditions as we pass slowly up the St. Lawrence from its mouth, and try to see what manner of region this is which has witnessed so much of romance and has brought together and kept together the new and the old—the Europe of three centuries ago and the America of today. From Percé and its memories of a naval battle in 1776, when two American ships were sunk, we pass along a shore devoted with undying allegiance to codfish, and possessing at Mont Ste. Anne one of the finest scenic views in eastern Canada. At Gaspé, the chief place in the peninsula—the farthest point of Quebec on the south shore of the St. Lawrence—there are abundant salmon and fruitful inland fields. Here Cartier once landed, took possession of vast unknown regions for the king of France, and erected a cross thirty feet high which flew the fleur-de-lis, also, as a mark of ownership; near here, Admiral Kirke defeated a large French fleet. Then comes Cape Gaspé with its towering rampart of sandstone, nearly 700 feet high, and many succeeding miles of rocky walls and lofty cliffs. Near Cape Chatte, another English and French naval fight took place, and near here, also, runs into the St. Lawrence the Matane River, famous for its trout and salmon, while the great river itself stretches thirty-five miles across to its northern shores.

Tadousac

Thence, one goes up the river to Tadousac, the ancient village on the north shore, which nestles at the black jaws of the Saguenay and seems unafraid of all the majesty and mystery of the scene, of all the weird tales and fables which centuries have woven around it, of the dark depths which go down into the bowels of the earth, and of shores which are bleak, inaccessible, and perpendicular walls of soaring rock. A little higher up on the other side of the St. Lawrence are Rivière du Loup and Cacouna—the latter a fashionable summer resort perched on a rocky peninsula many feet above the water. Back on the north shore is Murray Bay—the Malle Baie of Champlain, now famous for its fishing and bathing. Not far up the river, which here is fifteen miles wide, are the picturesque village and mountain of Les Éboulements with Isle aux Coudrés and its medieval population out in the center of the river. As the modern traveler passes on up to Quebec City he realizes something of what scenery is in Canada. On the north, for a time, there is visible a region of splendid vistas, a country of volcanic origin where rocks and mountains seem to roll into one another and commingle in the wildest fantasies of nature's strangest mood.

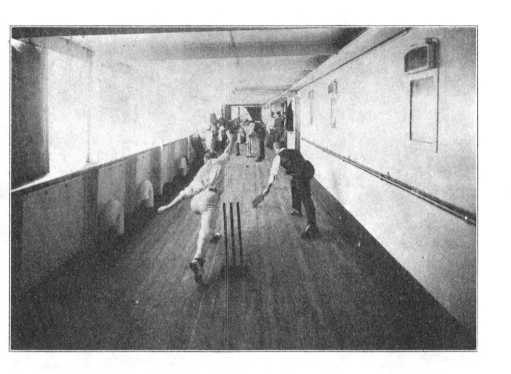

DECK SPORTS

Playing cricket on the deck of the *Empress of Ireland*. One of the favorite amusements of the male passengers. The broad decks and steadiness of the great liner made the game possible on all except the very rough days.

A NOOK IN THE MUSIC-ROOM

A cozy spot for a quiet hour on the *Empress of Ireland*.

Cap Tourmente

Then comes Cap Tourmente, towering 2,000 feet from the water's edge, and other massed piles of granite jutting out into the river, with the Isle of Orléans green and beautiful in the sunlight, with the St. Lawrence jewel-bright and showing glimpses of the white curtain of Montmorency Falls in the distance, with the naked, somber heights of the Laurentides to the north. Everywhere, indeed, along the north shore, from far down on the Labrador coast up to Cap Tourmente, there is this wall of mountains, like a sea of rolling rocks, cleft here and there by such recesses as Murray Bay or the Saguenay. Everywhere, also, are footprints of the early explorers. Here Cartier landed, there Champlain camped, here de Roberval is supposed to have disappeared forever between the wide walls of the Saguenay, there Pont-Gravé or Chauvin left traces of adventurous exploits.

Quebec

At Quebec there looms up the sentinel on the rock which overlooks all the pages of Canadian history and still stands as the most picturesque and impressive city of the New World. Here, on one side of the mile-wide river stand the green heights of Lévis; on the other are the grand outlines of Cape Diamond, crowned with the ramparts of Quebec and now embodying age and power as the graces of the Chateau Frontenac represent modern luxury and business. In the neighborhood of this once-famous walled city lie the Falls of Montmorency and the historic shrine of Ste. Anne de Beaupré; a succession of villages typical of the life of the old-time habitants and redolent of medieval Europe; ruins of famous chateaux embodying memories of history and politics, love and laughter, tragedy and crime.

History and Tradition

Passing from Quebec up the river to Montreal, the mouth of the Chaudière is seen with its splendid falls in the distance and the valley through which Benedict Arnold marched his disastrous expedition to the hoped-for capture of Quebec. At Pointe-aux-Trembles, farther on, there took place several encounters between French and English. Three Rivers stands at the mouth of the St. Maurice, which rises, with the Ottawa and the Saguenay, in a maze of lakes and streams hundreds of miles to the north. In the city lie varied historic memories running back to 1618 and including masses of legend and romantic tradition. Not far from here the St. Lawrence widens into Lake St. Peter and just above it the Richelieu pours its waters into the greater stream, and at this point stands Sorel, where in 1642 a fort was built by Monsieur de Montmagny.

Montreal

Montreal, with its modern population of 500,000 people, rests at the meeting place of the new and the old. It combines in itself the great and sometimes rival interests of church and commerce, the customs and methods of the English and French races, the streets and narrow passages of the past with the great financial thoroughfares and buildings of the present. It stands at a point where all the commercial and business ideals of English Canada meet and press upon the traditions, practices, and policy of French Canada; it preserves itself by combining these varied interests and maintaining a center of wealth, commerce, and transportation, while, so far as its French population is concerned, remaining devoted to racial instincts and loyal to one religious faith.

Geology of Country

Geologically this country of the French Canadian is of intense interest. It reaches back into the most ancient period of the world's evolution; it was a later product of titanic changes and movements of the earth's surface. The grinding, crushing flow of great masses of ice from the arctic regions had potent force in creating the vast basin of the St. Lawrence; upheavals of a volcanic character are obvious around Montreal, are clearly marked in the Lake St. John region, are found in the Laurentian ranges; evidence of earthquakes comes to us from within historic ages. Of the mountains in the Eastern Townships country, where the elemental struggles of geological antiquity must have been violent beyond description, Jesuit records at St. Francis describe an earthquake of September 5, 1732, so powerful as to destroy a neighboring Indian village. The better-known disturbance of 1663 along the lower St. Lawrence lasted for months and resulted in continuous landslides and a series of convulsions. The St. Lawrence was said to have run white as milk for a long distance because of the hills and vast masses of sand which were thrown into it, ranges of hills disappeared altogether, the forests, according to an Indian description, became as though they were drunk, vast fissures opened in the ground, and the courses of streams were changed. The whole of the Mount Royal region and valley shows clear evidences of volcanic action.

These latter disturbances were, however, only episodes in geologic ages of formation; there are no signs of a continuing character. Forever, so far as finite vision can see, the mighty piles of the Laurentian and other ranges of this part of the continent will stand as memorials of still more mighty world movements, as a somber environment for the history of the Indians and the early struggles of the French Canadian people, and as solemn witnesses of the civilization which has now taken possession of this inherited greatness and hopes in its own fleeting, fitful, fighting way to build upon and refine and cultivate nature's splendid storehouse for its own purposes and the advancement of its people.

20

The Tragic Story of the *Titanic* Disaster

"THE *TITANIC* IN COLLISION, BUT EVERYBODY SAFE"—ANOTHER
TRIUMPH SET DOWN TO WIRELESS TELEGRAPHY—THE WORLD
GOES TO SLEEP PEACEFULLY—THE SAD AWAKENING

L ike a bolt out of a clear sky came the wireless message on Monday, April 15, 1912, that on Sunday night the great *Titanic*, on her maiden voyage across the Atlantic, had struck a gigantic iceberg, but that all the passengers were saved. The ship had signaled her distress and another victory was set down to wireless. Twenty-one hundred lives saved!

Additional news was soon received that the ship had collided with a mountain of ice in the North Atlantic, off Cape Race, Newfoundland, at 10:25 Sunday evening, April 14. At 4:15 Monday morning the Canadian Government Marine Agency received a wireless message that the *Titanic* was sinking and that the steamers towing her were trying to get her into shoal water near Cape Race, for the purpose of beaching her.

Wireless dispatches up to noon Monday showed that the passengers of the *Titanic* were being transferred aboard the steamer *Carpathia*, a Cunarder, which left New York, April 13, for Naples. Twenty

FACTS ABOUT THE WRECK OF THE *TITANIC*

Number of persons aboard: 2,224

Number of lifeboats and rafts: 20

Capacity of each lifeboat: 50 passengers and crew of 8

Utmost capacity of lifeboats and rafts: about 1,100

Number of lifeboats wrecked in launching: 4

Capacity of lifeboats safely launched: 928

Total number of persons taken in lifeboats: 717

Number who died in lifeboats: 6

Total number saved: 711

Total number of *Titanic*'s company lost: 1,513

The cause of the disaster was a collision with an iceberg in latitude 41.46 north, longitude 50.14 west. The *Titanic* had had repeated warnings of the presence of ice in that part of the course. Two official warnings had been received defining the position of the ice fields. It had been calculated on the *Titanic* that she would reach the ice fields about eleven o'clock Sunday night. The collision occurred at 11:40. At that time the ship was driving at a speed of 21 to 23 knots, or about 26 miles, an hour.

There had been no details of seamen assigned to each boat.

Some of the boats left the ship without seamen enough to man the oars.

Some of the boats were not more than half full of passengers.

The boats had no provisions, some of them had no water stored, some were without sail equipment or compasses.

In some boats, which carried sails wrapped and bound, there was not a person with a knife to cut the ropes. In some boats the plugs in the bottom had been pulled out and the women passengers were compelled to thrust their hands into the holes to keep the boats from filling and sinking.

The captain, E. J. Smith, admiral of the White Star fleet, went down with his ship.

boatloads of the *Titanic*'s passengers were said to have been transferred to the *Carpathia* then, and allowing forty to sixty persons as the capacity of each lifeboat, some 800 or 1,200 persons had already been transferred from the damaged liner to the *Carpathia*. They were reported as being taken to Halifax, whence they would be sent by train to New York.

Another liner, the *Parisian*, of the Allan Company, which sailed from Glasgow for Halifax on April 6, was said to be close at hand and assisting in the work of rescue. The *Baltic*, *Virginian*, and *Olympic* were also near the scene, according to the information received by wireless.

While badly damaged, the giant vessel was reported as still afloat, but whether she could reach port or shoal water was uncertain. The White Star officials declared that the *Titanic* was in no immediate danger of sinking, because of her numerous watertight compartments.

"While we are still lacking definite information," Mr. Franklin, vice president of the White Star Line, said later in the afternoon, "we believe the *Titanic*'s passengers will reach Halifax, Wednesday evening. We have received no further word from Captain Haddock, of the *Olympic*, or from any of the ships in the vicinity, but are confident that there will be no loss of life."

With the understanding that the survivors would be taken to Halifax, the line arranged to have thirty Pullman cars, two diners, and many passenger coaches leave Boston Monday night for Halifax to get the passengers after they were landed. Mr. Franklin made a guess that the *Titanic*'s passengers would get into Halifax on Wednesday. The Department of Commerce and Labor notified the White Star Line that customs and immigration inspectors would be sent from Montreal to Halifax in order that there would be as little delay as possible in getting the passengers on trains.

Monday night the world slept in peace and assurance. A wireless message had finally been received, reading:

"All *Titanic*'s passengers safe."

It was not until nearly a week later that the fact was discovered that this message had been wrongly received in the confusion of messages flashing through the air, and that in reality the message should have read:

"Are all *Titanic*'s passengers safe?"

With the dawning of Tuesday morning came the awful news of the true fate of the *Titanic*.

21

The Most Sumptuous Palace Afloat

DIMENSIONS OF THE *TITANIC*—CAPACITY—PROVISIONS FOR THE
COMFORT AND ENTERTAINMENT OF PASSENGERS—MECHANICAL
EQUIPMENT—THE ARMY OF ATTENDANTS REQUIRED

T he statistical record of the great ship has news value at this
time.

Early in 1908 officials of the White Star Company announced
that they would eclipse all previous records in shipbuilding with a
vessel of staggering dimensions. The *Titanic* resulted.

The keel of the ill-fated ship was laid in the summer of 1909
at the Harland & Wolff yards, Belfast. Lord Pirrie, considered one
of the best authorities on shipbuilding in the world, was the designer.
The leviathan was launched on May 31, 1911, and was completed in
February 1912, at a cost of $10 million.

Sister Ship of *Olympic*

The *Titanic*, largest liner in commission, was a sister ship of the *Olympic*. The registered tonnage of each vessel is estimated as 45,000, but

officers of the White Star Line say that the *Titanic* measured 45,328 tons. The *Titanic* was commanded by Captain E. J. Smith, the White Star admiral, who had previously been on the *Olympic*.

She was 882½ feet long, or about four city blocks, and was 5,000 tons bigger than a battleship twice as large as the dreadnought *Delaware*.

Like her sister ship, the *Olympic*, the *Titanic* was a four-funneled vessel, and had eleven decks. The distance from the keel to the top of the funnels was 175 feet. She had an average speed of twenty-one knots.

The *Titanic* could accommodate 2,500 passengers. The steamship was divided into numerous compartments, separated by fifteen bulkheads. She was equipped with a gymnasium, swimming pool, hospital with operating room, and a grill and palm garden.

Carried Crew of 860

The registered tonnage was 45,000, and the displacement tonnage 66,000. She was capable of carrying 2,500 passengers and the crew numbered 860.

The largest plates employed in the hull were 36 feet long, weighing 4½ tons each, and the largest steel beam used was 92 feet long, the weight of this double beam being 4 tons. The rudder, which was operated electrically, weighed 100 tons, the anchors 15½ tons each, the center (turbine) propeller 22 tons, and each of the two "wing" propellers 38 tons each. The after "boss-arms," from which were suspended the three propeller shafts, tipped the scales at 73½ tons, and the forward "boss-arms" at 45 tons. Each link in the anchor chains weighed 175 pounds. There were more than 2,000 sidelights and windows to light the public rooms and passenger cabins.

Nothing was left to chance in the construction of the *Titanic*.

Three million rivets (weighing 1,200 tons) held the solid plates of steel together. To ensure stability in binding the heavy plates in the double bottom, half a million rivets, weighing about 270 tons, were used.

All the plating of the hulls was riveted by hydraulic power, driving seven-ton riveting machines, suspended from traveling cranes. The double bottom extended the full length of the vessel, varying from five feet three inches to six feet three inches in depth, and lent added strength to the hull.

Most Luxurious Steamship

Not only was the *Titanic* the largest steamship afloat but it was the most luxurious. Elaborately furnished cabins opened onto her eleven decks, and some of these decks were reserved as private promenades that were engaged with the best suites. One of these suites was sold for $4,350 for the boat's maiden and only voyage. Suites similar, but which were without the private promenade decks, sold for $2,300.

The *Titanic* differed in some respects from her sister ship. The *Olympic* has a lower promenade deck, but in the *Titanic*'s case the staterooms were brought out flush with the outside of the superstructure, and the rooms themselves made much larger. The sitting rooms of some of the suites on this deck were fifteen-by-fifteen feet.

The restaurant was much larger than that of the *Olympic* and it had a novelty in the shape of a private promenade deck on the starboard side, to be used exclusively by its patrons. Adjoining it was a reception room, where hosts and hostesses could meet their guests.

Two private promenades were connected with the two most luxurious suites on the ship. The suites were situated about amidships, one on either side of the vessel, and each was about fifty feet long. One of the suites comprised a sitting room, two bedrooms, and a bath.

These private promenades were expensive luxuries. The cost figured out something like forty dollars a front foot for a six days' voyage. They, with the suites to which they are attached, were the most expensive transatlantic accommodations yet offered.

The Engine Room

The engine room was divided into two sections, one given to the reciprocating engines and the other to the turbines. There were two sets of the reciprocating kind, one working each of the wing propellers through a four-cylinder triple-expansion, direct-acting inverted engine. Each set could generate 15,000 indicated horsepower at seventy-five revolutions a minute. The Parsons-type turbine takes steam from the reciprocating engines, and by developing a horsepower of 16,000 at 165 revolutions a minute works the third of the ship's propellers, the one directly under the rudder. Of the four funnels of the vessel three were connected with the engine room, and the fourth or after funnel for ventilating the ship including the gallery.

Practically all of the space on the *Titanic* below the upper deck was occupied by steam-generating plant, coal bunkers, and propelling machinery. Eight of the fifteen watertight compartments contained the mechanical part of the vessel. There were, for instance, twenty-four double-end and five single-end boilers, each sixteen feet nine inches in diameter, the larger twenty feet long and the smaller eleven feet nine inches long. The larger boilers had six fires under each of them and the smaller three furnaces. Coal was stored in bunker space along the side of the ship between the lower and middle decks, and was first shipped from there into bunkers running all the way across the vessel in the lowest part. From there the stokers handed it into the furnaces.

One of the most interesting features of the vessel was the refrigerating plant, which comprised a huge ice-making and refrigerating machine and a number of provision rooms on the after part of the lower and orlop decks. There were separate cold rooms for beef, mutton, poultry, game, fish, vegetables, fruit, butter, bacon, cheese, flowers, mineral water, wine, spirits, and champagne, all maintained at different temperatures most suitable to each. Perishable freight had a compartment of its own, also chilled by the plant.

Comfort and Stability

Two main ideas were carried out in the *Titanic.* One was comfort and the other stability. The vessel was planned to be an ocean ferry. She was to have only a speed of twenty-one knots, far below that of some other modern vessels, but she was planned to make that speed, blow high or blow low, so that if she left one side of the ocean at a given time she could be relied on to reach the other side at almost a certain minute of a certain hour.

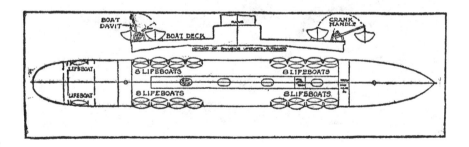

LIFEBOAT AND DAVITS ON THE *TITANIC*

This diagram shows very clearly the arrangement of the lifeboats and the manner in which they were launched.

LIFEBOATS AS SEEN FROM THE CARPATHIA

Photographs taken from the rescue ship as she reached the first boats carrying the *Titanic*'s sufferers.

CORNER OF THE MAIN SALOON

Showing the well and dome from the cafe, and giving an idea of the beautiful decorations on the lost liner.

One who has looked into modern methods for safeguarding a vessel of the *Titanic* type can hardly imagine an accident that could cause her to founder. No collision such as has been the fate of any ship in recent years, it has been thought up to this time, could send her down, nor could running against an iceberg do it unless such an accident were coupled with the remotely possible blowing out of a boiler. She would sink at once, probably, if she were to run over a submerged rock or derelict in such manner that both her keel plates and her double bottom were torn away for more than half her length; but such a catastrophe was so remotely possible that it did not even enter the field of conjecture.

The reason for all this is found in the modern arrangement of watertight steel compartments into which all ships now are divided and of which the *Titanic* had fifteen so disposed that half of them, including the largest, could be flooded without impairing the safety of the vessel. Probably it was the working of these bulkheads and the watertight doors between them as they are supposed to work that saved the *Titanic* from foundering when she struck the iceberg.

These bulkheads were of heavy sheet steel and started at the very bottom of the ship and extended right up to the topside. The openings in the bulkheads were just about the size of the ordinary doorway, but the doors did not swing as in a house, but fitted into watertight grooves above the opening. They could be released instantly in several ways, and once closed formed a barrier to the water as solid as the bulkhead itself.

In the *Titanic*, as in other great modern ships, these doors were held in place above the openings by friction clutches. On the bridge was a switch which connected with an electric magnet at the side of the bulkhead opening. The turning of this switch caused the magnet to draw down a heavy weight, which instantly released the friction clutch, and allowed the door to fall or slide down over the opening in a second. If, however, through accident the bridge switch was rendered useless, the doors would close automatically in a few seconds. This was arranged by means of large metal floats at the side of the doorways, which rested just above the level of the double bottom, and as the water entered the compartments these floats would rise to it and directly release the clutch holding the door open. These clutches could also be released by hand.

It was said of the *Titanic* that her compartments could be flooded as far back or as far forward as the engine room and she would float, though she might take on a heavy list, or settle considerably at one end. To provide against just such an accident as she is said to have encountered, she had set back a good distance from the bows an extra-heavy cross partition known as the collision bulkhead, which would prevent water getting in amidships, even though a good part of her bow should be torn away. What a ship can stand and still float was shown a few years ago when the *Suevic* of the White Star Line went on the rocks on the British coast. The wreckers could not move the forward part of her, so they separated her into two sections by the use of dynamite, and after putting in a temporary bulkhead floated off the after half of the ship, put it in dry dock, and built a new forward part for her. More recently the battleship *Maine*, or what was left of her, was floated out to sea, and kept on top of the water by her watertight compartments only.

22

The *Titanic* Strikes an Iceberg!

TARDY ATTENTION TO WARNING RESPONSIBLE FOR ACCIDENT—
THE DANGER NOT REALIZED AT FIRST—AN INTERRUPTED CARD
GAME—PASSENGERS JOKE AMONG THEMSELVES—THE REAL TRUTH
DAWNS—PANIC ON BOARD—WIRELESS CALLS FOR HELP

Sunday night the magnificent ocean liner was plunging through a comparatively placid sea, on the surface of which there was much mushy ice and here and there a number of comparatively harmless-looking floes. The night was clear and stars visible. First Officer William T. Murdock was in charge of the bridge. The first intimation of the presence of the iceberg that he received was from the lookout in the crow's nest.

Three warnings were transmitted from the crow's nest of the *Titanic* to the officer on the doomed steamship's bridge fifteen minutes before she struck, according to Thomas Whiteley, a first saloon steward.

Whiteley, who was whipped overboard from the ship by a rope while helping to lower a lifeboat, finally reported on the *Carpathia* aboard one of the boats that contained, he said, both the crow's-nest lookouts. He heard a conversation between them, he asserted, in

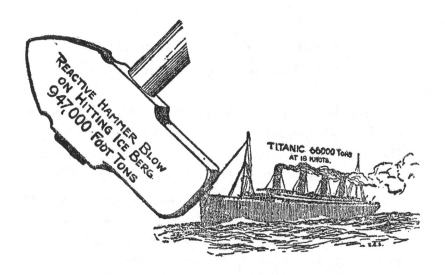

A GRAPHIC ILLUSTRATION OF THE FORCE WITH WHICH
A VESSEL STRIKES AN ICEBERG

which they discussed the warnings given to the *Titanic*'s bridge of the presence of the iceberg.

Whiteley did not know the names of either of the lookout men and believed that they returned to England with the majority of the surviving members of the crew.

"I heard one of them say that at 11:15 o'clock, fifteen minutes before the *Titanic* struck, he had reported to First Officer Murdock, on the bridge, that he fancied he saw an iceberg," said Whiteley. "Twice after that, the lookout said, he warned Murdock that a berg was ahead. They were very indignant that no attention was paid to their warnings."

Tardy Attention to Warning Responsible for Accident

Murdock's tardy answering of a telephone call from the crow's nest is assigned by Whiteley as the cause of the disaster.

When Murdock answered the call he received the information that the iceberg was due ahead. This information was imparted just a few seconds before the crash, and had the officer promptly answered the ring of the bell it is probable that the accident could have been avoided, or at least, been reduced by the lowered speed.

The lookout saw a towering "blue berg" looming up in the sea path of the *Titanic* and called the bridge on the ship's telephone. When, after the passing of those two or three fateful minutes, an officer on the bridge lifted the telephone receiver from its hook to answer the lookout, it was too late. The speeding liner, cleaving a calm sea under a star-studded sky, had reached the floating mountain of ice, which the theoretically "unsinkable" ship struck a crashing, if glancing, blow with her starboard bow.

Murdock Paid with Life

Had Murdock, according to the account of the tragedy given by two of the *Titanic*'s seamen, known how imperative was that call from the lookout man, the men at the wheel of the liner might have swerved the great ship sufficiently to avoid the berg altogether. At the worst the vessel would probably have struck the mass of ice with her stern.

Murdock, if the tale of the *Titanic* sailor be true, expiated his negligence by shooting himself within sight of all alleged victims huddled in lifeboats or struggling in the icy seas.

When at last the danger was realized, the great ship was so close upon the berg that it was practically impossible to avoid collision with it.

Vain Trial to Clear Berg

The first officer did what other startled and alert commanders would have done under similar circumstances, that is, he made an effort by going full speed ahead on the starboard propeller and reversing his port propeller, simultaneously throwing his helm over, to make a rapid turn and clear the berg. The maneuver was not successful. He succeeded in saving his bows from crashing into the ice cliff, but nearly the entire length of the underbody of the great ship on the starboard side was ripped. The speed of the *Titanic*, estimated to be at least twenty-one knots, was so terrific that the knife-like edge of the iceberg's spur protruding under the sea cut through her like a can opener.

The *Titanic* was in 41.46 north latitude and 50.14 west longitude when she was struck, very near the spot on the wide Atlantic where the *Carmania* encountered a field of ice, studded with great bergs, on her voyage to New York which ended on April 14. It was really an ice pack, due to an unusually severe winter in the North Atlantic. No fewer than twenty-five bergs, some of great height, were counted.

The shock was almost imperceptible. The first officer did not apparently realize that the great ship had received her death wound, and none of the passengers had the slightest suspicion that anything more than a usual minor sea accident had happened. Hundreds who had gone to their berths and were asleep were unawakened by the vibration.

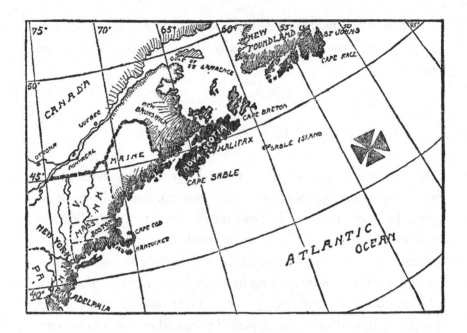

THE LOCATION OF THE DISASTER

Bridge Game Not Disturbed

To illustrate the placidity with which practically all the men regarded the accident, it is related that Pierre Maréchal, son of the vice admiral of the French navy, Lucien Smith, Paul Chevré, a French sculptor, and A. F. Ormont, a cotton broker, were in the Café Parisien playing bridge.

The four calmly got up from the table and after walking on deck and looking over the rail returned to their game. One of them had left his cigar on the card table, and while the three others were gazing out on the sea he remarked that he couldn't afford to lose his smoke, returned for his cigar, and came out again.

They remained only for a few moments on deck, and then resumed their game under the impression that the ship had stopped for reasons best known to the captain and not involving any danger to her. Later, in describing the scene that took place, Monsieur Maréchal, who was among the survivors, said: "When three-quarters of a mile away we stopped, the spectacle before our eyes was in its way magnificent. In a very calm sea, beneath a sky moonless but sown with millions of stars, the enormous *Titanic* lay on the water, illuminated from the waterline to the boat deck. The bow was slowly sinking into the black water."

The tendency of the whole ship's company except the men in the engine department, who were made aware of the danger by the inrushing water, was to make light of and in some instances even to ridicule the thought of danger to so substantial a fabric.

The Captain on Deck

When Captain Smith came from the chart room onto the bridge, his first words were, "Close the emergency doors."

"They're already closed, sir," Mr. Murdock replied.

"Send to the carpenter and tell him to sound the ship," was the next order. The message was sent to the carpenter, but the carpenter never came up to report. He was probably the first man on the ship to lose his life.

The captain then looked at the communicator, which shows in what direction the ship is listing. He saw that she carried five degrees list to starboard.

The ship was then rapidly settling forward. All the steam sirens were blowing. By the captain's orders, given in the next few minutes, the engines were put to work at pumping out the ship, distress signals were sent by the Marconi, and rockets were sent up from the bridge by Quartermaster Rowe. All hands were ordered on deck.

Passengers Not Alarmed

The blasting shriek of the sirens had not alarmed the great company of the *Titanic*, because such steam calls are an incident of travel in seas where fogs roll. Many had gone to bed, but the hour, 11:40 P.M., was not so late for the friendly contact of saloons and smoking rooms. It was Sunday night and the ship's concert had ended, but there were many hundreds up and moving among the gay lights, and many on deck with their eyes strained toward the mysterious west, where home lay. And in one jarring, breath-sweeping moment all of these, asleep or awake, were at the mercy of chance. Few among the more than 2,000 aboard could have had a thought of danger. The man who had stood up in the smoking room to say that the *Titanic* was vulnerable or that in a few minutes two-thirds of her people would be face-to-face with death, would have been considered a fool or a lunatic. No ship ever sailed the seas that gave her passengers more confidence, more cool security.

Within a few minutes stewards and other members of the crew were sent round to arouse the people. Some utterly refused to get up. The stewards had almost to force the doors of the staterooms to make the somnolent appreciate their peril, and many of them, it is believed, were drowned like rats in a trap.

Astor and Wife Strolled on Deck

Colonel and Mrs. Astor were in their room and saw the ice vision flash by. They had not appreciably felt the gentle shock and supposed that nothing out of the ordinary had happened. They were both dressed and came on deck leisurely. William T. Stead, the London journalist, wandered on deck for a few minutes, stopping to talk to Frank Millet.

"What do they say is the trouble?" he asked.

"Icebergs," was the brief reply.

"Well," said Stead, "I guess it is nothing serious. I'm going back to my cabin to read."

From end to end on the mighty boat officers were rushing about without much noise or confusion, but giving orders sharply. Captain Smith told the third officer to rush downstairs and see whether the water was coming in very fast. "And," he added, "take some armed guards along to see that the stokers and engineers stay at their posts."

In two minutes the officer returned. "It looks pretty bad, sir," he said. "The water is rushing in and filling the bottom. The locks of the watertight compartments have been sprung by the shock."

"Give the command for all passengers to be on deck with life belts on."

Through the length and breadth of the boat, upstairs and down-stairs, on all decks, the cry rang out: "All passengers on deck with life preservers."

A Sudden Tremor of Fear

For the first time there was a feeling of panic. Husbands sought for wives and children. Families gathered together. Many who were asleep hastily caught up their clothing and rushed on deck. A moment before the men had been joking about the life belts, according to the story told by Mrs. Vera Dick, of Calgary, Canada. "Try this one," one man said to her. "They are the very latest thing this season. Every-body's wearing them now."

Another man suggested to a woman friend, who had a fox terrier in her arms, that she should put a lifesaver on the dog. "It won't fit," the woman replied, laughing. "Make him carry it in his mouth," said the friend.

Confusion Among the Immigrants

Below, on the steerage deck, there was intense confusion. About the time the officers on the first deck gave the order that all men should stand to one side and all women should go below to deck B, taking the children with them, a similar order was given to the steerage passengers. The women were ordered to the front, the men to the rear. Half a dozen healthy, husky immigrants pushed their way forward and tried to crowd into the first boat.

"Stand back," shouted the officers who were manning the boat. "The women come first."

Shouting curses in various foreign languages, the immigrant men continued their pushing and tugging to climb into the boats. Shots rang out. One big fellow fell over the railing into the water. Another dropped to the deck, moaning. His jaw had been shot away. This was the story told by the bystanders afterward on the pier. One husky Italian told the writer on the pier that the way in which the men were shot down was horrible. His sympathy was with the men who were shot.

"They were only trying to save their lives," he said.

Wireless Operator Died at His Post

On board the *Titanic*, the wireless operator, with a life belt about his waist, was hitting the instrument that was sending out CQD messages, "Struck on iceberg, CQD."

"Shall I tell captain to turn back and help?" flashed a reply from the *Carpathia*.

"Yes, old man," the *Titanic* wireless operator responded. "Guess we're sinking."

An hour later, when the second wireless man came into the box-like room to tell his companion what the situation was, he found a black stoker creeping up behind the operator and saw him raise a knife over his head. He said afterward—he was among those rescued—that he realized at once that the man intended to kill the operator in order to take his life belt from him. The second operator pulled out his revolver and shot him dead.

"What was the trouble?" asked the operator.

"That man was going to kill you and steal your life belt," the second man replied.

"Thanks, old man," said the operator. The second man went on deck to get some more information. He was just in time to jump overboard before the *Titanic* went down. The wireless operator and the body of the man who tried to steal his belt went down together.

On the deck where the first-class passengers were quartered, known as deck A, there was none of the confusion that was taking place on the lower decks. The *Titanic* was standing without much rocking. The captain had given an order and the band was playing.

23

"Women and Children First!"

COOL-HEADED OFFICERS AND CREW BRING ORDER OUT OF
CHAOS—FILLING THE LIFEBOATS—HEARTRENDING SCENES AS
FAMILIES ARE PARTED—FOUR LIFEBOATS LOST—INCIDENTS OF
BRAVERY—"THE BOATS ARE ALL FILLED!"

O nce on the deck, many hesitated to enter the swinging lifeboats. The glassy sea, the starlit sky, the absence, in the first few moments, of intense excitement, gave them the feeling that there was only some slight mishap; that those who got into the boats would have a chilly half hour below and might, later, be laughed at.

It was such a feeling as this, from all accounts, which caused John Jacob Astor and his wife to refuse the places offered them in the first boat and to retire to the gymnasium. In the same way H. J. Allison, a Montreal banker, laughed at the warning, and his wife, reassured by him, took her time dressing. They and their daughter did not reach the *Carpathia*. Their son, less than two years old, was carried into a lifeboat by his nurse and was taken in charge by Major Arthur Peuchen.

The Lifeboats Lowered

The admiration felt by the passengers and crew for the matchlessly appointed vessel was translated, in those first few moments, into a confidence which for some proved deadly. The pulsing of the engines had ceased, and the steamship lay just as though she were awaiting the order to go on again after some trifling matter had been adjusted. But in a few minutes the canvas covers were lifted from the lifeboats and the crews allotted to each standing by, ready to lower them to the water.

Nearly all the boats that were lowered on the port side of the ship touched the water without capsizing. Four of the others lowered to starboard, including one collapsible, were capsized. All, however, who were in the collapsible boats that practically went to pieces, were rescued by the other boats.

Presently the order was heard: "All men stand back and all women retire to the deck below." That was the smoking room deck, or the B deck. The men stood away and remained in absolute silence, leaning against the rail or pacing up and down the deck slowly. Many of them lighted cigars or cigarettes and began to smoke.

Loading the Boats

The boats were swung out and lowered from the A deck above. The women were marshaled quietly in lines along the B deck, and when the boats were lowered down to the level of the latter the women were assisted to climb into them.

As each of the boats was filled with its quota of passengers the word was given and it was carefully lowered down to the dark surface of the water.

Nobody seemed to know how Mr. Ismay got into a boat, but it was assumed that he wished to make a presentation of the case of the *Titanic* to his company. He was among those who apparently realized that the splendid ship was doomed. All hands in the lifeboats, under instructions from officers and men in charge, were rowed a considerable distance from the ship herself in order to get far away from the possible suction that would follow her foundering.

Coolest Men on Board

Captain Smith and Major Archibald Butt, military aide to the president of the United States, were among the coolest men on board. A number of steerage passengers were yelling and screaming and fighting to get to the boats. Officers drew guns and told them that if they moved toward the boats they would be shot dead. Major Butt had a gun in his hand and covered the men who tried to get to the boats.

The following story of his bravery was told by Mrs. Henry B. Harris, wife of the theatrical manager:

"The world should rise in praise of Major Butt. That man's conduct will remain in my memory forever. The American army is honored by him and the way he taught some of the other men how to behave when women and children were suffering that awful mental fear of death. Major Butt was near me and I noticed everything that he did.

"When the order to man the boats came, the captain whispered something to Major Butt. The two of them had become friends. The major immediately became as one in supreme command. You would have thought he was at a White House reception. A dozen or more women became hysterical all at once, as something connected with a lifeboat went wrong.

"Major Butt stepped over to them and said: 'Really, you must not act like that; we are all going to see you through this thing.' He helped the sailors rearrange the rope or chain that had gone wrong and lifted some of the women in with a touch of gallantry. Not only was there a complete lack of any fear in his manner, but there was the action of an aristocrat.

"When the time came he was a man to be feared. In one of the earlier boats fifty women, it seemed, were about to be lowered, when a man, suddenly panic-stricken, ran to the stern of it. Major Butt shot one arm out, caught him by the back of the neck, and jerked him backward like a pillow. His head cracked against a rail and he was stunned.

"'Sorry,' said Major Butt, 'women will be attended to first or I'll break every damned bone in your body.'"

Forced Men Usurping Places to Vacate

"The boats were lowered one by one, and as I stood by, my husband said to me, 'Thank God for Archie Butt.' Perhaps Major Butt heard it, for he turned his face toward us for a second and smiled. Just at that moment a young man was arguing to get into a lifeboat, and Major Butt had a hold of the lad by the arm, like a big brother, and was telling him to keep his head and be a man.

"Major Butt helped those poor frightened steerage people so wonderfully, so tenderly, and yet with such cool and manly firmness that he prevented the loss of many lives from panic. He was a soldier to the last. He was one of God's greatest noblemen, and I think I can say he was an example of bravery even to men on the ship."

ON THE BRIDGE OF THE *EMPRESS OF IRELAND*

The ship's officers are taking the noon observation to ascertain the position of the ship. At the right are the engine-room and wheel-house "telegraphs." By moving the levers the officers controlled the movements of the ship with absolute precision.

SCENE ON DECK

Showing the spacious decks and easy steamer chairs. It was not far from this point that the *Storstad* struck the death-blow.

Last Words of Major Butt

Miss Marie Young, who was a music instructor to President Roosevelt's children and had known Major Butt during the Roosevelt occupancy of the White House, told this story of his heroism.

"Archie himself put me into the boat, wrapped blankets about me, and tucked me in as carefully as if we were starting on a motor ride. He himself entered the boat with me, performing the little courtesies as calmly and with as smiling a face as if death were far away, instead of being but a few moments removed from him.

"When he had carefully wrapped me up he stepped upon the gunwale of the boat and, lifting his hat, smiled down at me. 'Good-bye, Miss Young,' he said. 'Good luck to you, and don't forget to remember me to the folks back home.' Then he stepped back and waved his hand to me as the boat was lowered. I think I was the last woman he had a chance to help, for the boat went down shortly after we cleared the suction zone."

Colonel Astor Another Hero

Colonel Astor was another of the heroes of the awful night. Effort was made to persuade him to take a place in one of the lifeboats, but he emphatically refused to do so until every woman and child on board had been provided for, not excepting the women members of the ship's company.

One of the passengers describing the consummate courage of Colonel Astor said:

"He led Mrs. Astor to the side of the ship and helped her to the lifeboat to which she had been assigned. I saw that she was prostrated and said she would remain and take her chances with him,

THE NATURE OF THE INJURY SUSTAINED BY THE *TITANIC*

but Colonel Astor quietly insisted and tried to reassure her in a few words. As she took her place in the boat her eyes were fixed upon him. Colonel Astor smiled, touched his cap, and when the boat moved safely away from the ship's side he turned back to his place among the men."

Mrs. Ida S. Hippach and her daughter Jean, survivors of the *Titanic,* said they were saved by Colonel John Jacob Astor, who forced the crew of the last lifeboat to wait for them.

"We saw Colonel Astor place Mrs. Astor in a boat and assure her that he would follow later," said Mrs. Hippach.

"He turned to us with a smile and said, 'Ladies, you are next.' The officer in charge of the boat protested that the craft was full, and the seamen started to lower it.

"Colonel Astor exclaimed, 'Hold that boat,' in the voice of a man accustomed to be obeyed, and they did as he ordered. The boat had been lowered past the upper deck and the colonel took us to the deck below and put us in the boat, one after the other, through a porthole."

Heartbreaking Scenes

There were some terrible scenes. Fathers were parting from their children and giving them an encouraging pat on the shoulders; men were kissing their wives and telling them that they would be with them shortly. One man said there was absolutely no danger, that the boat was the finest ever built, with watertight compartments, and that it could not sink. That seemed to be the general impression.

A few of the men, however, were panic-stricken even when the first of the fifty-six-foot lifeboats was being filled. Fully ten men threw themselves into the boats already crowded with women and children. These men were dragged back and hurled sprawling across the deck. Six of them, screaming with fear, struggled to their feet and made a second attempt to rush to the boats.

About ten shots sounded in quick succession. The six cowardly men were stopped in their tracks, staggered, and collapsed one after another. At least two of them vainly attempted to creep toward the boats again. The others lay quite still. This scene of bloodshed served its purpose. In that particular section of the deck there was no further attempt to violate the rule of "women and children first."

"I helped fill the boats with women," said Thomas Whiteley, who was a waiter on the *Titanic*. "Collapsible boat No. 2 on the starboard jammed. The second officer was hacking at the ropes with a knife and I was being dragged around the deck by that rope when I looked up and saw the boat, with all aboard, turn turtle. In some way I got overboard myself and clung to an oak dresser. I wasn't more than sixty feet from the *Titanic* when she went down. Her big stern rose up in the air and she went down bow first. I saw all the machinery drop out of her."

Henry B. Harris

Henry B. Harris, of New York, a theatrical manager, was one of the men who showed superb courage in the crisis. When the lifeboats were first being filled, and before there was any panic, Mr. Harris went to the side of his wife before the boat was lowered away.

"Women first," shouted one of the ship's officers. Mr. Harris glanced up and saw that the remark was addressed to him.

"All right," he replied coolly. "Good-bye, my dear," he said as he kissed his wife, pressed her a moment to his breast, and then climbed back to the *Titanic*'s deck.

Three Explosions

Up to this time there had been no panic; but about one hour before the ship plunged to the bottom there were there separate explosions of bulkheads as the vessel filled. These were at intervals of about fifteen minutes. From that time there was a different scene. The rush for the remaining boats became a stampede.

The stokers rushed up from below and tried to beat a path through the steerage men and women and through the sailors and officers, to get into the boats. They had their iron bars and shovels, and they struck down all who stood in their way.

The first to come up from the depths of the ship was an engineer. From what he is reported to have said it is probable that the steam fittings were broken and many were scalded to death when the *Titanic* lifted. He said he had to dash through a narrow place beside a broken pipe and his back was frightfully scalded.

Right at his heels came the stokers. The officers had pistols, but they could not use them at first for fear of killing the women and children. The sailors fought with their fists and many of them took the stoke bars and shovels from the stokers and used them to beat back the others.

Many of the coal passers and stokers who had been driven back from the boats went to the rail, and whenever a boat was filled and lowered several of them jumped overboard and swam toward it trying to climb aboard. Several of the survivors said that men who swam to the sides of their boats were pulled in or climbed in.

Dozens of the cabin passengers were witnesses of some of the frightful scenes on the steerage deck. The steerage survivors said that ten women from the upper decks were the only cool passengers in the lifeboat, and they tried to quiet the steerage women, who were nearly all crazed with fear and grief.

Other Heroes

Among the chivalrous young heroes of the *Titanic* disaster were Washington A. Roebling, 2d, and Howard Case, London representative of the Vacuum Oil Company. Both were urged repeatedly to take places in lifeboats, but scorned the opportunity, while working against time to save the women aboard the ill-fated ship. They went to their death, it is said by survivors, with smiles on their faces.

Both of these young men aided in the saving of Mrs. William T. Graham, wife of the president of the American Can Company, and Mrs. Graham's nineteen-year-old daughter, Margaret.

Afterward relating some of her experiences, Mrs. Graham said: "There was a rap at the door. It was a passenger whom we had met shortly after the ship left Liverpool, and his name was Roebling— Washington A. Roebling, 2d. He was a gentleman and a brave man. He warned us of the danger and told us that it would be best to be prepared for an emergency. We heeded his warning, and I looked out of my window and saw a great big iceberg facing us. Immediately I knew what had happened and we lost no time after that to get out into the saloon.

"In one of the gangways I met an officer of the ship.

"'What is the matter?' I asked him.

"'We've only burst two pipes,' he said. 'Everything is all right, don't worry.'

"'But what makes the ship list so?' I asked.

"'Oh, that's nothing,' he replied, and walked away.

"Mr. Case advised us to get into a boat.

"'And what are you going to do?' we asked him.

"'Oh,' he replied, 'I'll take a chance and stay here.'

"Just at that time they were filling up the third lifeboat on the port side of the ship. I thought at the time that it was the third boat which had been lowered, but I found out later that they had lowered other boats on the other side, where the people were more excited because they were sinking on that side.

"Just then Mr. Roebling came up, too, and told us to hurry and get into the third boat. Mr. Roebling and Mr. Case bustled our party of three into that boat in less time than it takes to tell it. They were both working hard to help the women and children. The boat was fairly crowded when we three were pushed into it, and a few men jumped in at the last moment, but Mr. Roebling and Mr. Case stood at the rail and made no attempt to get into the boat.

"They shouted goodbye to us. What do you think Mr. Case did then? He just calmly lighted a cigarette and waved us goodbye with his hand. Mr. Roebling stood there, too—I can see him now. I am sure that he knew that the ship would go to the bottom. But both just stood there."

In the Face of Death

Scenes on the sinking vessel grew more tragic as the remaining passengers faced the awful certainty that death must be the portion of the majority, death in the darkness of a wintry sea studded with its ice monuments like the marble shafts in some vast cemetery.

In that hour, when cherished illusions of possible safety had all but vanished, manhood and womanhood aboard the *Titanic* rose to their sublimest heights. It was in that crisis of the direst extremity that many brave women deliberately rejected life and chose rather to remain and die with the men whom they loved.

Death Fails to Part Mr. and Mrs. Straus

"I will not leave my husband," said Mrs. Isidor Straus. "We are old; we can best die together," and she turned from those who would have forced her into one of the boats and clung to the man who had been the partner of her joys and sorrows. Thus they stood hand in hand and heart to heart, comforting each other until the sea claimed them, united in death as they had been through a long life.

"Greater love hath no man than this, that a man lay down his life for his friends."

Miss Elizabeth Evans fulfilled this final test of affection laid down by the Divine Master. The girl was the niece of the wife of Magistrate Cornell, of New York. She was placed in the same boat with many other women. As it was about to be lowered away it was found that the craft contained one more than its full quota of passengers.

The grim question arose as to which of them should surrender her place and her chance of safety. Beside Miss Evans sat Mrs. J. J. Brown, of Denver, the mother of several children. Miss Evans was the first to volunteer to yield to another.

Girl Steps Back to Doom

"Your need is greater than mine," said she to Mrs. Brown. "You have children who need you, and I have none."

So saying, she arose from the boat and stepped back upon the deck. The girl found no later refuge and was one of those who went down with the ship. She was twenty-five years old and was beloved by all who knew her.

Mrs. Brown thereafter showed the spirit which had made her also volunteer to leave the boat. There were only three men in the boat and but one of them rowed. Mrs. Brown, who was raised on the water, immediately picked up one of the heavy sweeps and began to pull.

In the boat which carried Mrs. Cornell and Mrs. Appleton there were places for seventeen more than were carried. This, too, was undermanned and the two women at once took their places at the oars.

The countess of Rothes was pulling at the oars of her boat, likewise undermanned because the crew preferred to stay behind.

Miss Bentham, of Rochester, showed splendid courage. She happened to be in a lifeboat which was very much crowded—so much so that one sailor had to sit with his feet dangling in the icy cold water, and as time went on the sufferings of the man from the cold were apparent. Miss Bentham arose from her place and had the man turn around while she took her place with her feet in the water.

Scarcely any of the lifeboats were properly manned. Two, filled with women and children, capsized immediately, while the collapsible boats were only temporarily useful. They soon filled with water. In one boat eighteen or twenty persons sat in water above their knees for six hours.

Eight men in this boat were overcome, died, and were thrown overboard. Two women were in this boat, and one succumbed after a few hours and one was saved.

The accident was reported as entirely the result of carelessness and lack of necessary equipment. There were boats for only one-third of the passengers, there were no searchlights; the lifeboats were not supplied with food or safety appliances; there were no lanterns on the lifeboats; there was no way to raise sails, as there was no one who understood managing a sailboat.

Mrs. Hogeboom explained that the new equipment of masts and sails in the boats was carefully wrapped and bound with twine. The men undertook to unfasten them, but found it necessary to cut the ropes. They had no knives, and in their frenzy they went about asking the ill-clad women if they had knives. The sails were never hoisted.

The Money Boat

Thomas Whiteley, a first-saloon steward, in telling of various experiences of the disaster that had come to his knowledge, said that on one of the first boats lowered the only passengers aboard were a man whom he was told was an American millionaire, his wife, child, and two valets. The others in the boat were firemen and coal trimmers, he said, seven in number, whom the man had promised to pay well if they would man the lifeboat. They made only thirteen in all.

"I do not know the man's name," said Whiteley. "I heard it, but have forgotten it. But I saw an order for five pounds which this man gave to each of the crew of his boat after they got aboard the *Carpathia*. It was on a piece of ordinary paper addressed to the Coutts Bank of England.

"We called that boat the 'money boat.' It was lowered from the starboard side and was one of the first off. Our orders were to load the lifeboats beginning forward on the port side, working aft and then back on the starboard. This man paid the firemen to lower a starboard boat before the officers had given the order."

Whiteley's own experience was a hard one. When the uncoiling rope, which entangled his feet, threw him into the sea, it furrowed the flesh of his leg, but he did not feel the pain until he was safe aboard the *Carpathia*.

"I floated on my life preserver for several hours," he said, "then I came across a big oak dresser with two men clinging to it. I hung on to this till daybreak and the two men dropped off. When the sun came up I saw the collapsible raft in the distance, just black with men. They were all standing up, and I swam to it—almost a mile, it seemed to me—and they would not let me aboard. Mr. Lightoller, the second officer, was one of them.

"'It's thirty-one lives against yours,' he said. 'You can't come aboard. There's not room.'

"I pleaded with him in vain, and then I confess I prayed that somebody might die, so I could take his place. It was only human. And then someone did die, and they let me aboard.

"By and by, we saw seven lifeboats lashed together, and we were taken into them."

Men Shot Down

The officers had to assert their authority by force, and three foreigners from the steerage who tried to force their way in among the women and children were shot down without mercy.

Robert Daniel, a Philadelphia passenger, told of terrible scenes at this period of the disaster. He said men fought and bit and struck one another like madmen, and exhibited wounds upon his face to prove the assertion. Mr. Daniel said that he was picked up naked from the ice-cold water and almost perished from exposure before he was rescued. He and others told how the *Titanic*'s bow was completely torn away by the impact with the berg.

K. Whiteman, of Palmyra, New Jersey, the *Titanic*'s barber, was lowering boats on deck after the collision, and declared that the officers on the bridge, one of them First Officer Murdock, promptly worked the electrical apparatus for closing the watertight compartments. He believed the machinery was in some way so damaged by the crash that the front compartments failed to close tightly, although the rear ones were secure.

Whiteman's manner of escape was unique. He was blown off the deck by the second of the two explosions of the boilers, and was in the water more than two hours before he was picked up by a raft.

"The explosions," Whiteman said, "were caused by the rushing in of the icy water on the boilers. A bundle of deck chairs, roped together, was blown off the deck with me, and I struck my back, injuring my spine, but it served as a temporary raft.

"The crew and passengers had faith in the bulkhead system to save the ship and we were lowering a collapsible boat, all confident the ship would get through, when she took a terrific dip forward and the water swept over the deck and into the engine rooms.

"The bow went clean down, and I caught the pile of chairs as I was washed up against the rim. Then came the explosions which blew me fifteen feet.

"After the water had filled the forward compartments, the ones at the stern could not save her, although they did delay the ship's going down. If it wasn't for the compartments hardly anyone could have got away."

A Sad Message

One of the *Titanic*'s stewards, Johnson by name, carried this message to the sorrowing widow of Benjamin Guggenheim:

"When Mr. Guggenheim realized that there was grave danger," said the room steward, "he advised his secretary, who also died, to dress fully and he himself did the same. Mr. Guggenheim, who was cool and collected as he was pulling on his outer garments, said to the steward:

Prepared to Die Bravely

"'I think there is grave doubt that the men will get off safely. I am willing to remain and play the man's game, if there are not enough boats for more than the women and children. I won't die here like a beast. I'll meet my end as a man.'

"There was a pause and then Mr. Guggenheim continued:

"'Tell my wife, Johnson, if it should happen that my secretary and I both go down and you are saved, tell her I played the game out straight and to the end. No woman shall be left aboard this ship because Ben Guggenheim was a coward.

"'Tell her that my last thoughts will be of her and of our girls, but that my duty now is to these unfortunate women and children on this ship. Tell her I will meet whatever fate is in store for me, knowing she will approve of what I do.'"

In telling the story, the room steward said the last he saw of Mr. Guggenheim was when he stood fully dressed upon the upper deck talking calmly with Colonel Astor and Major Butt.

Before the last of the boats got away, according to some of the passengers' narratives, there were more than fifty shots fired upon the decks by officers or others in the effort to maintain the discipline that until then had been well preserved.

The Sinking Vessel

Richard Norris Williams Jr., one of the survivors of the *Titanic*, saw his father killed by being crushed by one of the tremendous funnels of the sinking vessel.

"We stood on deck watching the lifeboats of the *Titanic* being filled and lowered into the water," said Mr. Williams. "The water was nearly up to our waists and the ship was about at her last. Suddenly one of the great funnels fell. I sprang aside, endeavoring to pull father with me. A moment later the funnel was swept overboard and the body of father went with it.

"I sprang overboard and swam through the ice to a life raft, and was pulled aboard. There were five men and one woman on the raft. Occasionally we were swept off into the sea, but always managed to crawl back.

"A sailor lighted a cigarette and flung the match carelessly among the women. Several screamed, fearing they would be set on fire. The sailor replied: 'We are going to hell anyway and we might as well be cremated now as then.'"

A huge cake of ice was the means of aiding Emile Portaleppi, of Italy, in his hairsbreadth escape from death when the *Titanic* went down. Portaleppi, a second-class passenger, was awakened by the explosion of one of the bulkheads of the ship. He hurried to the deck, strapped a life preserver around him, and leaped into the sea. With the aid of the preserver and by holding to a cake of ice he managed to keep afloat until one of the lifeboats picked him up. There were thirty-five other people in the boat, he said, when he was hauled aboard.

The Coward

Somewhere in the shadow of the appalling *Titanic* disaster slinks— still living by the inexplicable grace of God—a cur in human shape, today the most despicable human being in all the world.

In that grim midnight hour, already great in history, he found himself hemmed in by the band of heroes whose watchword and countersign rang out across the deep: "Women and children first!"

What did he do? He scuttled to the stateroom deck, put on a

A VIEW OF THE OLYMPIC

The sister-ship of the Titanic, showing the damage done to her hull in the collision with British war vessel *Hawke* in the British Channel.

VESSEL WITH BOTTOM OF HULL RIPPED OPEN

A view of the torpedo destroyer *Tiger*, taken in drydock after her collision with the Portland Breakwater in 1911; the damage to the *Tiger*, which is plainly shown in the photograph, is of the same character, though on a smaller scale, as that which was done to the *Titanic*.

woman's skirt, a woman's hat, and a woman's veil, and picking his crafty way back among the brave and chivalric men who guarded the rail of the doomed ship, he filched a seat in one of the lifeboats and saved his skin.

His name is on that list of branded rescued men who were neither picked up from the sea when the ship went down nor were in the boats under orders to help get them safe away. His identity is not yet known, though it will be in good time. So foul an act as that will out like murder.

The eyes of strong men who have read this crowded record of golden deeds, who have read and reread that deathless roll of honor of the dead, are still wet with tears of pity and of pride. This man still lives. Surely he was born and saved to set for men a new standard by which to measure infamy and shame.

It is well that there was sufficient heroism on board the *Titanic* to neutralize the horrors of the cowardice. When the first order was given for the men to stand back, there were a dozen or more who pushed forward and said that men would be needed to row the lifeboats and that they would volunteer for the work.

The officers tried to pick out the ones who volunteered merely for service and to eliminate those who volunteered merely to save their own lives. This elimination process, however, was not wholly successful.

The Doomed Men

As the ship began to settle to starboard, heeling at an angle of nearly forty-five degrees, those who had believed it was all right to stick by the ship began to have doubts, and a few jumped into the sea. They were followed immediately by others, and in a few minutes there were scores swimming around. Nearly all of them wore life preservers. One man, who had a Pomeranian dog, leaped overboard with it and, striking a piece of wreckage, was badly stunned. He recovered after a few minutes and swam toward one of the lifeboats and was taken aboard.

Said one survivor, speaking of the men who remained on the ship: "There they stood—Major Butt, Colonel Astor waving a farewell to his wife; Mr. Thayer, Mr. Case, Mr. Clarence Moore, Mr. Widener, all multimillionaires, and hundreds of other men, bravely smiling at us all. Never have I seen such chivalry and fortitude. Such courage in the face of fate horrible to contemplate filled us even then with wonder and admiration."

Why were men saved? ask others who seek to make the occasional male survivor a hissing scorn; and yet the testimony makes it clear that for a long time during that ordeal the more frightful position seemed to many to be in the frail boats in the vast relentless sea, and that some men had to be tumbled into the boats under orders from the officers. While others express the deepest indignation that 210 sailors were rescued, the testimony shows that most of these sailors were in the welter of ice and water into which they had been thrown from the ship's deck when she sank; they were human beings and so were picked up and saved.

"Women and Children First"

The one alleviating circumstance in the otherwise immitigable tragedy is the fact that so many of the men stood aside really without the necessity for the order "Women and children first," and insisted that the weaker sex should first have places in the boats.

There were men whose word of command swayed boards of directors, governed institutions, disposed of millions. They were accustomed merely to pronounce a wish to have it gratified. Thousands "posted at their bidding"; the complexion of the market altered hue when they nodded; they bought what they wanted, and for one of the humblest fishing smacks or a dory they could have given the price that was paid to build and launch the ship that has become the most imposing mausoleum that ever housed the bones of men since the Pyramids rose from the desert sands.

But these men stood aside—one can see them!—and gave place not merely to the delicate and the refined, but to the scared Czech woman from the steerage, with her baby at her breast; the Croatian with a toddler by her side, coming through the very gate of Death and out of the mouth of hell to the imagined Eden of America.

To many of those who went it was harder to go than to stay there on the vessel gaping with its mortal wounds and ready to go down. It meant that tossing on the waters they must wait in suspense, hour after hour even after the lights of the ship were engulfed in appalling darkness, hoping against hope for the miracle of a rescue dearer to them than their own lives.

It was the tradition of Anglo-Saxon heroism that was fulfilled in the frozen seas during the black hours of Sunday night. The heroism was that of the women who went, as well as of the men who remained!

24

Left to Their Fate

COOLNESS AND HEROISM OF THOSE LEFT TO PERISH—SUICIDE OF
MURDOCK—CAPTAIN SMITH'S END—THE SHIP'S BAND PLAYS A
NOBLE HYMN AS THE VESSEL GOES DOWN

The general feeling aboard the ship after the boats had left her
sides was that she would not survive, but the passengers who
remained aboard displayed the utmost heroism.

William T. Stead, the famous English journalist, was so little
alarmed that he calmly discussed with one of the passengers the
probable height of the iceberg after the *Titanic* had shot into it.

Confidence in the ability of the *Titanic* to remain afloat doubt-
lessly led many of the passengers to death. The theory that the great
ship was unsinkable remained with hundreds who had entrusted
themselves to the gigantic hulk, long after the officers knew that the
vessel could not survive.

The captain and officers behaved with superb gallantry, and
there was perfect order and discipline among those who were
aboard, even after all hope had been abandoned for the salvation of
the ship.

Many women went down, steerage women who were unable to
get to the upper decks where the boats were launched, maids who
were overlooked in the confusion, cabin passengers who refused to

desert their husbands or who reached the decks after the last of the lifeboats was gone and the ship was settling for her final plunge to the bottom of the Atlantic.

Narratives of survivors do not bear out the supposition that the final hours upon the vessel's decks were passed in darkness. They say the electric lighting plant held out until the last, and that even as they watched the ship sink, from their places in the floating lifeboats, her lights were gleaming in long rows as she plunged under by the head. Just before she sank, some of the refugees say, the ship broke in two abaft the engine room after the bulkhead explosions had occurred.

Colonel Astor's Death

To Colonel Astor's death Philip Mock bears this testimony:

"Many men were hanging on to rafts in the sea. William T. Stead and Colonel Astor were among them. Their feet and hands froze and they had to let go. Both were drowned."

The last man among the survivors to speak to Colonel Astor was K. Whiteman, the ship's barber.

"I shaved Colonel Astor Sunday afternoon," said Whiteman. "He was a pleasant, affable man, and that awful night when I found myself standing beside him on the passenger deck, helping to put the women into the boats, I spoke to him.

"'Where is your life belt?' I asked him.

"'I didn't think there would be any need of it,' he said.

"'Get one while there is time,' I told him. 'The last boat is gone, and we are done for.'

"'No,' he said, 'I think there are some lifeboats to be launched, and we may get on one of them.'

"'There are no life rafts,' I told him, 'and the ship is going to sink.

I am going to jump overboard and take a chance on swimming out and being picked up by one of the boats. Better come along.'

"'No, thank you,' he said calmly, 'I think I'll have to stick.'

"I asked him if he would mind shaking hands with me. He said, 'With pleasure,' gave me a hearty grip, and then I climbed up on the rail and jumped overboard. I was in the water nearly four hours before one of the boats picked me up."

Captain Washed Overboard

Murdock's last orders were to Quartermaster Moody and a few other petty officers who had taken their places in the rigid discipline of the ship and were lowering the boats. Captain Smith came up to him on the bridge several times and then rushed down again. They spoke to one another only in monosyllables.

There were stories that Captain Smith, when he saw the ship actually going down, had committed suicide. There is no basis for such tales. The captain, according to the testimony of those who were near him almost until the last, was admirably cool. He carried a revolver in his hand, ready to use it on anyone who disobeyed orders.

"I want every man to act like a man for manhood's sake," he said, "and if they don't, a bullet awaits the coward."

With the revolver in his hand—a fact that undoubtedly gave rise to the suicide theory—the captain moved up and down the deck. He gave the order for each lifeboat to make off and he remained until every boat was gone. Standing on the bridge, he finally called out the order: "Each man save himself." At that moment all discipline fled. It was the last call of death. If there had been any hope among those on board before, the hope now had fled.

The bearded admiral of the White Star Line fleet, with every lifesaving device launched from the decks, was returning to the deck to perform the sacred office of going down with his ship when a wave dashed over the side and tore him from the ladder.

The *Titanic* was sinking rapidly by the head, with the twisting sidelong motion that was soon to aim her on her course two miles down. Murdock saw the skipper swept out, but did not move. Captain Smith was but one of a multitude of lost at that moment. Murdock may have known that the last desperate thought of the gray mariner was to get upon his bridge and die in command. That the old man could not have done this may have had something to do with Murdock's suicidal inspiration. Of that no man say or safely guess.

The wave that swept the skipper out bore him almost to the thwart of a crowded lifeboat. Hands reached out, but he wrenched himself away, turned, and swam back toward the ship.

Some say that he said, "Good-bye, I'm going back to the ship."

He disappeared for a moment, then reappeared where a rail was slipping underwater. Cool and courageous to the end, loyal to his duty under the most difficult circumstances, he showed himself a noble captain, and he died a noble death.

Saw Both Officers Perish

Quartermaster Moody saw all this, watched the skipper scramble aboard again onto the submerged decks and then vanish altogether in a great billow.

As Moody's eye lost sight of the skipper in this confusion of waters it again shifted to the bridge, and just in time to see Murdock take his life. The man's face was turned toward him, Moody said, and he could not mistake it. There were still many gleaming lights on the ship, flickering out like little groups of vanishing stars, and with the clear starshine on the waters there was nothing to cloud or break the quartermaster's vision.

"I saw Murdock die by his own hand," said Moody, "saw the flash from his gun, heard the crack that followed the flash and then saw him plunge over on his face."

Others report hearing several pistol shots on the decks below the bridge, but amid the groans and shrieks and cries, shouted orders, and all that vast orchestra of sounds that broke upon the air they must have been faint periods of punctuation.

Band Played Its Own Dirge

The band had broken out in the strains of "Nearer, My God, to Thee," some minutes before Murdock lifted the revolver to his head, fired, and toppled over on his face. Moody saw all this in a vision that filled his brain while his ears drank in the tragic strain of the beautiful hymn that the band played as their own dirge, even to the moment when the waters sucked them down.

Wherever Murdock's eye swept the water in that instant, before he drew his revolver, it looked upon veritable seas of drowning men and women. From the decks there came to him the shrieks and groans of the caged and drowning, for whom all hope of escape was utterly vanished. He evidently never gave a thought to the possibility of saving himself, his mind freezing with the horrors he beheld and having room for just one central idea—swift extinction.

The strains of the hymn and the frantic cries of the dying blended in a symphony of sorrow.

Led by the green light, under the light of stars, the boats drew away, and the bow, then the quarter, then the stacks, and last the stern of the marvel ship of a few days before passed beneath the waters. The great force of the ship's sinking was unaided by any

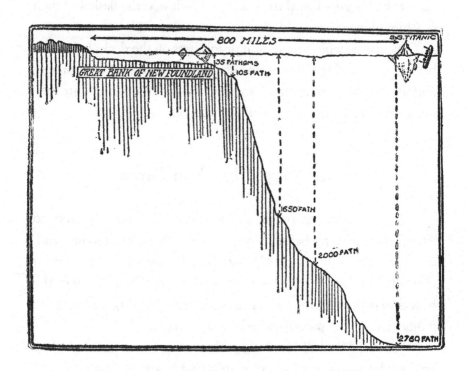

DEPTH OF OCEAN WHERE THE *TITANIC* WENT DOWN

The above etching shows a diagram of the ocean depths between the shore of Newfoundland (shown at the top the the left, by the heavily shaded part) to 800 miles out, where the *Titanic* struck an iceberg and sank. Over the Great Bank of Newfoundland the greatest depth is about 35 fathoms, or 210 feet. Then there is a sudden drop to 105 fathoms, or 630 feet, and then there is a falling away to 1650 fathoms or 9900 feet, then 2000 fathoms or 12,000 feet, and about where the *Titanic* sank 2760 fathoms or 16,560 feet.

violence of the elements, and the suction, not so great as had been feared, rocked but mildly the group of boats now a quarter of a mile distant from it.

Just before the *Titanic* disappeared from view men and women leaped from the stern. More than a hundred men, according to Colonel Gracie, jumped at the last. Gracie was among the number and he and the second officer were of the very few who were saved.

As the vessel disappeared, the waves drowned the majestic hymn which the musicians played as they went to their watery grave. The most authentic accounts agree that this hymn was not "Nearer, My God, to Thee," which it seems had been played shortly before, but "Autumn," which is found in the Episcopal hymnal and which fits appropriately the situation on the *Titanic* in the last moments of pain and darkness there. One line, "Hold me up in mighty waters," particularly may have suggested the hymn to some minister aboard the doomed vessel, who, it has been thought, thereupon asked the remaining passengers to join in singing the hymn, in a last service aboard the sinking ship, soon to be ended by death itself.

Following is the hymn:

God of mercy and compassion!
Look with pity on my pain:
Hear a mournful, broken spirit
Prostrate at Thy feet complain;
Many are my foes, and mighty;
Strength to conquer I have none!
Nothing can uphold my goings
But Thy blessed Self alone.

Savior, look on Thy beloved;
Triumph over all my foes;
Turn to heavenly joy my mourning,

Turn to gladness all my woes;
Live or die, or work or suffer,
Let my weary soul abide,
In all changes whatsoever
Sure and steadfast by Thy side.

When temptations fierce assault me,
When my enemies I find,
Sin and guilt, and death and Satan,
All against my soul combined,
Hold me up in mighty waters,
Keep my eyes on things above,
Righteousness, divine Atonement,
Peace, and everlasting Love.

It was a little lame schoolmaster, Tyrtaeus, who aroused the Spartans by his poetry and led them to victory against the foe.

It was the musicians of the band of the *Titanic*—poor men, paid a few dollars a week—who played the music to keep up the courage of the souls aboard the sinking ship.

"The way the band kept playing was a noble thing," says the wireless operator. "I heard it first while we were working the wireless, when there was a ragtime tune for us, and the last I saw of the band, when I was floating, struggling in the icy water, it was still on deck, playing 'Autumn.' How those brave fellows ever did it I cannot imagine."

Perhaps that music, made in the face of death, would not have satisfied the exacting critical sense. It may be that the chilled fingers faltered on the pistons of the cornet or at the valves of the French horn, that the time was irregular, and that by an organ in a church, with a decorous congregation, the hymns they chose would have been better played and sung. But surely that music went up to God from the souls of drowning men, and was not less acceptable than the song of songs no mortal ear may hear, the harps of the seraphs and the choiring cherubim. Under the sea the musicmakers lie, still in their fingers clutching the broken and battered means of melody; but over the strident voice of warring winds and the sound of many waters there rises their chant eternally; and though the musicians lie hushed and cold at the sea's heart, their music is heard forevermore.

25

The Call for Help Heard

THE VALUE OF THE WIRELESS—OTHER SHIPS ALTER THEIR
COURSE—RESCUERS ON THE WAY

W e have struck an iceberg. Badly damaged. Rush aid."
Seaward and landward, J. G. Phillips, the *Titanic*'s wireless man, had hurled the appeal for help. By fits and starts—for the wireless was working unevenly and blurringly—Phillips reached out to the world, crying the *Titanic*'s peril. A word or two, scattered phrases, now and then a connected sentence, made up the message that sent a thrill of apprehension for a thousand miles east, west, and south of the doomed liner.

The early dispatches from St. John's, Cape Race, and Montreal, told graphic tales of the race to reach the *Titanic*, the wireless appeals for help, the interruption of the calls, then what appeared to be a successful conclusion of the race when the *Virginian* was reported as having reached the giant liner.

Many Lines Hear the Call

Other rushing liners besides the *Virginian* heard the call and became on the instant something more than cargo carriers and passenger greyhounds. The big *Baltic*, 200 miles to the eastward and west-bound, turned again to save life, as she did when her sister of the White Star fleet, the *Republic*, was cut down in a fog in January 1909. The *Titanic's* mate, the *Olympic*, the mightiest of the seagoers save the *Titanic* herself, turned in her tracks. All along the northern lane the miracle of the wireless worked for the distressed and sinking White Star ship. The Hamburg-American *Cincinnati*, the *Parisian* from Glasgow, the North German Lloyd *Prinz Friedrich Wilhelm*, the Hamburg-American liners *Prinz Adelbert* and *Amerika*, all heard the CQD and the rapid, condensed explanation of what had happened.

Virginian in Desperate Haste

But the *Virginian* was nearest, barely 170 miles away, and was the first to know of the *Titanic's* danger. She went about and headed under forced draft for the spot indicated in one of the last of Phillips's messages—latitude 41.46 N. and longitude 50.14 W. She is a fast ship, the Allan liner, and her wireless has told the story of how she stretched through the night to get up to the *Titanic* in time. There was need for all the power of her engines and all the experience and skill of her captain. The final fluttering Marconigrams that were released from the *Titanic* made it certain that the great ship with 2,340 souls aboard was filling and in desperate peril.

Farther out at sea was the Cunarder, *Carpathia*, which left New York for the Mediterranean on April 13. Round she went and plunged back westward to take a hand in saving life. And the third steamship within short sailing of the *Titanic* was the Allan liner *Parisian* away to the eastward, on her way from Glasgow to Halifax.

While they sped in the night with all the drive that steam could give them, the *Titanic's* call reached to Cape Race and the startled

THE TITANIC

The largest and finest steamship in the world; on her maiden voyage loaded with a human freight of over 2,300 souls, she collided with a huge iceberg 600 miles southeast of Halifax, at 11:40 P.M., Sunday, April 14, 1912, and sank two and a half hours later, carrying over 1,600 of her passengers and crew with her.

LOWERING THE LIFEBOATS FROM THE *TITANIC*

Fortunately the sea was calm on the night of the disaster, for otherwise the loss of life might have been much greater in the terrible descent of more than 60 feet from the boat deck to the water. As it was, four of the lifeboats were wrecked in launching.

operator there heard at midnight a message which quickly reached New York:

"Have struck an iceberg. We are badly damaged. *Titanic* latitude 41.46 N., 50.14 W."

Cape Race threw the appeal broadcast wherever his apparatus could carry.

Then for hours, while the world waited for a crumb of news as to the safety of the great ship's people, not one thing more was known save that she was drifting, broken and helpless and alone in the midst of a waste of ice. And it was not until seventeen hours after the *Titanic* had sunk that the words came out of the air as to her fate. There was a confusion and tangle of messages—a jumble of rumors. Good tidings were trodden upon by evil. And no man knew clearly what was taking place in that stretch of waters where the giant icebergs were making a mockery of all that the world knew best in shipbuilding.

Titanic Sent Out No More News

It was at 12:17 A.M., while the *Virginian* was still plunging eastward, that all communication from the *Titanic* ceased. The *Virginian*'s operator, with the *Virginian*'s captain at his elbow, fed the air with blue flashes in a desperate effort to know what was happening to the crippled liner, but no message came back. The last word from the *Titanic* was that she was sinking. Then the sparking became fainter. The call was dying to nothing. The *Virginian*'s operator labored over a blur of signals. It was hopeless. So the Allan ship strove on, fearing that the worst had happened.

It was this ominous silence that so alarmed the other vessels hurrying to the *Titanic* and that caused so much suspense here.

26

In the Drifting Lifeboats

SORROW AND SUFFERING—THE SURVIVORS SEE THE *TITANIC*
GO DOWN WITH THEIR LOVED ONES ON BOARD—A NIGHT OF
AGONIZING SUSPENSE—WOMEN HELP TO ROW—HELP ARRIVES—
PICKING UP THE LIFEBOATS

S ixteen boats were in the procession which entered on the terrible hours of rowing, drifting, and suspense. Women wept for
lost husbands and sons, sailors sobbed for the ship which had been
their pride. Men choked back tears and sought to comfort the wid-
owed. Perhaps, they said, other boats might have put off in another
direction. They strove, though none too sure themselves, to con-
vince the women of the certainty that a rescue ship would appear.

In the distance the *Titanic* looked an enormous length, her great
bulk outlined in black against the starry sky, every porthole and
saloon blazing with light. It was impossible to think anything could
be wrong with such a leviathan, were it not for that ominous tilt
downward in the bows, where the water was now up to the lowest
row of portholes. Presently, about 2 A.M., as near as can be determined, those in the lifeboats observed her settling very rapidly, with
the bows and the bridge completely underwater, and concluded it
was now only a question of minutes before she went. So it proved.
She slowly tilted straight on end with the stern vertically upward,

and as she did, the lights in the cabins and saloons, which until then had not flickered for a moment, died out, came on again for a single flash, and finally went altogether. At the same time the machinery roared down through the vessel with a rattle and a groaning that could be heard for miles, the weirdest sound surely that could be heard in the middle of the ocean, a thousand miles away from land. But this was not yet quite the end.

Titanic Stood Upright

To the amazement of the awed watchers in the lifeboats, the doomed vessel remained in that upright position for a time estimated at five minutes; some in the boat say less, but it was certainly some minutes that at least 150 feet of the *Titanic* towered up above the level of the sea and loomed black against the sky.

Saw Last of Big Ship

Then with a quiet, slanting dive she disappeared beneath the waters, and the eyes of the helpless spectators had looked for the last time upon the gigantic vessel on which they had set out from Southampton. And there was left to the survivors only the gently heaving sea, the lifeboats filled with men and women in every conceivable condition of dress and undress, above the perfect sky of brilliant stars with not a cloud, all tempered with a bitter cold that made each man and woman long to be one of the crew who toiled away with the oars and kept themselves warm thereby—a curious, deadening, bitter cold unlike anything they had felt before.

"One Long Moan"

And then with all these there fell on the ear the most appalling noise that human being has ever listened to—the cries of hundreds of fellow beings struggling in the icy cold water, crying for help with a cry that could not be answered.

Third Officer Herbert John Pitman, in charge of one of the boats, described this cry of agony in his testimony before the Senatorial Investigating Committee, under the questioning of Senator Smith:

"I heard no cries of distress until after the ship went down," he said.

"How far away were the cries from your lifeboat?"

"Several hundred yards, probably, some of them."

"Describe the screams."

"Don't, sir, please! I'd rather not talk about it."

"I'm sorry to press it, but what was it like? Were the screams spasmodic?"

"It was one long continuous moan."

The witness said the moans and cries continued an hour.

Those in the lifeboats longed to return and pick up some of the poor drowning souls, but they feared this would mean swamping the boats and a further loss of life.

Some of the men tried to sing to keep the women from hearing the cries, and rowed hard to get away from the scene of the wreck, but the memory of those sounds will be one of the things the rescued will find it difficult to forget.

The waiting sufferers kept a lookout for lights, and several times it was shouted that steamers' lights were seen, but they turned out to be either a light from another boat or a star low down on the horizon. It was hard to keep up hope.

Women Tried to Commit Suicide

"Let me go back—I want to go back to my husband—I'll jump from the boat if you don't," cried an agonized voice in one lifeboat.

"You can do no good by going back—other lives will be lost if you try to do it. Try to calm yourself for the sake of the living. It may be that your husband will be picked up somewhere by one of the fishing boats."

The woman who pleaded to go back, according to Mrs. Vera Dick, of Calgary, Canada, later tried to throw herself from the lifeboat. Mrs. Dick, describing the scenes in the lifeboats, said there were half a dozen women in that one boat who tried to commit suicide when they realized that the *Titanic* had gone down.

"Even in Canada, where we have such clear nights," said Mrs. Dick, "I have never seen such a clear sky. The stars were very bright and we could see the *Titanic* plainly, like a great hotel on the water. Floor after floor of the lights went out as we watched. It was horrible, horrible. I can't bear to think about it. From the distance, as we rowed away, we could hear the band playing 'Nearer, My God, to Thee.'

"Among the lifeboats themselves, however, there were scenes just as terrible, perhaps, but to me nothing could outdo the tragic grandeur with which the *Titanic* went to its death. To realize it, you would have to see the *Titanic* as I saw it the day we set sail—with the flags flying and the bands playing. Everybody on board was laughing and talking about the *Titanic* being the biggest and most luxurious boat on the ocean and being unsinkable. To think of it then and to think of it standing out there in the night, wounded to death and gasping for life, is almost too big for the imagination.

Scantily Clad Women in Lifeboats

"The women on our boat were in nightgowns and bare feet—some of them—and the wealthiest women mingled with the poorest immigrants. One immigrant woman kept shouting, 'My God, my poor father! He put me in this boat and would not save himself. Oh, why didn't I die, why didn't I die? Why can't I die now?'

"We had to restrain her, else she would have jumped overboard. It was simply awful. Some of the men apparently had said they could row just to get into the boats. We paid no attention to cowardice, however. We were all busy with our own troubles. My heart simply bled for the women who were separated from their husbands.

"The night was frightfully cold, although clear. We had to huddle together to keep warm. Everybody drank sparingly of the water and ate sparingly of the bread. We did not know when we would be saved. Everybody tried to remain cool, except the poor creatures who could think of nothing but their own great loss. Those with the most brains seemed to control themselves best."

Philadelphia Women Heroines

How Mrs. George D. Widener, whose husband and son perished after kissing her goodbye and helping her into one of the boats, rowed when exhausted seamen were on the verge of collapse, was told by Emily Geiger, maid of Mrs. Widener, who was saved with her.

The girl said Mrs. Widener bravely toiled throughout the night and consoled other women who had broken down under the strain.

Mrs. William E. Carter and Mrs. John B. Thayer were in the same lifeboat and worked heroically to keep it free from the icy menace. Although Mrs. Thayer's husband remained aboard the *Titanic* and sank with it, and although she had no knowledge of the safety of her son until they met, hours later, aboard the *Carpathia*, Mrs. Thayer bravely labored at the oars throughout the night.

In telling of her experience, Mrs. Carter said:

"When I went over the side with my children and got in the boat there were no seamen in it. Then came a few men, but there were oars with no one to use them. The boat had been filled with passengers, and there was nothing else for me to do but to take an oar.

"We could see now that the time of the ship had come. She was sinking, and we were warned by cries from the men above to pull away from the ship quickly. Mrs. Thayer, wife of the vice president of the Pennsylvania Railroad, was in my boat, and she, too, took an oar.

"It was cold and we had no time to clothe ourselves with warm overcoats. The rowing warmed me. We started to pull away from the ship. We could see the dim outlines of the decks above, but we could not recognize anybody."

Many Women Rowing

Mrs. William R. Bucknell's account of the part women played in the rowing is as follows:

"There were thirty-five persons in the boat in which the captain placed me. Three of these were ordinary seamen, supposed to manage the boat, and a steward.

"One of these men seemed to think that we should not start away from the sinking ship until it could be learned whether the other boats would accommodate the rest of the women. He seemed to think that more could be crowded into ours, if necessary.

"'I would rather go back and go down with the ship than leave under these circumstances,' he cried.

"The captain shouted to him to obey orders and to pull for a little light that could just be discerned miles in the distance. I do not know what this little light was. It may have been a passing fishing vessel, which, of course could not know our predicament. Anyway, we never reached it.

"We rowed all night, I took an oar and sat beside the Countess de Rothes. Her maid had an oar and so did mine. The air was freezing cold, and it was not long before the only man that appeared to know anything about rowing commenced to complain that his hands were freezing. A woman back of him handed him a shawl from about her shoulders.

"As we rowed we looked back at the lights of the *Titanic*. There was not a sound from her, only the lights began to get lower and lower, and finally she sank. Then we heard a muffled explosion and a dull roar caused by the great suction of water.

"There was not a drop of water on our boat. The last minute before our boat was launched Captain Smith threw aboard a bag of bread. I took the precaution of taking a good drink of water before we started, so I suffered no inconvenience from thirst."

Mrs. Lucien Smith, whose young husband perished, was another heroine. It is related by survivors that she took turns at the oars, and then, when the boat was in danger of sinking, stood ready to plug a hole with her finger if the cork stopper became loose.

In another boat Mrs. Cornell and her sister, who had a slight knowledge of rowing, took turns at the oars, as did other women.

The boat in which Mrs. J. J. Brown, of Denver, Colorado, was saved contained only three men in all, and only one rowed. He was a half-frozen seaman who was tumbled into the boat at the last minute. The woman wrapped him in blankets and set him at an oar to start his blood. The second man was too old to be of any use. The third was a coward.

Strange to say, there was room in this boat for ten other people.

Ten brave men would have received the warmest welcome of their lives if they had been there. The coward, being a quartermaster and the assigned head of the boat, sat in the stern and steered. He was terrified, and the women had to fight against his pessimism while they tugged at the oars.

The women sat two at each oar. One held the oar in place, the other did the pulling. Mrs. Brown coached them and cheered them on. She told them that the exercise would keep the chill out of their veins, and she spoke hopefully of the likelihood that some vessel would answer the wireless calls. Over the frightful danger of the situation the spirit of this woman soared.

The Pessimist

And the coward sat in his stern seat, terrified, his tongue loosened with fright. He assured them there was no chance in the world. He had had fourteen years' experience, and he knew. First, they would have to row one and a half miles at least to get out of the sphere of the suction, if they did not want to go down. They would be lost, and nobody would ever find them.

"Oh, we shall be picked up sooner or later," said some of the braver ones. No, said the man, there was no bread in the boat, no water; they would starve—all that big boatload wandering the high seas with nothing to eat, perhaps for days.

"Don't," cried Mrs. Brown. "Keep that to yourself, if you feel that way. For the sake of these women and children, be a man. We have a smooth sea and a fighting chance. Be a man."

But the coward only knew that there was no compass and no chart aboard. They sighted what they thought was a fishing smack on the horizon, showing dimly in the early dawn. The man at the rudder steered toward it, and the women bent to their oars again. They covered several miles in this way—but the smack faded into the distance. They could not see it any longer. And the coward said that everything was over.

They rowed back nine weary miles. Then the coward thought they must stop rowing, and lie in the trough of the waves until the *Carpathia* should appear. The women tried it for a few moments, and felt the cold creeping into their bodies. Though exhausted from the hard physical labor, they thought work was better than freezing.

"Row again!" commanded Mrs. Brown.

"No, no, don't," said the coward.

"We shall freeze," cried several of the women together. "We must row. We have rowed all this time. We must keep on or freeze."

When the coward still demurred, they told him plainly and once for all that if he persisted in wanting them to stop rowing, they were going to throw him overboard and be done with him for good. Something about the look in the eye of that Mississippi-bred oarswoman, who seemed such a force among her fellows, told him that he had better capitulate. And he did.

Countess Rothes an Expert Oarswoman

Miss Alice Farnam Leader, a New York physician, escaped from the *Titanic* on the same boat which carried the Countess Rothes. "The countess is an expert oarswoman," said Dr. Leader, "and thoroughly at home on the water. She practically took command of our boat when it was found that the seaman who had been placed at the oars could not row skillfully. Several of the women took their place with the countess at the oars and rowed in turns, while the weak and unskilled stewards sat quietly in one end of the boat."

Men Could Not Row

"With nothing on but a nightgown I helped row one of the boats for three hours," said Mrs. Florence Ware, of Bristol, England.

"In our boat there were a lot of women, a steward, and a fireman. None of the men knew anything about managing a small boat, so some of the women who were used to boats took charge.

"It was cold and I worked as hard as I could at an oar until we were picked up. There was nothing to eat or drink on our boat."

Deaths on the Lifeboats

"The temperature must have been below freezing," testified another survivor, "and neither men nor women in my boat were warmly clothed. Several of them died. The officer in charge of the lifeboat decided it was better to bury the bodies. Soon they were weighted so they would sink and were put overboard. We could also see similar burials taking place from other lifeboats that were all around us."

Gamblers Were Polite

In one boat were two cardsharps. With the same cleverness that enabled them to win money on board they obtained places in the boats with the women.

In the boat with the gamblers were women in their nightgowns and women in evening dress. None of the boats were properly equipped with food, but all had enough bread and water to keep the rescued from starving until the expected arrival of help.

To the credit of the gamblers who managed to escape, it should be said that they were polite and showed the women every courtesy. All they wanted was to be sure of getting in a boat. That once accomplished, they reverted to their habitual practice of politeness and suavity. They were even willing to do a little manual labor, refusing to let women do any rowing.

The people on that particular boat were a sad group. Fathers had kissed their daughters goodbye and husbands had parted from their wives. The cardsharps, however, philosophized wonderfully about the will of the Almighty and how strange His ways. They said that one must be prepared for anything, that good always came from evil, and that every cloud had a silvery lining.

"Who knows?" said one. "It may be that everybody on board will be saved." Another added: "Our duty is to the living. You women owe it to your relatives and friends not to allow this thing to wreck your reason or undermine your health." And they took pains to see that all the women who were on the lifeboat had plenty of covering to keep them from the icy blasts of the night.

Help in Sight

The survivors were in the lifeboats until about 5:30 A.M. About 3 A.M. faint lights appeared in the sky and all rejoiced to see what was supposed to be the coming dawn, but after watching for half an hour and seeing no change in the intensity of the light, the disappointed sufferers realized it was the Northern Lights. Presently low down on the horizon they saw a light which slowly resolved itself into a double light, and they watched eagerly to see if the two lights would separate and so prove to be only two of the boats, or whether these lights would remain together, in which case they should expect them to be the lights of a rescuing steamer.

To the inexpressible joy of all, they moved as one! Immediately the boats were swung around and headed for the lights. Someone shouted, "Now, boys, sing!" and everyone not too weak broke into song with "Row for the shore, boys." Tears came to the eyes of all as they realized that safety was at hand. The song was sung, but it was a very poor imitation of the real thing, for quavering voices make poor songs. A cheer was given next, and that was better—you can keep in tune for a cheer.

The "Lucky Thirteen"

"Our rescuer showed up rapidly, and as she swung round we saw her cabins all alight, and knew she must be a large steamer. She was now motionless and we had to row to her. Just then day broke, a beautiful quiet dawn with faint pink clouds just above the horizon, and a new moon whose crescent just touched the horizon. 'Turn your money over, boys,' said our cheery steersman, 'that is, if you have any with you,' he added.

"We laughed at him for his superstition at such a time, but he countered very neatly by adding: 'Well, I shall never say again that 13 is an unlucky number; boat 13 has been the best friend we ever had.' Certainly the 13 superstition is killed forever in the minds of those who escaped from the *Titanic* in boat 13.

"As we neared the *Carpathia* we saw in the dawning light what we thought was a full-rigged schooner standing up near her, and presently behind her another, all sails set, and we said: 'They are fisher boats from the Newfoundland bank and have seen the steamer lying to and are standing by to help.' But in another five minutes the light shone pink on them and we saw they were icebergs towering many feet in the air, huge, glistening masses, deadly white, still, and peaked in a way that had easily suggested a schooner. We glanced round the horizon and there were others wherever the eye could reach.

HEARTBREAKING FAREWELLS

Both men and women were loaded into the first boats, but soon the cry of "Women first" was raised. Then came the real note of tragedy. Husbands and wives clung to each other in farewell; some refused to be separated.

PASSENGERS LEAVING THE *TITANIC* IN THE LIFEBOATS

The agony and despair which possessed the occupants of these boats as they were carried away from the doomed giant, leaving husbands and brothers behind, is almost beyond description. It is little wonder that the strain of these moments, with the physical and mental suffering which followed during the early morning hours, left many of the women still hysterical when they reached New York.

The steamer we had to reach was surrounded by them and we had to make a detour to reach her, for between her and us lay another huge berg."

A Wonderful Dawn

Speaking of the moment when the *Carpathia* was sighted, Mrs. J. J. Brown, who had cowed the driveling quartermaster, said: "Then, knowing that we were safe at last, I looked about me. The most wonderful dawn I have ever seen came upon us. I have just returned from Egypt. I have been all over the world, but I have never seen anything like this. First the gray and then the flood of light. Then the sun came up in a ball of red fire. For the first time we saw where we were. Near us was open water, but on every side was ice. Ice ten feet high was everywhere, and to the right and left and back and front were icebergs. Some of them were mountain high. This sea of ice was forty miles wide, they told me. We did not wait for the *Carpathia* to come to us, we rowed to it. We were lifted up in a sort of nice little sling that was lowered to us. After that it was all over. The passengers of the *Carpathia* were so afraid that we would not have room enough that they gave us practically the whole ship to ourselves."

It had been learned that some of the passengers, in fact all of the women passengers of the *Titanic* who were rescued, refer to "Lady Margaret," as they called Mrs. Brown, as the strength of them all.

Transferring the Rescued

Officers of the *Carpathia* report that when they reached the scene of the *Titanic*'s wreck there were fifty bodies or more floating in the sea. Only one mishap attended the transfer of the rescued from the lifeboats. One large collapsible lifeboat, in which thirteen persons were seated, turned turtle just as they were about to save it, and all in it were lost.

The Dog Hero

Not the least among the heroes of the *Titanic* disaster was Rigel, a big black Newfoundland dog, belonging to the first officer, who went down with the ship. But for Rigel the fourth boat picked up might have been run down by the *Carpathia*. For three hours he swam in the icy water where the *Titanic* went down, evidently looking for his master, and was instrumental in guiding the boatload of survivors to the gangway of the *Carpathia*.

Jonas Briggs, a seaman abroad the *Carpathia*, now has Rigel and told the story of the dog's heroism. The *Carpathia* was moving slowly about, looking for boats, rafts, or anything which might be afloat. Exhausted with their efforts, weak from lack of food and exposure to the cutting wind, and terror-stricken, the men and women in the fourth boat had drifted under the *Carpathia*'s starboard bow. They were dangerously close to the steamship, but too weak to shout a warning loud enough to reach the bridge.

The boat might not have been seen were it not for the sharp barking of Rigel, who was swimming ahead of the craft, and valiantly announcing his position. The barks attracted the attention of Captain Rostron, and he went to the starboard end of the bridge to see where they came from and saw the boat. He immediately ordered the engines stopped, and the boat came alongside the starboard gangway.

Care was taken to get Rigel aboard, but he appeared little affected by his long trip through the ice-cold water. He stood by the rail and barked until Captain Rostron called Briggs and had him take the dog below.

A Thrilling Account of Rescue

Mr. Wallace Bradford, of San Francisco, a passenger aboard the *Carpathia*, gave the following thrilling account of the rescue of the *Titanic*'s passengers.

"Since half past four this morning I have experienced one of those never-to-be-forgotten circumstances that weighs heavy on my soul and which shows most awfully what poor things we mortals are. Long before this reaches you the news will be flashed that the *Titanic* has gone down and that our steamer, the *Carpathia*, caught the wireless message when seventy-five miles away, and so far we have picked up twenty boats estimated to contain about 750 people.

"None of us can tell just how many, as they have been hustled to various staterooms and to the dining saloons to be warmed up. I was awakened by unusual noises and imagined that I smelled smoke. I jumped up and looked out of my porthole, and saw a huge iceberg looming up like a rock offshore. It was not white, and I was positive that it was a rock, and the thought flashed through my mind, how in the world can we be near a rock when we are four days out from New York in a southerly direction and in midocean.

"When I got out on deck the first man I encountered told me that the *Titanic* had gone down and we were rescuing the passengers. The first two boats from the doomed vessel were in sight making toward us. Neither of them was crowded. This was accounted for later by the fact that it was impossible to get many to leave the steamer, as they would not believe that she was going down. It was a glorious, clear morning and a quiet sea. Off to the starboard was a white area of ice plain, from whose even surface rose mammoth forts, castles, and pyramids of solid ice almost as real as though they had been placed there by the hand of man.

"Our steamer was hove to about two and a half miles from the edge of this huge iceberg. The *Titanic* struck about 11:20 P.M. and did not go down until two o'clock. Many of the passengers were in evening dress when they came aboard our ship, and most of these were in a most bedraggled condition. Near me as I write is a girl about eighteen years old in a fancy-dress costume of bright colors, while in another seat near by is a woman in a white dress trimmed with lace and covered with jaunty blue flowers.

"As the boats came alongside after the first two all of them contained a very large proportion of women. In fact, one of the boats had women at the oars, one in particular containing, as near as I could estimate, about forty-five women and only about six men. In this boat two women were handling one of the oars. All of the engineers went down with the steamer. Four bodies have been brought aboard. One is that of a fireman, who is said to have been shot by one of the officers because he refused to obey orders. Soon after I got on deck I could, with the aid of my glasses, count seven boats headed our way, and they continued to come up to half past eight o'clock. Some were in sight for a long time and moved very slowly, showing plainly that the oars were being handled by amateurs or by women.

"No baggage of any kind was brought by the survivors. In fact, the only piece of baggage that reached the *Carpathia* from the *Titanic* is a small closed truck about twenty-four inches square, evidently the property of an Irish female immigrant. While some seemed fully dressed, many of the men having their overcoats and the women sealskin and other coats, others came just as they had jumped from their berths, clothed in their pajamas and bathrobes."

The Sorrow of the Living

Of the survivors in general it may be said that they escaped death and they gained life. Life is probably sweet to them as it is to everyone, but what physical and mental torture has been the price of life to those who were brought back to land on the *Carpathia*—the hours in lifeboats, amid the crashing of ice, the days of anguish that have succeeded, the horrors of body and mind still experienced and never to be entirely absent until death affords them its relief.

The thought of the nation today is for the living. They need our sympathy, our consolation more than do the dead, and, perhaps, in the majority of the cases they need our protecting care as well.

27

The Tragic Homecoming

THE *CARPATHIA* REACHES NEW YORK—AN INTENSE AND
DRAMATIC MOMENT—HYSTERICAL REUNIONS AND CRUSHING
DISAPPOINTMENTS AT THE DOCK—CARING FOR THE SUFFERERS—
FINAL REALIZATION THAT ALL HOPE FOR OTHERS IS FUTILE—
LIST OF SURVIVORS—ROLL OF THE DEAD

I t was a solemn moment when the *Carpathia* heaved in sight. There
she rested on the water, a blur of black—huge, mysterious, awe-
inspiring—and yet withal a thing to send thrills of pity and then of
admiration through the beholder.

It was a few minutes after seven o'clock when she arrived at the
entrance to Ambrose Channel. She was coming fast, steaming at
better than fifteen knots an hour, and she was sighted long before
she was expected. Except for the usual side and masthead lights she
was almost dark, only the upper cabins showing a glimmer here and
there.

Then began a period of waiting, the suspense of which proved
almost too much for the hundreds gathered there to greet friends
and relatives or to learn with certainty at last that those for whom
they watched would never come ashore.

There was almost complete silence on the pier. Doctors and

nurses, members of the Women's Relief Committee, city and government officials, as well as officials of the line, moved nervously about.

Seated where they had been assigned beneath the big customs letters corresponding to the initials of the names of the survivors they came to meet, sat the mass of 2,000 on the pier.

Women wept, but they wept quietly, not hysterically, and the sound of the sobs made many times less noise than the hum and bustle which is usual on the pier among those awaiting an incoming liner.

Slowly and majestically the ship slid through the water, still bearing the details of that secret of what happened and who perished when the *Titanic* met her fate.

Convoying the *Carpathia* was a fleet of tugs bearing men and women anxious to learn the latest news. The Cunarder had been as silent for days as though it, too, were a ship of the dead. A list of survivors had been given out from its wireless station and that was all. Even the approximate time of its arrival had been kept a secret.

Nearing Port

There was no response to the hail from one tug, and as others closed in, the steamship quickened her speed a little and left them behind as she swung up the channel.

There was an exploding of flashlights from some of the tugs, answered seemingly by sharp stabs of lightning in the northwest that served to accentuate the silence and absence of light aboard the rescue ship. Five or six persons, apparently members of the crew or the ship's officers, were seen along the rail, but otherwise the boat appeared to be deserted.

Off quarantine, the *Carpathia* slowed down and, hailing the immigration inspection boat, asked if the health officer wished to board. She was told that he did, and came to a stop while Dr. O'Connell and two assistants climbed on board. Again the newspapermen asked for some word of the catastrophe to the *Titanic*, but there was no answer, and the *Carpathia* continued toward her pier.

As she passed the revenue cutter *Mohawk* and the derelict destroyer *Seneca* anchored off Tompkinsville, the wireless on the government vessels was seen to flash, but there was no answering spark from the *Carpathia*. Entering the North River, she laid her course close to the New Jersey side in order to have room to swing into her pier.

By this time the rails were lined with men and women. They were very silent. There were a few requests for news from those on board and a few answers to questions shouted from the tugs.

The liner began to slacken her speed, and the tugboat soon was alongside. Up above the inky blackness of the hull figures could be made out, leaning over the port railing, as though peering eagerly at the little craft which was bearing down on the *Carpathia*.

Some of them, perhaps, had passed through that inferno of the deep sea which sprang up to destroy the mightiest steamship afloat.

"*Carpathia*, ahoy!" was shouted through a megaphone.

There was an interval of a few seconds, and then, "Aye, aye," came the reply.

"Is there any assistance that can be rendered?" was the next question.

"Thank you, no," was the answer in a tone that carried emotion with it. Meantime the tugboat was getting nearer and nearer to the *Carpathia*, and soon the faces of those leaning over the railing could be distinguished.

Talk with Survivors

More faces appeared, and still more.

A woman who called to a man on the tugboat was asked, "Are you one the *Titanic* survivors?"

"Yes," said the voice hesitatingly.

"Do you need help?"

"No," after a pause.

"If there is anything you want done it will be attended to."

"Thank you. I have been informed that my relatives will meet me at the pier."

"Is it true that some of the lifeboats sank with the *Titanic*?"

"Yes. There was some trouble in manning them. They were not far enough away from her."

All of this questioning and receiving replies was carried on with the greatest difficulty. The pounding of the liner's engines, the washing of the sea, the tugboat's engines, made it hard to understand the woman's replies.

All Cared for on Board

"Were the women properly cared for after the crash?" she was asked.

"Oh, yes," came the shrill reply. "The men were brave—very brave." Here her voice broke and she turned and left the railing, to reappear a few moments later and cry: "Please report me as saved."

"What name?" was asked. She shouted a name that could not be understood, and, apparently believing that it had been, turned away again and disappeared.

"Nearly all of us are very ill," cried another woman. Here several other tugboats appeared, and those standing at the railing were besieged with questions.

"Did the crash come without warning?" a voice on one of the smaller boats megaphoned.

"Yes," a woman answered. "Most of us had retired. We saved a few of our belongings."

"How long did it take the boat to sink?" asked the voice.

Titanic Crew Heroes

"Not long," came the reply. "The crew and the men were very brave. Oh, it is dreadful—dreadful to think of!"

"Is Mr. John Jacob Astor on board?"

"No."

"Did he remain on the *Titanic* after the collision?"

"I do not know."

Questions of this kind were showered at the few survivors who stood at the railing, but they seemed too confused to answer them intelligibly, and after replying evasively to some, they would disappear.

Rushes onto Dock

"Are you going to anchor for the night?" Captain Rostron was asked by megaphone as his boat approached Ambrose Light. It was then raining heavily.

"No," came the reply. "I am going into port. There are sick people on board."

"We tried to learn when she would dock," said Dr. Walter Kennedy, head of the big ambulance corps on the mist-shrouded pier, "and we were told it would not be before midnight and that most probably it would not be before dawn tomorrow. The childish deception that has been practiced for days by the people who are responsible for the *Titanic* has been carried up to the very moment of the landing of the survivors."

She proceeded past the Cunard pier, where 2,000 persons were awaiting her, and steamed to a spot opposite the White Star piers at Twenty-first Street.

The ports in the big enclosed pier of the Cunard Line were opened, and through them the waiting hundreds, almost frantic with anxiety over what the *Carpathia* might reveal, watched her as with nerve-destroying leisure she swung about in the river, dropping over the lifeboats of the *Titanic* that they might be taken to the piers of the White Star Line.

The *Titanic* Lifeboats

It was dark in the river, but the lowering away of the lifeboats could be seen from the *Carpathia*'s pier, and a deep sigh arose from the multitude there as they caught this first glance of anything associated with the *Titanic*.

Then the *Carpathia* started for her own pier. As she approached it the ports on the north side of pier 54 were closed that the *Carpathia* might land there, but through the two left open to accommodate the forward and after gangplanks of the big liner the watchers could see her looming larger and larger in the darkness till finally she was directly alongside the pier.

As the boats were towed away the picture taking and shouting of questions began again. John Badenoch, a buyer for Macy & Co., called down to a representative of the firm that neither Mr. nor Mrs. Isidor Straus was among the rescued on board the *Carpathia*. An officer of the *Carpathia* called down that 710 of the *Titanic*'s passengers were on board, but refused to reply to other questions.

The heavy hawsers were made fast without the customary shouting of ship's officers and pier hands. From the crowd on the pier came a long, shuddering murmur. In it were blended sighs and hundreds of whispers. The burden of it all was: "Here they come."

Anxious Men and Women

About each gangplank a portable fence had been put in place, marking off some fifty feet of the pier, within which stood one hundred or more customs officials. Next to the fence, crowded close against it, were anxious men and women, their gaze strained for a glance of the first from the ship, their mouths opened to draw their breaths in spasmodic, quivering gasps, their very bodies shaking with suppressed excitement, excitement which only the suspense itself was keeping in subjection.

These were the husbands and wives, children, parents, sweethearts, and friends of those who had sailed upon the *Titanic* on its maiden voyage.

They pressed to the head of the pier, marking the boats of the wrecked ship as they dangled at the side of the *Carpathia* and were revealed in the sudden flashes of the photographers upon the tugs. They spoke in whispers, each group intent upon its own sad business. Newspaper writers, with pier passes showing in their hatbands, were everywhere.

A sailor hurried outside the fence and disappeared, apparently on a mission for his company. There was a deep-drawn sigh as he walked away, shaking his head toward those who peered eagerly at him. Then came a man and woman of the *Carpathia*'s own passengers, as their orderly dress showed them to be.

Again a sigh like a sob swept over the crowd, and again they turned back to the canopied gangplank.

The First Survivors

Several minutes passed and then out of the first cabin gangway, tunneled by a somber awning, streamed the first survivors. A young woman, hatless, her light brown hair disordered and the leaden weight of crushing sorrow heavy upon eyes and sensitive mouth, was in the van. She stopped perplexed, almost ready to drop with terror and exhaustion, and was caught by a customs official.

"A survivor?" he questioned rapidly, and a nod of the head answering him, he demanded: "Your name."

The answer given, he started to lead her toward that section of the pier where her friends would be waiting.

When she stepped from the gangplank there was quiet on the pier. The answers of the woman could almost be heard by those fifty feet away, but as she staggered rather than walked toward the waiting throng outside the fence, a low wailing sound arose from the crowd.

"Dorothy, Dorothy!" cried a man from the number. He broke through the double line of customs inspectors as though it was composed of wooden toys and caught the woman to his breast. She opened her lips inarticulately, weakly raised her arms, and would have pitched forward upon her face had she not been supported. Her fair head fell weakly to one side as the man picked her up in his arms and, with tears streaming down his face, stalked down the long avenue of the pier and down the long stairway to a waiting taxicab.

The wailing of the crowd—its cadences, wild and weird—grew steadily louder and louder till they culminated in a mighty shriek, which swept the whole big pier as though at the direction of some master hand.

Rumors Afloat

The arrival of the *Carpathia* was the signal for the most sensational rumors to circulate through the crowd on the pier.

First, Mrs. John Jacob Astor was reported to have died at 8:06 o'clock, when the *Carpathia* was on her way up the harbor.

Captain Smith and the first engineer were reported to have shot themselves when they found that the *Titanic* was doomed to sink. Afterward it was learned that Captain Smith and the engineer went down with their ship in perfect courage and coolness.

Major Archibald Butt, President Taft's military aide, was said to have entered into an agreement with George D. Widener, Colonel John Jacob Astor, and Isidor Straus to kill them first and then shoot himself before the boat sank. It was said that this agreement had been carried out. Later it was shown that, like many other men on the ship, they had gone down without the exhibition of a sign of fear.

Mrs. Cornell Safe

Magistrate Cornell's wife and her two sisters were among the first to leave the ship. They were met at the first-cabin pier entrance by Magistrate Cornell and a party of friends. None of the three women had hats. One of those who met them was Magistrate Cornell's son. One of Mrs. Cornell's sisters was overheard to remark that "it would be a dreadful thing when the ship began really to unload."

The three women appeared to be in a very nervous state. Their hair was more or less disheveled. They were apparently fully dressed save for their hats. Clothing had been supplied them in their need and everything had been done to make them comfortable. One of the party said that the collision occurred at 9:45.

Following closely the Cornell party was H. J. Allison, of Montreal, who came to meet his family. One of the party, who was weeping bitterly as he left the pier, explained that the only one of the family who was rescued was the young brother.

Mrs. Astor Appeared

In a few minutes young Mrs. Astor with her maid appeared. She came down the gangplank unassisted. She was wearing a white sweater. Vincent Astor and William Dobbyn, Colonel Astor's secretary, greeted her and hurried her to a waiting limousine which contained clothing and other necessaries of which it was thought she might be in need. The young woman was white-faced and silent. Nobody cared to intrude upon her thoughts. Her stepson said little to her. He did not feel like questioning her at such a time, he said.

Last Seen of Colonel Astor

Walter M. Clark, a nephew of the senator, said that he had seen Colonel Astor put his wife in a boat, after assuring her that he would soon follow her in another. Mr. Clark and others said that Colonel and Mrs. Astor were in their suite when the crash came, and that they appeared quietly on deck a few minutes afterward.

Here and there among the passengers of the *Carpathia* and from the survivors of the *Titanic* the story was gleaned of the rescue. Nothing in life will ever approach the joy felt by the hundreds who were waiting in little boats on the spot where the *Titanic* foundered when the lights of the *Carpathia* were first distinguished. That was at four o'clock on Monday morning.

Dr. Frauenthal Welcomed

Efforts were made to learn from Dr. Henry Frauenthal something about the details of how he was rescued. Just then, or as he was leaving the pier, beaming with evident delight, he was surrounded by a big crowd of his friends.

"There's Harry! There he is!" they yelled and made a rush for him.

All the doctor's face that wasn't covered with red beard was aglow with smiles as his friends hugged him and slapped him on the back. They rushed him off bodily through the crowd and he too was whirled home.

A Sad Story

How others followed—how heartrending stories of partings and of thrilling rescues were poured out in an amazing stream—this has all been told over and over again in the news that for days amazed, saddened, and angered the entire world.

It is the story of a disaster that nations, it is hoped, will make impossible in the years to come.

In the stream of survivors were a peer of the realm, Sir Cosmo Duff Gordon, and his secretary, side by side with plain Jack Jones, of Birmingham, able seaman, millionaires and paupers, women with bags of jewels and others with nightgowns their only property.

More Than Seventy Widows

More than seventy widows were in the weeping company. The only large family that was saved in its entirety was that of the Carters, of Philadelphia. Contrasting with this remarkable salvage of wealthy Pennsylvanians was the sleeping eleven-month-old baby of the Allisons, whose father, mother, and sister went down to death after it and its nurse had been placed in a lifeboat.

Millionaire and pauper, titled grandee and weeping immigrant, Ismay, the head of the White Star Company, and Jack Jones from the stoke hole were surrounded instantly. Some would gladly have escaped observation. Every man among the survivors acted as though it were first necessary to explain how he came to be in a lifeboat. Some of the stories smacked of Münchausen. Others were as plain and unvarnished as a pikestaff. Those that were most sincere and trustworthy had to be fairly pulled from those who gave their sad testimony.

Far into the night the recitals were made. They were told in the rooms of hotels, in the wards of hospitals, and upon trains that sped toward saddened homes. It was a symposium of horror and heroism, the like of which has not been known in the civilized world since man established his dominion over the sea.

Steerage Passengers

The two hundred and more steerage passengers did not leave the ship until eleven o'clock. They were in a sad condition. The women were without wraps and the few men there were wore very little clothing. A poor Syrian woman who said she was Mrs. Habush, bound for Youngstown, Ohio, carried in her arms a six-year-old baby girl. This woman had lost her husband and three brothers. "I lost four of my menfolks," she cried.

Two Little Boys

Among the survivors who elicited a large measure of sympathy were two little French boys who were dropped, almost naked, from the deck of the sinking *Titanic* into a lifeboat. From what place in France did they come and to what place in the New World were they bound? There was not one iota of information to be had as to the identity of the waifs of the deep, the orphans of the *Titanic*.

The two baby boys, two and four years old, respectively, were in charge of Miss Margaret Hays, who is a fluent speaker of French, and she had tried vainly to get from the lisping lips of the two little ones some information that would lead to the finding of their relatives.

Miss Hays, also a survivor of the *Titanic*, took charge of the almost naked waifs on the *Carpathia*. She became warmly attached to the two boys, who unconcernedly played about, not understanding the great tragedy that had come into their lives.

The two little curly-heads did not understand it all. Had not their pretty nineteen-year-old foster mother provided them with pretty suits and little white shoes and playthings aplenty? Then, too, Miss Hays had a Pom dog that she brought with her from Paris and which she carried in her arms when she left the *Titanic* and held to her bosom through the long night in the lifeboat, and to which the children became warmly attached. All three became aliens on an alien shore.

Miss Hays, unable to learn the names of the little fellows, had dubbed the older Louis and the younger "Lump." "Lump" was all that his name implies, for he weighed almost as much as his brother.

They were dark-eyed and brown curly-haired children, who knew how to smile as only French children can.

On the fateful night of the *Titanic* disaster and just as the last boats were pulling away with their human freight, a man rushed to the rail holding the babes under his arms. He cried to the passengers in one of the boats and held the children aloft. Three or four sailors and passengers held up their arms. The father dropped the older boy. He was safely caught. Then he dropped the little fellow and saw him folded in the arms of a sailor. Then the boat pulled away.

The last seen of the father, whose last living act was to save his babes, he was waving his hand in a final parting. Then the *Titanic* plunged to the ocean's bed.

Baby Travers

Still more pitiable in one way was the lot of the baby survivor, eleven-month-old Travers Allison, the only member of a family of four to survive the wreck. His father, H. J. Allison, and mother and Lorraine, a child of three, were victims of the catastrophe. Baby Travers, in the excitement following the crash, was separated from the rest of the family just before the *Titanic* went down. With the party were two nurses and a maid.

Major Arthur Peuchen, of Montreal, one of the survivors, standing near the little fellow, who, swathed in blankets, lay blinking at his nurse, described the death of Mrs. Allison. She had gone to the deck without her husband, and, frantically seeking him, was directed by an officer to the other side of the ship.

She failed to find Mr. Allison and was quickly hustled into one of the collapsible lifeboats, and when last seen by Major Peuchen she was toppling out of the half-swamped boat. J. W. Allison, a cousin of

H. J. Allison, was at the pier to care for Baby Travers and his nurse. They were taken to the Manhattan Hotel.

Describing the details of the perishing of the Allison family, the rescued nurse said they were all in bed when the *Titanic* hit the berg.

"We did not get up immediately," said she, "for we had not thought of danger. Later we were told to get up, and I hurriedly dressed the baby. We hastened up on deck, and confusion was all about. With other women and children we clambered to the lifeboats, just as a matter of precaution, believing that there was no immediate danger. In about an hour there was an explosion and the ship appeared to fall apart. We were in the lifeboat about six hours before we were picked up."

The Ryerson Family

Probably few deaths have caused more tears than Arthur Ryerson's, in view of the sad circumstances which called him home from a lengthy tour in Europe. Mr. Ryerson's eldest son, Arthur Larned Ryerson, a Yale student, had been killed in an automobile accident Easter Monday, 1912.

A cablegram announcing the death plunged the Ryerson family into mourning and they boarded the first steamship for this country. If happened to be the *Titanic*, and the death note came near being the cause of the blotting out of the entire family.

The children who accompanied them were Miss Susan P. Ryerson, Miss Emily B. Ryerson, and John Ryerson. The latter is twelve years old.

They did not know their son intended to spend the Easter holidays at their home at Haverford, Pennsylvania, until they were informed of his death. John Lewis Hoffman, also of Haverford and a student of Yale, was killed with young Ryerson.

The two were hurrying to Philadelphia to escort a fellow student to his train. In turning out of the road to pass a cart, the motorcar crashed into a pole in front of the entrance to the estate of Mrs. B. Frank Clyde. The college men were picked up unconscious and died in the Bryn Mawr Hospital.

G. Heide Norris of Philadelphia, who went to New York to meet the surviving members of the Ryerson family, told of a happy incident at the last moment as the *Carpathia* swung close to the pier. There had been no positive information that young "Jack" Ryerson was among those saved—indeed, it was feared that he had gone down with the *Titanic*, like his father, Arthur Ryerson.

Mr. Norris spoke of the feeling of relief that came over him as, watching from the pier, he saw "Jack" Ryerson come from a cabin and stand at the railing. The name of the boy was missing from some of the lists and for two days it was reported that he had perished.

Captain Rostron's Report

Less than twenty-four hours after the Cunard Line steamship *Carpathia* came in as a rescue ship with survivors of the *Titanic* disaster, she sailed again for the Mediterranean cruise which she originally started upon the week before. Just before the liner sailed, H. S. Bride, the second Marconi wireless operator of the *Titanic*, who had both of his legs crushed on a lifeboat, was carried off on the shoulders of the ship's officers to St. Vincent's Hospital.

Captain A. H. Rostron, of the *Carpathia*, addressed an official report, giving his account of the *Carpathia*'s rescue work, to the general manager of the Cunard Line, Liverpool. The report read: "I beg to report that at 12:35 A.M. Monday 18th inst. I was informed of urgent message from *Titanic* with her position. I immediately ordered ship turned around and put her in course for that position, we being then 58 miles S. 52—E. 'T' from her; had heads of all departments called and issued what I considered the necessary orders, to be in preparation for any emergency.

"At 2:40 A.M. saw flare half a point on port bow. Taking this for granted to be ship, shortly after we sighted our first iceberg. I had previously had lookouts doubled, knowing that *Titanic* had struck ice, and so took every care and precaution. We soon found ourselves in a field of bergs, and had to alter course several times to clear bergs; weather fine, and clear, light air on sea, beautifully clear night, though dark.

"We stopped at 4 A.M., thus doing distance in three hours and a half, picking up the first boat at 4:10 A.M.; boat in charge of officer, and he reported that *Titanic* had foundered. At 8:30 A.M. last boat picked up. All survivors aboard and all boats accounted for, viz., fifteen lifeboats, one boat abandoned, two Berthon boats alongside (saw one floating upwards among wreckage), and according to second officer (senior officer saved) one Berthon boat had not been launched, it having got jammed, making sixteen lifeboats and four Berthon boats accounted for. By the time we had cleared first boat it was breaking day, and I could see all within area of four miles. We also saw that we were surrounded by icebergs, large and small, huge field of drift ice with large and small bergs in it, the ice field trending from N.W. round W. and S. to S.E., as far as we could see either way.

"At 8 A.M. the Leyland S.S. *California* came up. I gave him the principal news and asked him to search and I would proceed to New York; at 8:50 proceeded full speed while researching over vicinity of disaster, and while we were getting people aboard I gave orders to get spare hands along and swing in all our boats, disconnect the fall, and hoist up as many *Titanic* boats as possible in our davits; also get some on forecastle heads by derricks. We got thirteen lifeboats, six on forward deck and seven in davits. After getting all survivors aboard and while searching, I got a clergyman to offer a short prayer of thankfulness for those saved, and also a short burial service for their loss, in saloon.

"Before deciding definitely where to make for, I conferred with Mr. Ismay, and as he told me to do what I thought best, I informed him, I considered New York best. I knew we should require clean blankets, provisions, and clean linen, even if we went to the Azores, as most of the passengers saved were women and children, and they hysterical, not knowing what medical attention they might require. I thought it best to go to New York. I also thought it would be better for Mr. Ismay to go to New York or England as soon as possible, and knowing I should be out of wireless communication very soon if I proceeded to Azores, it left Halifax, Boston, and New York, so I chose the latter.

"Again, the passengers were all hysterical about ice, and I pointed out to Mr. Ismay the possibilities of seeing ice if I went to Halifax. Then I knew it would be best to keep in touch with land stations as best I could. We have experienced great difficulty in transmitting news, also names of survivors. Our wireless is very poor, and again we have had so many interruptions from other ships and also messages from shore (principally press, which we ignored). I gave instructions to send first all official messages, then names of passengers, then survivors' private messages. We had haze early Tuesday morning for several hours; again more or less all Wednesday from 5:30 A.M. to 5 P.M.; strong south-southwesterly winds and clear weather Thursday, with moderate rough sea.

"I am pleased to say that all survivors have been very plucky. The majority of women, first, second, and third class, lost their husbands, and, considering all, have been wonderfully well. Tuesday our doctor reported all survivors physically well. Our first-class passengers have behaved splendidly, given up their cabins voluntarily, and supplied the ladies with clothes, etc. We all turned out of our cabins

and gave them to survivors—saloon, smoking room, library, etc., also being used for sleeping accommodation. Our crew, also turned out to let the crew of the *Titanic* take their quarters. I am pleased to state that owing to preparations made for the comfort of survivors, none were the worse for exposure, etc. I beg to specially mention how willing and cheerful the whole of the ship's company behaved, receiving the highest praise from everybody. And I can assure you I am very proud to have such a company under my command."
—A. H. Rostron

The following list of the survivors and dead contains the latest revisions and corrections of the White Star Line officials, and was furnished by them exclusively for this book.

List of Survivors

First Cabin

Anderson, Harry.

Antoinette, Miss.

Appieranelt, Miss.

Appleton, Mrs. E. D.

Abbott, Mrs. Rose.

Allison, Master, and nurse.

Andrews, Miss Cornelia I.

Allen, Miss. E. W.

Astor, Mrs. John Jacob, and maid.

Aubeart, Mme. N., and maid.

Barratt, Karl B.

Besette, Miss.

Barkworth, A. H.

Bucknell, Mrs. W.

Bowerman, Miss E.

Brown, Mrs. J. J.

Burns, Miss C. M.

Bishop, Mr. and Mrs. D. H.

Blank, H.

Bessina, Miss A.

Baxter, Mrs. James.

Brayton, George.

Bonnell, Miss Lily.

Brown, Mrs. J. M.

Bowen, Miss G. C.

Beckwith, Mr. and Mrs. R. L.

Bisley, Mr. and Mrs.

Bonnell, Miss C.

Cassebeer, Mrs. H. A.

Cardeza, Mrs. J. W.

Candell, Mrs. Churchill.

Case, Howard B.

Camarion, Kenard.

Casseboro, Miss D. D.

Clark, Mrs. W. M.

Chibinace, Mrs. B. C.

Charlton, W. M.

Crosby, Mrs. E. G.

Carter, Miss Lucille.

Calderhead, E. P.

Chandanson, Miss Victorine.

Cavendish, Mrs. Turrell, and
maid.

Chafee, Mrs. H. I.

Cardeza, Mr. Thomas.

Cummings, Mrs. J.

Chevre, Paul.

Cherry, Miss Gladys.

Chambers, Mr. and Mrs. N. C.

Carter, Mr. and Mrs. W. E.

Carter, Master William.

Compton, Mrs. A. T.

Compton, Miss S. R.

Crosby, Mrs. E. G.

Crosby, Miss Harriet.

Cornell, Mrs. R. C.

Chibnall, Mrs. E.

Douglas, Mrs. Fred.

De Villiers, Mme.

Daniel, Miss Sarah.

Daniel, Robert W.

Davidson, Mr. and Mrs.
Thornton, and family.

Douglas, Mrs. Walter, and maid.

Dodge, Miss Sarah.

Dodge, Mrs. Washington,
and son.

Dick, Mr. and Mrs. A. A.

Daniell, H. Haren.

Drachensted, A.

Daly, Peter D.

Endres, Miss Caroline.

Ellis, Miss.

Earnshaw, Mrs. Boulton.

Eustis, Miss E.

Emmock, Philip E.

Flagenheim, Mrs. Antoinette.

Franicatelli, Miss.

Flynn, J. I.

Fortune, Miss Alice.

Fortune, Miss Ethel.

Fortune, Mrs. Mark.

Fortune, Miss Mabel.

Frauenthal, Dr. and Mrs. H. W.

Frauenthal, Mr. and Mrs. T. G.

Frolicher, Miss Margaret.

Frolicher, Max and Mrs.

Frolicher, Miss N.

Futrelle, Mrs. Jacques.

Gracie, Colonel Archibald.

Graham, Mr. and Mrs. William.

Graham, Miss M.

Gordon, Sir Cosmo Duff.

Gordon, Lady.

Gibson, Miss Dorothy.

Goldenberg, Mr. and Mrs. Samuel.

Goldenberg, Miss Ella.

Greenfield, Mrs. L. P.

Greenfield, G. B.

Greenfield, William.

Gibson, Mrs. Leonard.

Googht, James.

Haven, Mr. Henry B.

Harris, Mrs. H. B.

Holverson, Mrs. Alex.

Hogeboom, Mrs. J. C.

Hawksford, W. J.

Harper, Henry, and manservant.

Harper, Mrs. H. S.

Hold, Miss J. A.

Hope, Nina.

Hoyt, Mr. and Mrs. Fred.

Horner, Henry R.

Harder, Mr. and Mrs. George.

Hays, Mrs. Charles M., and daughter.

Hippach, Miss Jean.

Hippach, Mrs. Ida S.

Ismay, J. Bruce.

Jenasco, Mrs. J.

Kimball, Mr. and Mrs. Ed. N.

Kennyman, F. A.

Kenchen, Miss Emile.

Longley, Miss G. F.

Leader, Mrs. A. F.

Leahy, Miss Nora.

Lavory, Miss Bertha.

Lines, Mrs. Ernest.

Lines, Miss Mary.

Lindstrom, Mrs. Singird.

Lesneur, Gustave, Jr.

Madill, Miss Georgette A.

Mahan, Mrs.

Melicard, Mme.

Menderson, Miss Letta.

Maimy, Miss Roberta.

Marvin, Mrs. D. W.

Marechell, Pierre.

Maroney, Mrs. R.

Meyer, Mrs. E. I.

Mock, Mr. P. E.

Middle, Mme. M. Olive.

Minahan, Miss Daisy.

Minahan, Mrs. W. E.

McGough, James.

Newell, Miss Alice.

Newell, Miss Madeline.

Newell, Washington.

Newson, Miss Helen.

O'Connell, Miss R.

Ostby, E. C.

Osrby, Miss Helen.

Omund, Fieunam.

Panhart, Miss Ninette.

Pears, Mrs. E.

Pomroy, Miss. Ellen.

Potter, Mrs. Thomas, Jr.

Peuchen, Major Arthur.

Peercault, Miss A.

Ryerson, John.

Renago, Mrs. Mamam.

Ranelt, Miss Appie.

Rothschild, Mrs. Lord Martin.

Rosenbaum, Miss Edith.

Rheims, Mr. and Mrs George.

Rosible, Miss H.

Rothes, Countess.

Robert, Mrs. Edna.

Rolmane, C.

Ryerson, Miss Susan P.

Ryerson, Miss Emily.

Ryerson, Mrs. Arthur, and maid.

Stone, Mrs. George M.

Skeller, Mrs. William.

Segesser, Miss Emma.

Seward, Fred K.

Shutter, Miss.

Sloper, William T.

Swift, Mrs. F. Joel.

Schabert, Mrs. Paul.

Sheddel, Robert Douglass.

Snyder, Mr. and Mrs. John.

Serepeca, Miss Augusta.

Silverthorn, R. Spencer.

Saalfeld, Adolf.

Stahelin, Max.

Simoinus, Alfonsius.

Smith, Mrs. Lucien P.

Stephenson, Mrs. Walter.

Solomon, Abraham.

Silvey, Mrs. William B.

Stenmel, Mr. and Mrs. Heleery.

Spencer, Mrs. W. A., and maid.

Slayter, Miss Hilda.

Spedden, Mr. and Mrs. F. O., and child.

Steffanson, H. B.

Straus, Mrs., maid of.

Schabert, Mrs. Emma.

Slinter, Mrs. E.

Simmons, A.

Taylor, Miss.

Tucker, Mrs., and maid.

Thayer, Mrs. J. B.

Thayer, J. B., Jr.

Taussig, Miss Ruth.

Taussig, Mrs. E.

Thor, Miss Ella.

Thorne, Mrs. G.

Taylor, Mr. and Mrs. E. Z.

Trout, Miss Jessie.

Tucker, Gilbert.

Woolner, Hugh.

Ward, Miss Anna.

Williams, Richard M., Jr.

Warren, Mrs. F.

Wilson, Miss Helen A.

Williard, Miss C.

Wick, Miss Mary.

Wick, Geo.

Widener, valet of.

Widener, Mrs. George D., and maid.

White, Mrs. J. Stuart.

Young, Miss Marie.

List of Survivors—Second Cabin

Abesson, Mrs. Hanna.

Abbott, Mrs. R.

Abgenia, Mrs. and two children.

Angel, F.

Angle, William.

Baumthorpe, Mrs. L.

Balls, Mrs. Ada E.

Buss, Miss Kate.

Becker, Mrs. A. O., and three children.

Beane, Edward.

Beane, Mrs. Ethel.

Bryhl, Miss D.

Beesley, Mr. L.

Brown, Mr. T.W.S.

Brown, Miss E.

Brown, Mrs.

Benthan, Lillian W.

Bystron, Karolina.

Bright, Dagmar.

Bright, Daisy.

Clarke, Mrs. Ada.

Cameron, Miss C.

Caldwell, Albert F.

Caldwell, Mrs. Sylvan.

Caldwell, Alden, infant.

Cristy, Mr. and Mrs.

Collyer, Mrs. Charlotte.

Collyer, Miss Marjorie.

Christy, Mrs. Alice.

Collet, Stuart.

Christa, Miss Ducia.

Charles, William.

Croft, Millie Mall.

Doling, Mrs. Elsie.

Drew, Mrs. Lulu.

Davis, Mrs. Agnes.

Davis, Miss Mary.

Davis, John M.

Duvan, Florentine.

Duvan, Miss A.

Davidson, Miss Mary.

Doling, Miss Ada.

Driscoll, Mrs. B.

Deystrom, Caroline.

Emcarmacion, Mrs. Rinaldo.

Faunthorpe, Mrs. Lizzie.

Formery, Miss Ellen.

Garside, Ethel.

Gerrecai, Mrs. Marcy.

Genovese, Angere.

Hart, Mrs. Esther.

Hrat, Eva.

Harris, George.

Hewlett, Mrs. Mary.

Hebber, Miss S.

Hoffman, Lola.

Hoffman, Louis.

Harper, Nina.

Hold, Stephen.

Hold, Mrs. Anna.

Hosono, Masabumi.

Hocking, Mr. and Mrs. George

Hocking, Miss Nellie.

Herman, Mrs. Jane, and two
daughters.

Healy, Nora.

Hanson, Jennie.

Hamatainen, W.

Hamatainen, Anna.

Harnlin, Anna, and child.

Ilett, Bertha.

Jackson, Mrs. Amy.

Juliet, Luwche.

Jerwan, Mary.

Juhon, Podro.

Jacobson, Mrs.

Keane, Miss Nora H.

Kelly, Mrs. F.

Kantar, Mrs. S.

Leitch, Jessie.

Laroche, Mrs. and Miss
Simmone.

Laroche, Miss Louise.

Lehman, Bertha.

Lauch, Mrs. Alex.

Laniore, Amelia.

Lystrom, Mrs. C.

Mellinger, Elizabeth.

Mellinger, child.

Marshall, Mrs. Kate.

Mallett, A.

Mallett, Mrs., and child.

Mange, Paula.

Mare, Mrs. Florence.

Mellor, W. J.

McDearmont, Miss Lela.

McGowan, Anna.

Nye, Elizabeth.

Nasser, Mrs. Delia.

Nussa, Mrs. A.

Oxenham, Percy J.

Phillips, Alice.

Pallas, Emilio.

Padro, Julian.

Prinsky, Rosa.

Portaluppi, Emilio.

Parsh, Mrs. L.

Plett, B.

Quick, Mrs. Jane.

Quick, Mrs. Vera W.

Quick, Miss Phyllis.

Reinardo, Miss E.

Ridsdale, Lucy.

Renouf, Mrs. Lily.

Rugg, Miss Emily.

Richards, M.

Rogers, Miss Selina.

Richards, Mrs. Emilia, two boys,
and Mr. Richards, Jr.

Simpson, Miss.

Sincock, Miss Maude.

Sinkkonnen, Anna.

Smith, Miss Marion.

Silven, Lylle.

Trant, Mrs J.

Toomey, Miss E.

Troutt, Miss E.

Troutt, Miss Cecelia.

Ware, Miss H.

Watter, Miss N.

Wilhelm, Chas.

Wat, Mrs. A., and two children.

Williams, Richard M., Jr.

Weisz, Mathilde.

Webber, Miss Susie.

Wright, Miss Marion.

Watt, Miss Bessie.

Watt, Miss Bertha.

West, Mrs. E. A.

West, Miss Constance.

West, Miss Barbara.

Wells, Addie.

Wells, Master.

Wells, Miss.

A list of surviving third cabin passengers and crew is omitted owing to the impossibility of obtaining the correct names of many.

Roll of the Dead

First Cabin

Allison, H. J.

Allison, Mrs., and maid.

Allison, Miss.

Andrews, Thomas.

Artagaveytia, Mr. Ramon.

Astor, Col. J. J., and servant.

Anderson, Walker.

Beattie, T.

Brandeis, E.

Bucknell, Mrs. William, maid of.

Baumann, J.

Baxter, Mr. and Mrs. Quigg.

Bjornstrom, H.

Birnbaum, Jacob.

Blackwell, S. W.

Borebank, J. J.

Bowen, Miss.

Brady, John B.

Brewe, Arthur J.

Butt, Major A.

Clark, Walter M.

Clifford, George Q.

Colley, E. P.

Cardeza, T. D. M., servant of.

Cardeza, Mrs. J. W., maid of.

Carlson, Frank.

Corran, F. M.

Corran, J. P.

Chafee, Mr. H. I.

Chisholm, Robert.

Compton, A. T.

Crafton, John B.

Crosby, Edward G.

Cummings, John Bradley.

Dulles, William C.

Douglas, W. D.

Douglas, Master R., nurse of.

Evans, Miss E.

Fortune, Mark.

Foreman, B. L.

Fortune, Charles.

Franklin, T. P.

Futrelle, J.

Gee, Arthur.

Goldenberg, E. L.

Goldschmidt, G. B.

Giglio, Victor.

Guggenheim, Benjamin.

Hays, Charles M.

Hays, Mrs. Charles, maid of.

Head, Christopher.

Hilliard, H. H.

Hipkins, W. E.

Hogenheim, Mrs. A.

Harris, Henry B.

Harp, Mr. and Mrs. Charles M.

Harp, Miss Margaret, and maid.

Holverson, A. M.

Isham, Miss A. E.

Ismay, J. Bruce, servant of.

Julian, H. F.

Jones, C. C.

Kent, Edward A.

Kenyon, Mr. and Mrs. F. R.

Klaber, Herman.

Lamberth, Williams, F. F.

Lawrence, Arthur.

Long, Milton.

Lewy, E. G.

Loring, J. H.

Lingrey, Edward.

Maguire, J. E.

McCaffry, T.

McCaffry, T., Jr.

McCarthy, T.

Middleton, J. C.

Millet, Frank D.

Minahan, Dr.

Meyer, Edgar J.

Molson, H. M.

Moore, C., servant.

Natsch, Charles.

Newall, Miss T.

Nicholson, A. S.

Ovies, S.

Ornout, Alfred T.

Parr, M.H.W.

Pears, Mr. and Mrs. Thomas.

Penasco, Mr. and Mrs. Victor.

Partner, M. A.

Payne, V.

Pond, Florence, and maid.

Porter, Walter.

Puffer, C. C.

Reuchlin, J.

Robert, Mrs. E., maid of.

Roebling, Washington A., 2d.

Rood, Hugh R.

Roes, J. Hugo.

Rothes, Countess, maid of.

Rothschild, M.

Rowe, Arthur.

Ryerson, A.

Silvey, William B.

Spedden, Mrs. F. O., maid of.

Spencer, W. A.

Stead, W. T.

Stehli, Mr. and Mrs. Max Frolicher.

Stone, Mrs. George, maid of.

Straus, Mr. and Mrs. Isidor.

Sutton, Frederick.

Smart, John M.

Smith, Clinch.

Smith, R. W.

Smith, L. P.

Taussig, Emil.

Thayer, Mrs., maid of.

Thayer, John B.

Thorne, G.

Vanderhoof, Wyckoff.

Walker, W. A.

Warren, F. M.

White, Percival A.

White, Richard F.

Widener, G. D.

Widener, Harry.

Wood, Mr. and Mrs. Frank P.

Weir, J.

Williams, Duane.

Wright, George.

Second Cabin

Abelson, Samson.

Andrew, Frank.

Ashby, John.

Aldworth, C.

Andrew, Edgar.

Bracken, James H.

Bracken, Mrs.

Banfield, Fred.

Bright, Narl.

Braily, bandsman.

Breicoux, bandsman.

Bailey, Percy.

Bainbridge, C. R.

Byles, the Reverend Thomas.

Beauchamp, H. J.

Berg, Miss E.

Benthan, I.

Bateman, Robert J.

Butler, Reginald.

Botsford, Hull.

Boweener, Solomon.

Berriman, William.

Clarke, Charles.

Clark, bandsman.

Corey, Mrs. C. P.

Carter, the Reverend Ernest.

Carter, Mrs.

Coleridge, Reginald.

Chapman, Charles.

Cunningham, Alfred.

Campbell, William.

Collyer, Harvey.

Corbett, Mrs. Irene.

Chapman, John H.

Chapman, Mrs. E.

Colander, Eric.

Cotterill, Harry.

Deacon, Percy.

Davis, Charles.

Dibben, William.

De Brito, Jose.

Denborny, H.

Drew, James.

Drew, Master M.

David, Master J. W.

Dounton, W. J.

Del Varlo, S.

Del Varlo, Mrs.

Enander, Ingvar.

Eitemiller, G. F.

Frost, A.

Fynnery, Mr.

Faunthorpe, H.

Fillbrook, C.

Funk, Annie.

Fahlstrom, A.

Fox, Stanley W.

Greenberg, S.

Giles, Ralph.

Gaskell, Alfred.

Gillespie, William.

Gilbert, William.

Gall, S.

Gill, John.

Giles, Edgar.

Giles, Fred.

Gale, Harry.

Gale, Phadruch.

Garvey, Lawrence.

Hickman, Leonard.

Hickman, Lewis.

Hume, bandsman.

Hickman, Stanley.

Hood, Ambrose.

Hodges, Henry P.

Hart, Benjamin.

Harris, Walter.

Harper, John.

Harbeck, W. H.

Hoffman, Mr.

Herman, Mrs. S.

Howard, B.

Howard, Mrs. E. T.

Hale, Reginald.

Hiltunen, M.

Hunt, George.

Jacobson, Mr.

Jacobson, Sydney.

Jeffery, Clifford.

Jeffery, Ernest.

Jenkin, Stephen.

Jarvis, John D.

Keane, Daniel.

Kirkland, the Reverend C.

Karnes, Mrs. F. G.

Keynaldo, Miss.

Krillner, J. H.

Krins, bandsman.

Karines, Mrs.

Kantar, Selna.

Knight, R.

Lengam, John.

Levy, R. J.

Lahtiman, William.

Lauch, Charles.

Leyson, R.W.N.

Laroche, Joseph.

Lamb, J. J.

McKane, Peter.

Milling, Jacob.

Mantoila, Joseph.

Malachard, Noll.

Moraweck, Dr.

Mangiovacchi, E.

McCrae, Arthur G.

McCrie, James M.

McKane, Peter D.

Mudd, Thomas.

Mack, Mrs. Mary.

Marshall, Henry.

Mayberg, Frank H.

Meyer, August.

Myles, Thomas.

Mitchell, Henry.

Matthews, W. J.

Nessen, Israel.

Nicholls, Joseph C.

Norman, Robert D.

Otter, Richard.

Phillips, Robert.

Ponesell, Martin.

Pain, Dr. Alfred.

Parkes, Frank.

Pengelly, F.

Pernot, Rene.

Peruschitz, the Reverend.

Parker, Clifford.

Pulbaum, Frank.

Renouf, Peter H.

Rogers, Harry.

Reeves, David.

Slemen, R. J.

Sobey, Hayden.

Slatter, Miss H. M.

Stanton, Ward.

Sword, Hans K.

Stokes, Philip J.

Sharp, Percival.

Sedgwick, Mr. F. W.

Smith, Augustus.

Sweet, George.

Sjostedt, Ernst.

Taylor, bandsman.

Turpin, William J.

Turpin, Mrs. Dorothy.

Turner, John H.

Troupiansky, M.

Tirvan, Mrs. A.

Veale, James.

Watson, E.

Woodward, bandsman.

Ware, William J.

Weisz, Leopold.

Wheadon, Edward.

Ware, John J.

West, E. Arthur.

Wheeler, Edwin.

Werman, Samuel.

The total death list was 1,635. Third-cabin passengers and crew are not included in the list here given owing to the impossibility of obtaining the exact names of many.

28

Other Great Marine Disasters

DEADLY DANGER OF ICEBERGS—THE *ARIZONA*—DOZENS OF SHIPS
PERISH IN COLLISION—OTHER DISASTERS.

T he danger of collision with icebergs has always been one of the most deadly that confront the mariner. Indeed, so well recognized is this peril of the Newfoundland Banks, where the Labrador current in the early spring and summer months floats southward its ghostly argosy of icy pinnacles detached from the polar ice caps, that the government hydrographic offices and the maritime exchanges spare no pains to collate and disseminate the latest bulletins on the subject.

The *Arizona*

A most remarkable case of an iceberg collision is that of the Guion liner *Arizona*, in 1879. She was then the greyhound of the Atlantic,

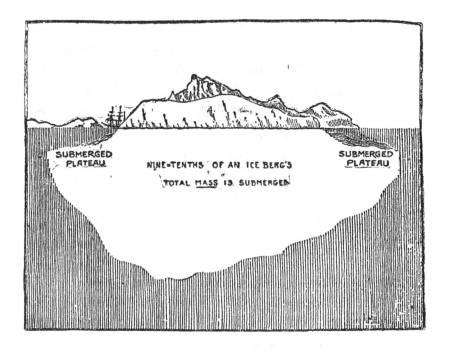

THE SHAPE OF AN ICEBERG

Showing the bulk and formation under water and the consequent danger to vessels even without actual contact with the visible part of the iceberg.

and the largest ship afloat—5,750 tons—except for the *Great East-ern*. Leaving New York in November for Liverpool with 509 souls aboard, she was coursing across the Banks, with fair weather but dark, when, near midnight, about 250 miles east of St. John's, she rammed a monster ice island at full speed—eighteen knots. Terrific was the impact.

The welcome word was passed along that the ship, though sorely stricken, would still float until she could make harbor. The vast white terror had lain across her course, stretching so far each way that, when described, it was too late to alter the helm. Its giant shape filled the foreground, towering high above the masts, grim and gaunt and ghastly, immovable as the adamantine buttresses of a frowning seaboard, while the liner lurched and staggered like a wounded thing in agony as her engines slowly drew her back from the rampart against which she had flung herself.

She was headed for St. John's at slow speed, so as not to strain the bulkhead too much, and arrived there thirty-six hours later. That little port—the crippled ship's hospital—has seen many a strange sight come in from the sea, but never a more astounding spectacle than that which the *Arizona* presented the Sunday forenoon she entered there.

"Begob, Captain!" said the pilot as he swung himself over the rail. "I've heard of carrying coals to Newcastle, but this is the first time I've seen a steamer bringing a load of ice into St. John's."

They are a grim race, these sailors, and the danger over, the captain's reply was: "We were lucky, my man, that we didn't all go to the bottom in an icebox."

Dozens of Ships Perish

But to the one wounded ship that survives collision with a berg, a dozen perish. Presumably, when the shock comes, it loosens their bulkheads and they fill and founder, or the crash may injure the boilers or engines, which explode and tear out the sides, and the ship goes down like a plummet. As long ago as 1841, the steamer *President*, with 120 people aboard, crossing from New York to Liverpool in March, vanished from human ken. In 1854, in the same month, the *City of Glasgow* left Liverpool for Philadelphia with 480 souls, and was never again heard of. In February 1856, the *Pacific*, from Liverpool for New York, carrying 185 persons, passed away down to a sunless sea. In May 1870, the *City of Boston*, from that port for Liverpool, mustering 191 souls, met a similar fate. It has always been thought that these ships were sunk by collision with icebergs or floes. As shipping traffic has expanded the losses have been more frequent. In February 1892, the *Naronic*, from Liverpool for New York; in the same month in 1896, the *State of Georgia*, from Aberdeen for Boston; in February 1899, the *Alleghany*, from New York for Dover; and once more in February 1902, the *Huronian*, from Liverpool for St. John's—all disappeared without leaving a trace. Between February and May, the Grand Banks are most infested with ice, and collision therewith is the most likely explanation of the loss of these steamers, all well manned and in splendid trim, and meeting only the storms which scores of other ships have braved without a scathe.

Toll of the Sea

Among the important marine disasters recorded since 1866 are the following:

1866, Jan. 11—Steamer *London*, on her way to Melbourne, foundered in the Bay of Biscay; 220 lives lost.

1866, Oct. 3—Steamer *Evening Star*, from New York to New Orleans, foundered; about 250 lives lost.

1867, Oct. 29—Royal Mail steamers *Rhone* and *Wye* and about fifty other vessels driven ashore and wrecked at St. Thomas, West Indies, by a hurricane; about 1,000 lives lost.

1873, Jan. 22—British steamer *Northfleet* sunk in collision off Dungeness: 300 lives lost.

1873, Nov. 23—White Star liner *Atlantic* wrecked off Nova Scotia; 547 lives lost.

1873, Nov. 23—French line *Ville du Havre*, from New York to Havre, in collision with ship *Locharn* and sunk in sixteen minutes; 110 lives lost.

1874, Dec. 24—Emigrant vessel *Cospatrick* took fire and sank off Auckland; 476 lives lost.

1875, May 7—Hamburg mail steamer *Schiller* wrecked in fog on Scilly Islands; 200 lives lost.

1875, Nov. 4—American steamer *Pacific* in collision thirty miles southwest of Cape Flattery; 236 lives lost.

1878, March 24—British training ship *Eurydice*, a frigate, foundered near the Isle of Wight; 300 lives lost.

1878, Sept. 3—British iron steamer *Princess Alice* sunk in the Thames River; 700 lives lost.

1878, Dec. 18—French steamer *Byzantin* sunk in collision in the Dardanelles with the British steamer *Rinaldo*; 210 lives lost.

1879, Dec. 2—Steamer *Borussia* sank off the coast of Spain; 174 lives lost.

1880, Jan. 31—British trading ship *Atlanta* left Bermuda with 290 men and was never heard from.

1881, Aug. 30—Steamer *Teuton* wrecked off the Cape of Good Hope; 200 lives lost.

1883, July 3—Steamer *Daphne* turned turtle in the Clyde; 124 lives lost.

1884, Jan. 18—American steamer *City of Columbus* wrecked off Gay Head Light, Massachusetts; 99 lives lost.

1884, July 23—Spanish steamer *Gijon* and British steamer *Lux* in collision off Finisterre; 150 lives lost.

1887, Jan. 29—Steamer *Kapunda* in collision with bark *Ada Melore* off coast of Brazil; 300 lives lost.

1887, Nov. 15—British steamer *Wah Young* caught fire between Canton and Hong Kong; 400 lives lost.

1888, Sept. 13—Italian steamship *Sud America* and steamer *La France* in collision near the Canary Islands; 89 lives lost.

1889, March 16—United States warships *Trenton*, *Vandalia*, and *Nipsic* and German ships *Adler* and *Eber* wrecked on Samoan Islands; 147 lives lost.

1890, Jan. 2—Steamer *Persia* wrecked on Corsica; 130 lives lost.

1890, Feb. 17—British steamer *Duburg* wrecked in the China Sea; 400 lives lost.

1890, March 1—British steamship *Quetta* foundered in Torres Straits; 124 lives lost.

1890, Dec. 27—British steamer *Shanghai* burned in China Seas; 101 lives lost.

1891, March 17—Anchor liner *Utopia* in collision with British steamer *Anson* off Gibraltar and sunk; 574 lives lost.

1892, Jan. 13—Steamer *Namehow* wrecked in China Sea; 414 lives lost.

1892, Oct. 28—Anchor liner *Romania*, wrecked off Portugal; 113 lives lost.

1893, Feb. 8—Anchor liner *Trinairia*, wrecked off Spain: 115 lives lost.

1894, June 25—Steamer *Norge*, wrecked on Rockall Reef, in the North Atlantic; nearly 600 lives lost.

1895, Jan. 30—German steamer *Elbe* sunk in collision with British steamer *Crathie* in North Sea; 335 lives lost.

1898, July 4—French line steamer *La Bourgogne* in collision with British sailing vessel *Cromartyshire*; 571 lives lost.

1898, Nov. 27—American steamer *Portland*, wrecked off Cape Cod, Massachusetts; 157 lives lost.

1901, April 1—Turkish transport *Aslam* wrecked in the Red Sea; over 180 lives lost.

1902, July 21—Steamer *Primus* sunk in collision with the steamer *Hansa* on the Lower Elbe; 112 lives lost.

1903, June 7—French steamer *Libau* sunk in collision with steamer *Insulerre* near Marseilles; 150 lives lost.

1904, June 15—*General Slocum*, excursion steamboat, took fire going through Hell Gate, East River; more than 1,000 lives lost.

1906, Jan. 21—Brazilian battleship *Aquidaban* sunk near Rio de Janeiro by an explosion of the powder magazines; 212 lives lost.

1906, Jan. 22—American steamer *Valencia* lost off Cloose, Pacific Coast; 140 lives lost.

1906, Aug. 4—Italian emigrant ship *Sirio* struck a rock off Cape Palos; 350 lives lost.

1906, Oct. 21—Russian steamer *Variag*, on leaving Vladivostock, struck by a torpedo and sunk; 140 lives lost.

1907, Feb. 12—American steamer *Larchmond* sunk in collision off Rhode Island coast; 131 lives lost.

1907, July 20—American steamers *Columbia* and *San Pedro* collided on the Californian coast; 100 lives lost.

1907, Nov. 26—Turkish steamer *Kaptain* foundered in the North Sea; 110 lives lost.

1908, March 23—Japanese steamer *Mutsu Maru* sunk in collision near Hakodate; 300 lives lost.

1908, April 30—Japanese training cruiser *Matsu Shima* sunk off the Pescadores owing to an explosion; 200 lives lost.

1909, Jan. 24—Collision between the Italian steamer *Florida* and the White Star liner *Republic*, about 170 miles east of New York during a fog; a large number of lives were saved by the arrival of the steamer *Baltic*, which received the CQD, or distress signal sent up by wireless by the *Republic*

January 22. The *Republic* sank while being towed; six lives lost.

1910, Feb. 9—French line steamer *Général Chanzy* off Minorca; 200 lives lost.

1911, Sept. 25—French battleship *Liberté* sunk by explosion in Toulon harbor; 223 lives lost.

29

Development of Shipbuilding

EVOLUTION OF WATER TRAVEL—INCREASES IN SIZE OF
VESSELS—IS THERE ANY LIMIT?—ACHIEVEMENTS IN SPEED—
TITANIC NOT THE LAST WORD

T he origin of travel on water dates back to a very early period in human history, men beginning with the log, the inflated skin, the dugout canoe, and upward through various methods of flotation; while the paddle, the oar, and finally the sail served as means of propulsion. This was for inland water travel, and many centuries passed before the navigation of the sea was dreamed of by adventurous mariners.

The paintings and sculptures of early Egypt show us boats built of sawed planks, regularly constructed and moved both by oars and sails. At a later period we read of the Phoenicians, the most daring and enterprising of ancient navigators, who braved the dangers of the open sea, and are said by Herodotus to have circumnavigated Africa as early as 604 BC. Starting from the Red Sea, they followed the east coast, rounded the Cape, and sailed north along the west coast to the Mediterranean, reaching Egypt again in the third year of this enterprise.

The Carthaginians and Romans come next in the history of shipbuilding, confining themselves chiefly to the Mediterranean and using oars as the principal means of propulsion. Their galleys ranged from one to five banks of oars. The Roman vessels in the first Punic War were over 100 feet long and had 300 rowers, while they carried 120 soldiers. They did not use sails until about the beginning of the fourteenth century BC.

Portugal was the first nation to engage in voyages of discovery, using vessels of small size in these adventurous journeys. Spain, which soon became her rival in this field, built larger ships and long held the lead. Yet the ships with which Columbus made the discovery of America were of a size and character in which few sailors of the present day would care to venture far from land.

England was later in coming into the field of adventurous navigation, being surpassed not only by the Portuguese and Spanish, but by the Dutch, in ventures to far lands.

Europe long held the precedence in shipbuilding and enterprise in navigation, but the shores of America had not long been settled before the adventurous colonists had ships upon the seas. The first of these was built at the mouth of the Kennebec River in Maine. This was a staunch little two-masted vessel, which was named the *Virginia*, supposed to have been about sixty feet long and seventeen feet in beam. Next in time came the *Restless*, built in 1614 or 1615 at New York, by Adrian Blok, a Dutch captain whose ships had been burned while lying at Manhattan Island. This vessel, thirty-eight feet long and of eleven feet beam, was employed for several years in exploring the Atlantic coast.

With the advent of the nineteenth century a new ideal in naval architecture arose, that of the ship moved by steam power instead of wind power, and fitted to combat with the seas alike in storm and calm, with little heed as to whether the wind was fair or foul. The steamship appeared, and grew in size and power until such giants of the wave as the *Titanic* and *Olympic* were set afloat. To the development of this modern class of ships our attention must now be turned.

As the reckless cowboy of the West is fast becoming a thing of the past, so is the daring seaman of fame and story. In his place is coming a class of men miscalled sailors, who never reefed a sail or coiled a cable, who do not know how to launch a lifeboat or pull an oar, and in whose career we meet the ridiculous episode of the life-boats of the *Titanic*, where women were obliged to take the oars from their hands and row the boats. Thus has the old-time hero of the waves been transformed into one fitted to serve as a clown of the vaudeville stage.

The advent of steam navigation came early in the nineteenth century, though interesting steps in this direction were taken earlier. No sooner had the steam engine been developed than men began to speculate on it as a moving power on sea and land. Early among these were several Americans, Oliver Evans, one of the first to project steam railway travel, and James Rumsey and John Fitch, steamboat inventors of early date. There were several experimenters in Europe also, but the first to produce a practical steamboat was Robert Fulton, a native of Pennsylvania, whose successful boat, the *Clermont*, made its maiden trip up the Hudson in 1807. A crude affair was the *Clermont*, with a top speed of about seven miles an hour; but it was the dwarf from which the giant steamers of today have grown.

Boats of this type quickly made their way over the American rivers and before 1820 regular lines of steamboats were running between England and Ireland. In 1817 James Watt, the inventor of the practical steam engine, crossed in a steamer from England to Belgium. But these short voyages were far surpassed by an American enterprise, that of the first ocean steamship, the *Savannah*, which crossed the Atlantic from Savannah to Liverpool in 1819.

Twelve years passed before this enterprise was repeated, the next steam voyage being in 1831, when the *Royal William* crossed from Quebec to England. She used coal for fuel, having utilized her entire hold to store enough for the voyage. The *Savannah* had burned pitch pine under her engines, for in America wood was long used as fuel for steam-making purposes. As regards this matter, the problem of fuel was of leading importance, and it was seriously questioned if a ship could be built to cross the Atlantic depending solely upon steam power. Steam engines in those days were not very economical, needing four or five times as much fuel for the same power as the engines of recent date.

It was not until 1838 that the problem was solved. On April 23 of that year a most significant event took place. Two steamships dropped anchor in the harbor of New York, the *Sirius* and the *Great Western*. Both of these had made the entire voyage under steam, the *Sirius*, in eighteen and a half and the *Great Western* in fourteen and a half days, measuring from Queenstown. The *Sirius* had taken on board 450 tons of coal, but all this was burned by the time Sandy Hook was reached, and she had to burn her spare spars and forty-three barrels of rosin to make her way up the bay. The *Great Western*, on the contrary, had coal to spare.

Two innovations in shipbuilding were soon introduced. These were the building of iron instead of wooden ships and the replacing of the paddle wheel by the screw propeller. The screw propeller was first successfully introduced by the famous Swede John Ericsson in 1835. His propeller was tried in a small vessel, forty-five feet long and eight wide, which was driven at the rate of ten miles an hour, and towed a large packet ship at fair speed. Ericsson, not being appreciated in England, came to America to experiment. Other inventors were also at work in the same line.

Their experiments attracted the attention of Isambard Brunel, one of the greatest engineers of the period, who was then engaged in building a large paddlewheel steamer, the Great Britain. Appreciating the new idea, he had the engines of the new ship changed and a screw propeller introduced. This ship, a great one for the time, 322 feet long and of 3,443 tons, made her first voyage from Liverpool to New York in 1845, her average speed being 12¼ knots an hour, the length of the voyage 14 days and 21 hours.

By the date named, the crossing of the Atlantic by steamships had become a common event. In 1840 the British and Royal Mail Steam Packet Company was organized, its chief promoter being Samuel Cunard, of Halifax, Nova Scotia, whose name has long been attached to this famous line.

The first fleet of the Cunard Line comprised four vessels, the *Britannia, Acadia, Caledonia,* and *Columbia.* The *Unicorn,* sent out by this company as a pioneer, entered Boston harbor on June 2, 1840, being the first steamship from Europe to reach that port. Regular trips began with the *Britannia,* which left Liverpool on July 4, 1840. For a number of years later this line enjoyed a practical monopoly of the steam carrying trade between England and the United States. Then other companies came into the field, chief among them being the Collins Line, started in 1849, and of short duration, and the Inman Line, instituted in 1850.

We should say something here of the comforts and conveniences provided for the passengers on these early lines. They differed strikingly from those on the leviathans of recent travel and were little, if any, superior to those on the packet ships, the active rivals at that date of the steamers. Then there were none of the comfortable smoking rooms, well-filled libraries, drawing rooms, electric lights, and other modern improvements. The saloons and staterooms were in the extreme after part of the vessel, but the stateroom of that day was little more than a closet, with two berths, one above the other, and very little standing room between these and the wall. By paying nearly double fare a passenger might secure a room for himself, but the room given him did not compare well even with that of small and unpretentious modern steamers.

Other ocean steamship companies gradually arose, some of which are still in existence. But no especial change in shipbuilding was introduced until 1870, when the Oceanic Company, now known as the White Star Line, built the *Britannic* and *Germanic*. These were the largest of its early ships. They were 468 feet long and 35 feet wide, constituting a new type of extreme length as compared with their width. In the first White Star ship, the *Oceanic*, the improvements abovementioned were introduced, the saloons and staterooms being brought as near as possible to the center of the ship. All the principal lines built since that date have followed this example, thus adding much to the comfort of the first-class passengers.

Speed and economy in power also became features of importance, the tubular boiler and the compound engine being introduced. These have developed into the cylindrical, multitubular boiler and the triple-expansion engine, in which a greater percentage of the power of the steam is utilized and four or five times the work obtained from coal over that of the old system. The side wheel was continued in use in the older ships until this period, but after 1870 it disappeared.

It has been said that the life of iron ships, barring disasters at sea, is unlimited, that they cannot wear out. This statement has not been tested, but the fact remains that the older passenger ships have gone out of service and that steel has now taken the place of iron, as lighter and more durable.

Something should also be said here of the steam turbine engine, recently introduced in some of the greatest liners, and of proven value in several particulars, an important one of these being the doing away with the vibration, an inseparable accompaniment of the old-style engines. The *Olympic* and *Titanic* engines were a combination of the turbine and reciprocating types. In regard to the driving power, one of the recent introductions is that of the multiple propeller. The twin screw was first applied in the *City of New York*, of the Inman Line, and enabled her to make in 1890 an average speed of a little over six days from New York to Queenstown. The best record up to October 1891 was that of the *Teutonic*, of five days, sixteen hours, and thirty minutes. Triple-screw propellers have since then been introduced in some of the greater ships, and the record speed has been cut down to the four days and ten hours of the *Lusitania* in 1908 and the four days, six hours, and forty-one minutes of the *Mauretania* in 1910.

The *Titanic* was not built especially for speed, but in every other way she was the master product of the shipbuilders' art. Progress through the centuries has been steady, and perhaps the twentieth century will prepare a vessel that will be unsinkable as well as magnificent. Until the fatal accident the *Titanic* and *Olympic* were considered the last words on shipbuilding but much may still remain to be spoken.

30

Safety and Lifesaving Devices

WIRELESS TELEGRAPHY—WATERTIGHT BULKHEADS—SUBMARINE
SIGNALS—LIFEBOATS AND RAFTS—NIXON'S PONTOON—
LIFE PRESERVERS AND BUOYS—ROCKETS

The fact that there were any survivors of the *Titanic* left to tell the story of the terrible catastrophe is only another of the hundreds of instances on record of the value of wireless telegraphy in saving life on shipboard. Without Marconi's invention it is altogether probable that the world would never have known of the nature of the *Titanic*'s fate, for it is only barely within the realm of posibility that any of the *Titanic*'s passengers, poorly clad, without proper provisions of food and water, and exposed in the open boats to the frigid weather, would have survived long enough to have been picked up by a transatlantic liner in ignorance of the accident to the *Titanic*.

Speaking (since the *Titanic* disaster) of the part which wireless telegraphy has played in the salvation of distressed ships, Guglielmo Marconi, the inventor of this wonderful science, has said: "Fifteen years ago the curvature of the earth was looked upon as the one great obstacle to wireless telegraphy. By various experiments in the Isle of Wight and at St. John's I finally succeeded in sending the letter 2,000 miles.

"We have since found that the fog and the dull skies in the vicinity of England are exceptionally favorable for wireless telegraphy."

Then the inventor told of wireless messages being transmitted 2,500 miles across the Abyssinian desert, and of preparation for similar achievements.

"The one necessary requirement for continued success is that governments keep from being enveloped in political red tape," said he.

"The fact that a message can be flashed across the wide expanse of ocean in ten minutes has exceeded my fondest expectations. Some idea of the progress made may be had by citing the fact that in eleven years the range of wireless telegraphy has increased from 200 to 3,000 miles.

"Not once has wireless telegraphy failed in calling and securing help on the high seas. A recognition of this is shown in the attitude of the United States government in compelling all passenger-carrying vessels entering our ports to be equipped with wireless apparatus."

Of the *Titanic* tragedy, Marconi said:

"I know you will all understand when I say that I entertain a deep feeling of gratitude because of the fact that wireless telegraphy has again contributed to the saving of life."

Watertight Bulkheads

One of the most essential factors in making ships safe is the construction of proper bulkheads to divide a ship into watertight compartments in case of injury to her hull. Of the modern means of forming such compartments, and of the complete and automatic devices for operating the watertight doors which connect them, a full explanation has already been given in the description of the *Titanic*'s physical features, to which the reader is referred. A wise precaution usually taken in the case of twin- and triple-screw ships is to arrange the bulkheads so that each engine is in a separate compartment, as is also each boiler or bank of boilers and each coal bunker.

Submarine Signals

Then there are submarine signals to tell of nearby vessels or shores. This signal arrangement includes a small tank on either side of the vessel, just below the waterline. Within each is a microphone with wires leading to the bridge. If the vessel is near any other or approaching shore, the sounds conveyed through the water from the distant object are heard through the receiver of the microphone. These arrangements are called the ship's ears, and whether the sounds come from one side of the vessel or the other, the officers can tell the location of the shore or ship nearby. If both ears record, the object is ahead.

Lifeboats and Rafts

The construction of lifeboats adapts them for very rough weather. The chief essentials, of course, are ease in launching, strength in withstanding rough water and bumping when beached, also strength to withstand striking against wreckage or a ship's side, carrying capacity, and lightness. Those carried on board ship are lighter than those used in lifesaving service on shore. Safety is provided by airtight tanks which ensure buoyancy in case the boat is filled with water. They have also self-righting power in case of being overturned; likewise self-emptying power. Lifeboats are usually of the whaleboat type, with copper airtight tanks along the side beneath the thwarts, and in the ends.

Lifeboats range from twenty-four to thirty feet in length and carry from thirty to sixty persons. The rafts carry from twenty to forty persons. The old-fashioned round bar davits can be gotten for $100 to $150 a set. The new-style davits, quick launchers in type, come as low as $400 a set.

According to some naval constructors, an ocean steamship can carry in davits enough boats to take care of all the passengers and crew, it being simply a question as to whether the steamship owners are willing to take up that much deck room which otherwise would be used for lounging chairs or for a promenade.

Nowadays all lifeboats are equipped with air tanks to prevent sinking, with the result that metal boats are as unsinkable as wooden ones. The metal boats are considered in the United States Navy as superior to wooden ones, for several reasons: they do not break or collapse; they do not, in consequence of long storage on deck, open at the seams and thereby spring a leak; and they are not eaten by bugs, as is the case with wooden boats.

Comparatively few of the transatlantic steamships have adopted metal lifeboats. Most of the boats are of wood, according to the official United States government record of inspection. The records show that a considerable proportion of the entire number of so-called lifeboats carried by Atlantic Ocean liners are not actually lifeboats at all, but simply open boats, without air tanks or other special equipment or construction.

Life rafts are of several kinds. They are commonly used on large passenger steamers where it is difficult to carry sufficient lifeboats. In most cases they consist of two or more hollow metal or inflated

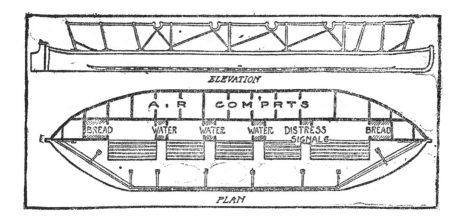

CHAMBERS COLLAPSIBLE LIFE RAFT

rubber floats which support a wooden deck. The small rafts are supplied with lifelines and oars, and the larger ones with lifelines only,
or with lifelines and sails.

The collapsible feature of the Chambers raft consists of canvas-
covered steel frames extending up twenty-five inches from the sides
to prevent passengers from being pitched off. When the rafts are not
in use these side frames are folded down on the raft.

The collapsible rafts are favored by the shipowners because such
boats take up less room, they do not have to be carried in the davits,
and they can be stowed to any number required. Some of the German lines stack their collapsible rafts one above another on deck.

Nixon's Pontoon

Lewis Nixon, the well-known ship designer, suggests the construction of a pontoon to be carried on the after end of the vessel and to

be made of sectional airtight compartments. One compartment would accommodate the wireless outfit. Another compartment would hold drinking water, and still another would be filled with food.

The pontoon would follow the line of the ship and seem to be a part of it. The means for releasing it before the sinking of the vessel present no mechanical problem. It would be too large and too buoyant to be sucked down with the wreck.

The pontoon would accommodate, not comfortably but safely, all those who failed to find room in the lifeboats.

It is Mr. Nixon's plan to install a gas engine in one of the compartments. With this engine the wireless instrument would remain in commission and direct the rescuers after the ship itself had gone down.

Life Preservers and Buoys

Life preservers are chiefly of the belt or jacket type, made to fit about the body and rendered buoyant by slabs of cork sewed into the garment or by rubber-lined airbags. The use of cork is usually considered preferable, as the inflated articles are liable to injury, and jackets are preferable to belts as they can be put on more quickly.

Life buoys are of several types, but those most common are of the ring type, varying in size from the small one designed to be thrown by hand to the large hollow metal buoy capable of supporting several people. The latter are usually carried by seagoing vessels and are fitted with lamps which are automatically lighted when the buoy is dropped into the water.

Rockets

American oceangoing steamers are required to have some approved means of firing lines to the shore. Cunningham rockets and the Hunt gun are largely used. The inaccuracy of the rocket is of less importance when fired from a ship than when fired from shore.

31

Seeking Safety at Sea

ONE MORE TRAGIC LESSON—RESULTS OF *TITANIC* DISASTER—
LONDON CONFERENCE ON SAFETY AT SEA—LIFE-BELT DRILL—
GIANT RAFTS—LIFESAVING SUIT—STORAGE BATTERIES FOR
LIGHTS—DOUBLE HULL ABOVE WATER—SUBMARINE BELL—
REGULATION OF TRAFFIC

W ith the sacrifice of another thousand human lives in the sinking of the *Empress of Ireland* the world has received one more
tragic lesson in solving the problem of achieving safety at sea. Dras-
tic rules governing navigation in narrow, much-frequented passages
in times of fog are expected to result. Perhaps, as George Uhler,
supervising inspector general in the service of the United States,
said, "There is only one safe way for vessels to navigate a fog, and
that is to stop until the weather clears."

Results of *Titanic* Disaster

The foundering of the *Titanic* in 1912 eclipsed all previous disasters
and led to much searching of heart as to the means of providing better security at sea. Inquiries were conducted in New York under Senator W. A. Smith of Michigan, and in London under Lord Mersey,

sitting as wreck commissioner with five experts as assessors. In both cases recommendations were made that liners should have boats for all, regular boat drill, more efficient wireless telegraphy arrangements, and improved subdivision in construction. Lord Mersey's report showed that six out of fifteen of the main compartments of the vessel were damaged, that the ship filled and went gradually down by the head without capsizing, and recommended improvements as mentioned and supervision of ship designs. The recommendations of improvements were generally endorsed by the Merchant Shipping Advisory Committee of the Board of Trade, who did not however concur in the matter of supervising ship designs. The Board of Trade appointed two committees—one (Bulkheads), with Dr. Denny of Dumbarton as chairman, to consider the best means of improving the subdivision of new ships, the second (Boats and Davits), with Professor Biles as chairman, to consider questions relating to design and handling of boats, supply of motorboats, etc. The Board of Trade also laid draft rules before Parliament requiring (1) great increases in the number and capacity of boats to be carried by all classes of passenger vessels, and (2) the submission of the designs of new ships for examination of stability, proposed subdivision, etc.; and the board also took steps to secure international agreement as to wireless telegraphy and all questions affecting safety at sea. The draft rules went considerably beyond the recommendation of the Advisory Committee, and met with very serious opposition from many quarters, but many steamship companies proceeded even before official action was taken to supply boats for all on board their vessels, while the White Star Company announced that improved subdivision would be built into the *Britannic*, and that the *Olympic* would be similarly improved.

London Conference on Safety at Sea

As a later result of the *Titanic* disaster a conference of maritime nations was called in London and a safety-at-sea treaty drawn up. The question of submarine signals between vessels, such as might have prevented the latter catastrophe, was discussed in the conference, but the treaty adopted does not require the equipment of ships with these devices.

An important decision of this conference was that a continuous watch should be kept by all vessels of over thirteen knots speed carrying more than 200 passengers and making voyages of more than 500 miles between two ports, and by all other passenger ships when more than 500 miles from land, and by all cargo boats on voyages that lead them more than a thousand miles from land.

When everything possible has been done to prevent accidents, it remains to reduce to a minimum the life and property loss attendant on such accidents as will happen even to the best of ships and navigators. There are three important items to be considered in this regard: first, means of calling help from shore or from other vessels; second, devices for escaping safely from a sinking vessel; and third, means of so constructing a vessel that it will not sink no matter how hard hit.

Each Tragedy Has Its Lesson

From each appalling tragedy of the sea we laboriously spell out some lessons which are to teach us how to escape these strokes of fate for the future. Then comes another tragedy, and shows us the futility of these dearly bought lessons. From the *Titanic*, we deduced that what is needed is a plentiful supply of lifeboats and life rafts. Given enough of these to easily carry all the passengers and crew, and so terrible a disaster as that which engulfed this peerless ship would, we believed, become impossible. Then came the tragedy of the burning *Volturno*, and practically all those who were "fortunate" enough to get into the lifeboats were drowned, and all who stayed with the burning ship were saved.

Thus was the chief lesson drawn from the *Titanic* shown within a year to be very much less—for all its value—than a certain security against wholesale death at sea. And now we have the frightful case of the *Empress of Ireland* to emphasize this point. The *Empress* had lifeboats; but so swiftly fell the shattering stroke—they could not be launched. The accident occurred in a quiet river, where, had there been time enough, these lifeboats could have saved every man, woman, and child on board in the most orderly fashion. In a word, the lifeboat "cure" would have been perfect had the conditions of the *Titanic* disaster obtained.

Life-Belt Drill

Now the cry is "life belts," and a universal knowledge of how to use them. We are told that very few of the bodies recovered from the *Empress* were encircled with life belts. Very probably if all the passengers who could get to the decks, and so were not carried down in their cabins, had worn life belts, most of them would have remained afloat in the water until rescued. But possibly they never thought of life belts; and it is a fair conjecture that many would not have known how to put them on if they had thought of them. Most passengers take the whole voyage on a "liner" without once studying out how best to attach to themselves the life belts which hang ready for them in their cabins.

A life-belt drill would be an excellent thing for the first day out. The passengers would find it entertaining, and they could each in this way learn that the particular life belt which belonged to him was in order, and what to do with it if an alarm came. A little instruction of this sort, and every passenger—at a midnight outcry—would be more anxious to get on his life belt than his clothes before he rushed up on deck to see what was the matter. If a lifeboat drill is necessary for the crew, a life belt drill is necessary for the passengers.

Mr. Nixon Suggests Remedy

This is only one of many suggestions arising out of the *Empress of Ireland* disaster. Mr. Lewis Nixon, the shipbuilder, believes that hundreds of lives might be spared in sea disasters with an efficient lifesaving suit that would keep persons warm when in the water. He said it was perfectly possible to have a lifesaving suit that would be comfortable for many hours in the coldest water.

Mr. Nixon declared that to jump from a deck high above the water filled most persons with terror, and he mapped out a safety slide which could be shot out from the deck of a vessel in a few minutes. Moreover, Mr. Nixon asserted that a light ray that will penetrate a fog must be worked upon by scientists, and he added that he had expected to see before this a direction indicator.

Giant Rafts

The shipbuilder asserted that he still thinks that vessels will be built with the upper after structure constructed after the fashion of a giant raft. He said that from what he had read there seemed to have been ample warning in the instance of the latest disaster to have prevented the crash if proper precaution had been taken.

"With every loss of a vessel we look for lessons, find them each time, and then ignore them," said Mr. Nixon. "The *Titanic* had one weak spot, the edge of a berg struck the vessel exactly there, a combination against which the odds were almost infinite. This lesson, it is true, was heeded, and later vessels will have double bottoms to above the waterline.

"But the slowness with which she sank misled in other directions. It is true more boats are now carried because the passenger is entitled to his chance, even if the combination of slow sinking and calm is not in the doctrine of probabilities likely to occur frequently. But more boats if they cannot be launched are an aggravation in a heavy sea and on a vessel with a heavy list.

Lifesaving Suit

"It's true we do not build vessels to collide with one another, yet we have had many collisions of late. We build to avoid fire, yet fire still stands out, to my mind, as the great peril at sea.

"But let us read our lesson from recent wrecks. In all, many have been lost who might have been saved with an efficient lifesaving suit.

"It is not only necessary to have the man in the water kept afloat until relief comes. We all know of the gruesome sight of numerous corpses floating on the ocean, dead from exposure, after the loss of the *Titanic*. It is perfectly possible to don a lifesaving suit that one can be comfortable in for many hours in an icy sea.

"It may be said that such a device is too bulky to be carried and that it will not often be used. Yet if such devices had been available the greater part of the passengers of the *Titanic* and the *Empress of Ireland* would now be alive.

"Boats are being improved all the time, and all will soon have power.

"Have you ever noticed a lot of people coming out of a theater where there were plenty of exits? Can you imagine what it would be to take them down in a number of elevators, even if the number of elevators were ample, in time of panic?

More Individualism in Saving

"Then think of a vessel, pitching and tossing, with passengers in terror, unused to ship passageways and stairways, and expect them to be embarked in orderly fashion in a short time. More and more is it impressed upon me that there should be more individualism in lifesaving.

"Recent happenings have shown that relief can usually be had as a result of calling by wireless.

"So the passenger, even though thrown or landed in the sea, could be buoyed up by the hope of ultimate relief if he felt reasonably safe from death by drowning or exposure during the time taken by the relief ship to come. So I think we must adopt a life suit which will keep one warm as well as afloat. There should be exhibitions daily on deck, where passengers should be shown how to don such suits, and those who had never done so should be required to don them.

Chutes Down Ships' Sides

"Since, under certain conditions, which have been of frequent occurrence of late, safety lies in getting afloat, there should be regular chutes down which one could slide and be delivered clear of the vessel. When one thinks of jumping from the deck of a vessel as high as a house, the terror of contemplation results in demoralization just at a moment when the keenest wit is needed. Of course, this does not argue that we must not have the best boat and boat-lowering equipment possible.

"The safe transfer of all passengers into the lifeboats is, of course, the most desirable outcome, but, as we see, this is not always possible.

"A side-wiping blow delivered by such a vessel as the *Storstad* would sink almost any vessel, though I am inclined to think that the heavy scantlings of large vessels like the *Lusitania*, the *Imperator*, or the *Vaterland*, would break off the stem of a vessel so much smaller and so localize the damage.

"Our aim must be of course to keep them apart. Years ago I endeavored to have experiments made with various kinds of light rays with a view to fixing the courses of Staten Island ferryboats in fogs.

"There may be found if not a light ray a dark one that will penetrate fog, and while we have no light-ray transformers like current transformers, if they do penetrate, their presence can in some way be made manifest.

"I have expected before this to see some direction indicator, to the end of which I called attention when the *Titanic* sank. But in this last accident there seems to have been ample warning of approach and enough knowledge of location to have prevented disaster, were proper precaution taken.

Storage Batteries for Lights

"Of course we must hear both sides, but personally I am far more disposed to lay blame when two vessels collide than when one collides with a berg or a derelict. In a channel where sea room is limited and currents due to enormous tidal rise exist, more than the usual care at sea should be exercised.

"There should be on all passenger vessels storage batteries that would light up enough lights in passageways and about the decks to enable passengers to move freely, and special colored lights, well understood, to show the means of reaching the upper deck.

"These are the lessons. They have all been known all the time, but heeding them can only be arrived at through crushing disaster that will hold the attention of travelers by sea long enough for them to show their appreciation of the lines which best safeguard life at sea.

"After all, the transatlantic lines will provide such safety as modern ingenuity may evolve, and they will install devices in deference to demands of the traveling public. The difficulty is that the greater part of such public are fatalists when they go to sea."

Double Hull Above Water

Alexander MacGregor, engineer commander, retired, Royal Naval Reserves, who lives in Inverness, Scotland, after a lifetime on the seas of all the world, declared that such an accident as befell the *Empress of Ireland* spells certain and quick destruction to any steamship of the prevailing type now engaged in passenger as well as cargo traffic.

"Double hulls extending well above the waterline are the only safeguard for the ship, and individual unsinkable garments for the passengers their only certain protection," Mr. MacGregor said. "I knew the *Empress of Ireland*. She was of the same construction type as the *Titanic*. She, and practically every other, except four of the largest passenger steamships out of New York, has only a double shell far below the waterline, a protection only from damage about the keel. It cost more than $1 million to reconstruct with a double hull one of the biggest transatlantic service steamships after the *Titanic* went down. The expense and great reduction of cargo capacity have been a bar to general adoption of that type.

"Under the rules of the sea, the *Empress of Ireland* appears to have been properly at a standstill and the collier steaming on in the dense fog against the rule. If the *Empress* had a double hull it would have been practically impossible for the other to have torn out both her shells, which usually are built four feet apart, and opened up all the bulkheads.

"Passenger vessels navigating narrow waters like the St. Lawrence should have lifesaving apparel close at hand for passengers. Boats are of no use if you can't get to them. Few men could last long in the icy waters of the St. Lawrence at this season."

Mr. MacGregor for eighteen years was marine superintendent of the Dominion Atlantic Railway, whose steamships plied between New York, Boston, and Nova Scotia. He retired a few years ago.

Submarine Bell

Another opinion is that the use of the submarine bell would have prevented the collision of the *Storstad* and the *Empress of Ireland*. The bell is in use on lightships, but seagoing vessels use only the receivers, and the utility of the warnings by sound underwater between approaching vessels is not appreciated. Many think that publication of the facts would aid in making the use of the apparatus compulsory, and point to the time when those who could spread the knowledge of the useful wireless system hesitated to "do anything that would advertise a patented article."

The report of the American Commissioners to the International Conference on Safety of Life at Sea, touching on submarine bells, says: "While the American delegation was convinced of the value of submarine bells, it did not press their compulsory use, as this bell is patented and sold only by one company. In the official recommendations (No. 5) the use of this bell is recommended by lightships on important outside stations where fog is frequent. Congress has appropriated money for this purpose in the United States."

The question has been raised by Mr. William Spiegel, whose patent on the submarine bell was granted in 1888, whether the fundamental invention is no longer protected by the patent laws. His patent was bought up about five months before its expiration in 1905. But whether or not subsequent and patentable improvements have been made, if the bell will prevent collisions in fog it should be used, and, if necessary, its use should be made compulsory.

Regulation of Traffic

It is probable that the wider investigation of the disaster will deal with traffic regulations or their absence which made the collision between the *Empress* and the *Storstad* possible. There are no regulations separating the paths of eastbound and westbound steamers in the St. Lawrence, although at the point where this collision occurred the river is nearly thirty miles wide and the depth of water ample for the whole distance across. The *Empress of Ireland* had gone out from Father Point and was proceeding down the river at a distance of three miles from shore, which is apparently the custom. The *Storstad*, with her

11,000 tons of coal, was steaming westward at about the same distance from shore, and this, too, seems to have been the custom. Cargo-carrying tramp steamers have equal rights with passenger ships in the St. Lawrence, and the path along the south shore off Father Point and Rimouski seems to be common to both classes of traffic both eastbound and westbound. It is not so long since the *Empress of Britain*, sister ship to the lost *Empress of Ireland*, ran into the collier *Helvetia*, but in that case the collier came off second best. Obviously, we must have more painstaking rules for the navigation of the Gulf and River.

AFTERWORD

The *Commision of Inquiry into Casualty to British Steamship "Empress of Ireland"* commenced in a Quebec courtroom on June 16, 1914. Presiding was John Bingham, first Viscount Mersey, a retired jurist who was just two years removed from his role heading the British Board of Trade's inquiry into the sinking of the RMS *Titanic*. Presumably it was this experience that caused John Douglas Hazen, the Canadian minister of marine and fisheries, to summon Lord Mersey from England. Rounding out the commission were two Canadian justices, Sir Adolphe Basile Routhier and the Honorable Ezekiel McLeod.

Together the three men faced the unenviable task of sorting out the testimonies of over sixty witnesses—none of whom seemed to offer matching stories. Not only were Captain Kendall of the *Empress* and Captain Andersen of the *Storstad* both equally adamant that the other was to blame for the accident, but many times witnesses from the same ship offered contradictory testimony. Hence different crewmen from the *Empress* estimated that the ship had stayed motionless anywhere from several seconds to almost ten minutes.

As the inquiry progressed it became apparent that, at best, incorrect recollections had solidified in the minds of the witnesses, or, at worst, some were knowingly lying and could not be shaken from their statements. Like Occam's razor, the three commissioners sought a way to cut through the complicated issues at hand. They realized that the central question was: which ship had changed its course prior to the collision? If they could answer this question, they would be able to assess blame.

Of course, even such a straightforward question as this was not easy to answer. Captain Kendall testified that he first spotted the *Storstad* at a distance of six miles. From his vantage point, it was clear that the ships would pass each other on their starboard sides. After a fogbank rolled in and reduced visibility, Kendall ordered the engines full speed astern. Suddenly out of the fogbank, the *Storstad* appeared headed directly at the *Empress* at a right angle.

On the other side, Chief Officer Toftenes told a very different story. He also saw the *Empress* at a distance of several miles. It seemed obvious to him that the two ships would pass *port to port* and not starboard to starboard as Kendall had testified. Toftenes slowed the *Storstad* and called Captain Andersen to the bridge. When he arrived the captain saw the lights of the other vessel cross their path. He immediately ordered full speed astern, but it was too late.

Faced with such different stories, there was nothing left to do but choose one. The commission reasoned that since the *Empress* had already steadied up for her voyage out to sea, it was unlikely that she would have been the turning ship. Therefore the *Storstad*, and specifically Chief Officer Toftenes, was to blame. Captain Andersen was so inflamed by this verdict that he swore to sue the commissioners, though he never did.

His was not an outrageous response. There was very little in the way of direct physical evidence, and, in fact, a later Norwegian inquiry would come to the opposite conclusion, blaming Kendall for not passing port to port as would be customary.

Throughout 1914 divers descended to the wreck, bringing up silver, mailbags, and, most importantly, the bodies of the dead. Finally, on August 20, they completed their work by saving the purser's safe. They had to blow a large hole in the side of the ship to get it out.

Captain Henry George Kendall continued to lead a life of adventure. Seemingly shuffled off to a desk job in Antwerp, he was soon presented with another challenge as the German invasion of Belgium caused the British embassy to be flooded with refugees. Kendall packed the refugees onto the only two ships available: an old command of his, the *Montrose*, and the *Montreal*, an aged steamer whose engines were not working. Once the refugees were loaded on the two ships, Kendall assumed command of the *Montrose* and used it to tow the *Montreal* back to London.

As a reward for his heroism, Kendall was assigned as second in command of the *Calgarian*. He spent the war crossing the ocean on this liner until it was sunk by a U-boat on March 1, 1918. Kendall was picked up by a trawler and survived.

When he died in 1965 his obituary in the *Times* of London never mentioned the *Empress of Ireland*. Instead, the focus was on another remarkable event in his maritime career.

In 1908 Kendall was in command of the *Montrose* crossing from Antwerp to Quebec when he recognized one of his passengers as the notorious fugitive murderer Dr. Hawley Harvey Crippen. The captain took the unprecedented step of alerting authorities by wireless telegram. The chief inspector in charge of the case raced across the ocean in a faster ship and was waiting for Crippen in Canada.

This was the first time that a criminal had ever been captured through the use of this new communication technology.

Captain Andersen remained in command of the *Storstad* until she also was sunk by a U-boat March 8, 1917. Andersen and all but four of his crew survived.

Every year, on a Sunday in May, the Salvation Army in Toronto holds a remembrance ceremony for the 159 Army members who died in the *Empress of Ireland* tragedy. One of the youngest survivors was seven-year-old Grace Hanagan. Both of her parents were Salvation Army members who drowned and Grace ultimately became the last living survivor of the tragedy until her passing on May 15, 1995.

Today the *Empress of Ireland* lies forty meters under the St. Lawrence River with the great gash in her starboard side buried in the silty bottom. The elegant liner is destined to remain there for eternity with the secret of her death never truly answered.

Printed in the United States
by Baker & Taylor Publisher Services